The Institute of British Geographers
Special Publications Series

26 The Making of the Urban Landscape

The Institute of British Geographers
Special Publications Series

EDITOR: N. J. Thrift
University of Bristol

The Making
of the
Urban Landscape

J. W. R. Whitehand

BLACKWELL
Oxford UK & Cambridge USA

J. W. R. Whitehand is hereby identified as author of this work in accordance with Section 77 of the Copyright, Designs and Patents Act 1988.

First published 1992

Basil Blackwell Ltd
108 Cowley Road, Oxford, OX4 1JF, UK

Basil Blackwell, Inc.
3 Cambridge Center
Cambridge, Massachusetts 02142, USA

Library of Congress Cataloging in Publication Data

Whitehand, J.W.R.
  The making of the urban landscape/J.W.R. Whitehand.
  p. cm. — (The Institute of British Geographers special
  publications series: 26)
  ISBN 0-631-17634-9
  1. City planning — Environmental aspects. 2. City planning —
  Great Britain — Case studies. 3. Urban ecology. 4. Urban ecology
  — Great Britain — Case studies. 5. Urban renewal. 6. Urban
  renewal — Great Britain — Case studies. I. Title. II. Series:
  Special publication series (Institute of British Geographers): 26.
  HQ166.W48 1992
  307.3'416—dc20   91-13425 CIP

British Library Cataloguing in Publication Data

A CIP catalogue record for this book is available from the British Library.

Typeset in 10½ on 12 pt Plantin
by Times Graphics, Singapore
Printed in Great Britain by Alden Press Ltd, Oxford

This book is printed on acid-free paper.

Contents

vi *Contents*

Preface

This monograph is a sequel to *The Changing Face of Cities* (1987), which was a previous volume in the Institute of British Geographers Special Publications Series. That earlier volume provided a perspective on the cyclical processes whereby cities change their form. In it little consideration was given to the people and organizations responsible for the making of the urban landscape. These 'makers' are a central concern of the present volume. Indeed, this monograph might well have been entitled 'The makers of the urban landscape', for attention is devoted as much to the agents responsible for creating urban landscapes as to the processes by which those landscapes are shaped.

For many years this topic has excited the interest of local historians, curious about the previous inhabitants of the places in which they live. Despite the long-standing interest of geographers in urban morphology, the actual agents responsible for the making of the urban landscape – the property owners, developers, builders and architects, to mention only a few of the more important – were for a long time neglected from a geographical standpoint. Since about 1980, however, a sizeable amount of geographical research on this topic has appeared in journals, collections of essays, theses and other forms. Most of this writing is on particular aspects and individual parts of urban areas. There is a need to begin the task of integration, even if the patchy nature of what has so far been accomplished precludes a balanced and rounded treatment. In this monograph a range of issues concerning the makers and the making of different parts of the urban landscape are brought together. The contents reflect a research frontier along which a number of explorations have been undertaken but large stretches of which remain uninvestigated. An attempt has been made to convey the depth of some of the investigations that have been carried out, and to relate their findings, rather than to provide representative coverage of the frontier. Some types of urban area, for example industrial landscapes and the housing that goes with them, receive little or no attention.

In endeavouring to write for English-speaking readers worldwide, compromises have been necessary in the use of terms. Problems stemming from the use of different words in America and Great Britain to describe urban settlements and their internal divisions are not readily resolved. In general, terms that are more likely to be understood in the same sense on both sides of the Atlantic have been preferred. For example, in most contexts the term 'urban landscape' has been preferred to 'townscape', which is a term rarely used by researchers in America, and 'commercial core' and 'central area', as well as 'town centre' and 'city centre', have been preferred to 'central business district' and 'downtown', which have strong American connotations. When referring to particular places, however, local terms have generally been used. Thus, Northampton, in the English Midlands, is referred to as a 'town', although the general term in America for such a place would be 'city'. Similarly, 'City of London' refers to the medieval core of London, now the principal financial area, which is only a tiny fraction of the present built-up area of London.

A good deal of the work described in this monograph has for some years been central to a rolling programme of research on the agents of urban landscape change being undertaken by the Urban Morphology Research Group at the University of Birmingham. Some of the more important seeds of this research began to germinate at the end of the 1970s. Aspinall (1977, 1982) demonstrated the scope for the systematic analysis of building firms, and he and a succession of research fellows and research students worked with me to uncover the firms and individuals responsible for a variety of geographical aspects of urban form. In the course of these researches the Urban Morphology Research Group grew to its present size of some 15 members. By no means all have been concerned with the research projects described here, but all have contributed to the regular discussions that have been, and continue to be, a feature of the Group's work. These acted as a forum that stimulated, criticized and helped to develop a number of the ideas that have shaped this volume. I am therefore indebted to all the members of the Group, past and present. Those whose membership came within the period of just over a decade during which the work described here was undertaken were, in order of date of joining, Dr T. R. Slater, Messrs P. J. Aspinall and A. J. Howson, Dr R. F. Broaderwick, Mr S. T. Delaney, Miss J. S. M. Kingston, Dr I. A. Thompson, Mr R. J. Pain, Mrs S. M. Whitehand, Drs M. Freeman, P. J. Larkham and N. D. Pompa, Messrs A. N. Jones and P. N. Booth, Miss J. C. Horn, Dr N. J. Baker, Miss H. J. Barrett, Mr K. S. Kropf, Miss H. C. Wright and Messrs D. J. Bell, T. R. Hall, P. J. Hubbard, K. D. Lilley and J. L. McGahey. The large majority of the Group's projects, including some described in this monograph, have been funded by the Economic and Social Research Council or its predecessor, the Social Science Research Council. In addition, grants have been received from the Leverhulme Trust, the British Academy, the Nuffield Foundation and the British Council.

Like *The Changing Face of Cities*, this volume draws on the contents of a number of papers that I have published elsewhere (Aspinall and Whitehand, 1980; Whitehand, 1983a, b, 1984a, b, c, 1988, 1989a, b, 1990a, b; Whitehand and Whitehand, 1983, 1984). It also contains information from unpublished theses and dissertations that·I have had the pleasure of supervising (Butcher, 1974; Ross, 1979; Pain, 1980; Broaderwick, 1981; Collier, 1981; Tate, 1983; MacGregor, 1984; Callis, 1986; Freeman, 1986; Larkham, 1986a; Thompson, 1987; Pompa, 1988; Booth, 1989) or for which I acted as external examiner (McNamara, 1985). I should like to thank the following for permission to reproduce and adapt copyright material: the Editor, *Area*, for figure 1.1 (from *Area*, 12 (1980), pp. 199–203); the Editor, *Geographical Journal*, for figures 4.3, 4.4, 4.6 and 4.7 (from *Geographical Journal*, 154 (1988), pp. 351–66); the Editor, *Journal of Cultural Geography*, for figures 2.12–2.17 (from *Journal of Cultural Geography*, 5 (1984), pp. 41–55); Academic Press for figures 2.5 and 2.7–2.11 (from *Journal of Historical Geography*, 10 (1984), pp. 174–200); the Editor, *Transactions of the Institute of British Geographers*, for figures 2.18–2.25 (from *Transactions* 8 (1983), pp. 483–507), figures 2.26–2.34 (from *Transactions* 9 (1984), pp. 231–47) and figures 4.8–4.11, tables 4.1–4.3 and table 4.17 (from *Transactions* 15 (1990), pp. 87–101); the Editor, *Town Planning Review*, for figures 4.5 and 4.12–4.15 and tables 4.4–4.16 (from the *Town Planning Review*, 60 (1989), pp. 403–21); the Editor, *Die Alte Stadt*, for figure 4.2 (from *Die Alte Stadt*, 16 (1989), pp. 24–38); the Editor, *Planning History*, for figures 3.12–3.18 (from *Planning History* 13, 2 (1991)); the Series Editor, University of Birmingham School of Georgraphy Occasional Publications, for figure 2.6 (from Occasional Publication 19 (1984)) and figures 6.1 and 6.2 (from Occasional Publication 28 (1989)); Leicester University Press for figures 5.1–5.6 and 5.8–5.10 (from *The Built Form of Western Cities*, edited by T. R. Slater, 1990); Martin Grant Homes for figure 5.7 (from the sales brochure of A. C. Frost & Co.); Dr I. A. Thompson for figures 2.2 and 2.3 (redrawn from his unpublished PhD thesis, University of Birmingham, 1987); Dr P. F. McNamara for figure 2.4 (redrawn from his unpublished PhD thesis, University of Edinburgh, 1985); and Dr R F Broaderwick for figures 3.1–3.4 (redrawn from his unpublished PhD thesis, University of Birmingham, 1981).

During the gestation period of this monograph I have received assistance from more people than it would be practicable individually to acknowledge here. Among the members, or former members, of the Urban Morphology Research Group already mentioned, I am particularly indebted to Mrs S. M. Whitehand, who helped to collect the data for the case studies that form the major part of chapter 2, and Dr P. J. Larkham, who has contributed in numerous ways to the progress of the Group generally, and in particular to a series of collaborative ventures with me personally, and who read and commented on a draft of this volume. Professor G. E. Cherry has been a source of much help and encouragement, and Professor M. R. G. Conzen has influenced my perspective more fundamentally than is formally apparent from my frequent references to his publications. Members of my family have not only contributed to the practical aspects of creating the manuscript but even, in a small way, found themselves as contributors to events that provided grist for my mill. The illustrations were prepared for publication by Messrs T. G. Grogan, H. Buglass, K. Burkhill, G. P Dowling, S. Restorick and V. Richardson, and most of the word processing was undertaken by Mrs G. Coldicott, Miss J.

Hadley and Mrs M. Richardson. The copy editing, by Mr S. J. D. Ryan, was of an exceptionally high standard.

A final category of indebtedness is that to people and organizations who either provided information or, more often, gave me access to it. This includes Mr K. B. Nunn, Dr P. F. McNamara, Barclays Bank, the Boots Co., Chas E. Goad, Chiltern District Council, Courtney Builders, Epsom and Ewell Borough Council, Fairbriar Homes, Martin Grant Homes, Midlands Postal Board, Northampton Borough Council, Northampton Central Library, the Prudential Assurance Co., J. Sainsbury & Co., the University of Birmingham, Watford Borough Council, Watford Central Library, the Whinney, Mackay Lewis Partnership, and the YWCA. These individuals and organizations, and many others, enabled me to get as close as is practicable to a large number of makers of the urban landscape.

J. W. R. Whitehand
University of Birmingham

Note: The author wishes to thank Virginia Sullivan, for kind permission to use the jacket flap photograph.

To Susan

1

Introduction

The physical form of urban areas, the urban landscape or townscape, has attracted the interest of scholars in a number of disciplines. Urban morphology, the name by which the study of this subject is widely known, is most firmly established in geography, although it has in recent decades enjoyed popularity among a limited coterie of architects. Within the discipline of history it is doubtful whether it would be recognized as a branch of the subject, though its subject matter has attracted the interest of many urban historians, usually as part of a broader study.

As an organized body of knowledge, urban morphology developed first within central European geography, nearly 100 years ago (Whitehand, 1981b). Its popularity, like that of most fields of inquiry, has varied over time and space. Furthermore, there has been no simple correlation between the various amounts of attention it has received within different disciplines. As interest in urban morphology was growing within architecture in the 1970s, largely in continental Europe (Samuels, 1985), the subject was in a state of quiescence within geography – being little studied outside the German-speaking world.

In geography, the drive for scientific respectability in the 1960s and early 1970s almost brushed aside urban morphology. The attributes of the urban landscape, often qualitative in character, were less obviously amenable to quantitative analysis than were social and economic data. Although the occasional attempts at a more scientific urban morphology processed impressive quantities of information (Corey, 1969; Openshaw, 1974), gains in the understanding of the urban landscape were relatively small.

In the 1980s urban morphology came back firmly on the geographical research agenda (Whitehand, 1987; Ley, 1988). This revival was not unconnected with a wider resurgence of interest in the character of places. A major part of the justification for urban morphology that was then put forward (Whitehand, 1987, p. 2) was grounded in much earlier arguments, especially those of M. R. G. Conzen (1966, 1975). That justification rested, and continues to rest, on the economic and social importance of the objects of study. First, most of the population of the industrial world lives in urban environments; the production and maintenance of the physical parts of that environment absorb a large part of the wealth of Western societies. Secondly, and more important, the built environment is a fundamental means by which individuals and societies orient themselves in time and space. It is both a means of functional efficiency and, through its embodiment of the endeavours of past societies, a cultural and educational resource of inestimable value (Conzen, 1966, 1975). To study the dynamics of the urban landscape, from its beginnings through generations of transformations to the decisions shaping its future, is thus an endeavour of major importance.

APPROACHES

Within geography there have been a number of approaches to urban morphology. Of fundamental importance is the morphogenetic tradition. This was developed in the German-speaking countries during the half-century before the Second World War, was brought to Great Britain and greatly enriched by Conzen (1958, 1960, 1962), and is still being actively pursued (Slater, 1990). Work in this tradition, especially by Conzen himself, has provided the basis for a variety of studies of wider aspects of urban form, especially the cyclical character of land utilization and building form. These draw not only on Conzen's concepts but upon at least two other types of work, by land economists and economic historians. Urban-rent theory and ideas on building cycles have thus been married to the morphogenetic tradition (Whitehand, 1974).

A more recent development has been the use of urban landscapes as a means of interpreting the societies that create them. In this perspective, rather than being viewed just as objects to be explained, urban landscapes are viewed much more as transmitters of signals about the societies that make them. They are 'texts' to be read for the ideas, practices and interests of those societies (Ley, 1988, p. 101). In this view the physical form of the urban area and the society creating it are synthesized: the urban landscape becomes a part of social geography. The interdisciplinary links of this perspective are well developed, especially with sociology, anthropology and art history. The interpretation of the bungalow by King (1984) is an example of this genre.

The approach to the urban landscape adopted in the present study is to focus attention on the people and organizations responsible for urban development. Within geographical research these agents of change have until recent years remained largely anonymous. A number of studies by historians, however, have helped to draw the attention of geographers to their significance (for example, Dyos, 1968; Hobhouse, 1971; Thompson, 1974). Moreover, quantitative analyses of the building process and the building industry, such as the study of residential development by Craven (1969) and that of the housebuilding industry by Aspinall (1982), though only indirectly concerned with the urban landscape, have made apparent to geographers the need for more-rigorous

analysis of the relationship between forms in the landscape and the organizations and individuals responsible for producing them. Attention has thus been
attracted to the enterprises that lie behind the anonymous forces and cyclical
processes whose role in shaping the urban landscape has for nearly two decades
been a prominent concern in geographical urban morphology. Harbingers of
the upsurge of research by geographers on the agents of change were the study
by Johns (1971) of two Devon towns and Carter's (1970) 'decision-making'
approach to town-plan analysis, although the latter was more concerned with
decision-making than with decision-makers. The more recent attempt by
Gordon (1981, 1984) to produce an organizational framework for urban
morphology in which decision-makers and decision-making are primary
elements generated further interest. The study of 150 years of office development in Toronto by Gad and Holdsworth (1984) has shown the kind of insights
that can be obtained when building form is related to both the activities of
individual organizations and the changing social and economic environment in
which they exist.

The focus on the agents of change in this monograph is viewed as a
complement to the cyclical approach which the author adopted in *The
Changing Face of Cities* (1987), which provides a springboard for some of the
ideas developed here. In the essentially historico-geographical perspective on
the physical form of urban areas developed in that work, stress was placed on
the economics of land use. At the centre of the theoretical framework were land
value, economic fluctuations and the adoption of innovations. Fluctuations in
urban development were related to land-value theory in a schema of urban
growth and internal change in which the creation and modification of elements
in the urban landscape were linked to pressures on land over time and space.
The rapid outward growth of urban areas in the form of high-density housing
took place during periods of relatively high land values associated with
housebuilding booms. The rapid adoption of innovations also occurred at such
times, each boom being characterized by the appearance in the landscape of a
particular admixture of innovations. Conversely, slow outward growth of the
built-up area, relatively low land values, and the creation of large plots for
extensive land use, especially for public and institutional purposes, were
associated with housebuilding slumps. These relationships have imparted a
roughly annular structure to urban areas. A number of factors, such as the
mutual attraction of similar land uses and various economic and social forces,
including planning, predisposed against radical change once this structure was
established. Thus the zones of differing character created by the process of
uneven outward growth have become deeply etched within the city's internal
structure.

The recognition of some kind of annular or zonal structure was characteristic
of earlier attempts to generalize the form of the city, though explanations were
couched in different terms. By far the best known zonal schema, that of Burgess
(1925), was social rather than economic in its underlying basis. Its popularity
was undoubtedly sustained by the appealing simplicity with which it could be

depicted diagrammatically. It should not be confused with the intellectual antecedents of the present study, which are primarily economic and morpho-genetic.

Annular schemata in general would appear to correspond less well morpho-graphically to the late-twentieth-century city than they did to the nineteenth-century city. A host of innovations have ensured in the 1990s a land-use pattern that is less oriented around the historical commercial core than it was a century ago and is in some respects less orderly than it was in the 1960s. In Great Britain, this change has occurred despite nearly half a century of heavy investment in local government planning, including the designation of 'green belts' around major cities. Although the lessening of the gravitational pull of the commercial core became evident first in North America, it is now becoming increasingly evident in Great Britain, with out-of-town shopping centres, 'high-tech' corridors, business parks and leisure complexes already adding a further dimension to British landscapes. Large-scale, sometimes multi-purpose, developments such as are taking place in numerous former docklands are evidence of the scale of change that is possible within a decade.

These recent changes and their rationale have yet to be incorporated fully in explanations of the landscape development of the late-twentieth-century city (Knox, 1991). It is important that they are not divorced from their historical and geographical context. In Great Britain, is in Europe as a whole, current urban developments are heavily constrained by physical forms inherited from the long period of industrial urban development before the Second World War. The fact that the basic lineaments of urban physical structure still strongly reflect developments of that period must be central to a balanced account of the urban landscape. Furthermore, in a world in which the pulse of fashion seems to have quickened and in which a sense of direction and purpose is sometimes elusive, the need for a firm grasp of enduring conceptions of the urban development process is greater than ever. Such conceptions provide anchorages for the organizing framework of our study.

AREAS, PROCESSES AND AGENTS

Against this background, and viewing the urban development process in the long term it is evident that some major internal variations in the landscapes of an urban area may be accounted for by employing familiar notions. Some differences between landscapes within an urban area are inherent in the different functions that different parts of that urban area perform; perhaps the most obvious difference of this type is between the central business district, or commercial core, and residential areas. Others relate to the different ways in which various types of development have been brought into being; for example, not only do areas of institutional and public buildings provide a function distinct from that of residential areas but their financial basis is often different (Whitehand, 1987). Still other differences between landscapes within an urban area relate to the switching of capital between different types of investment and different parts of the city. Some of these differences may be the geographical effects of alternations between housebuilding booms and slumps. Others may be the effects of government aid to particular industries or localities. These spatial variations suggest that a geographical division of an urban area based in particular on functional differences still affords a reasonable way of organizing an investigation of its physical configuration.

In addition to, and sometimes related to, this long-term geographical differentiation, there are important distinctions between, and dimensions to, the roles of the agents influencing the development of the urban landscape. Three of them are particularly relevant here.

First, a distinction can be made between corporate or public activities on the one hand and individual or private activities on the other (Conzen, 1988). These two types of activities occur simultaneously in the development of the urban landscape, but their relative importance has varied over time and space. For example, in his study of the town of Ludlow, Conzen (1988) makes a broad distinction between the layout of the medieval town, formed by predominantly corporate initiatives, and its transformation between late-medieval times and the late nineteenth century by predominantly individual initiatives. This transformation was a piecemeal, and in many ways uncoordinated, 'erosion' of earlier corporate creations.

Secondly, an essentially independent, though in practice often related, dimension is the degree of concentration of decision-making. It is a reasonable presumption that concentrated decision-making will yield greater landscape uniformity than dispersed decision-making. Carter (1970) draws parallels between the high concentrations of authority involved in the creation of the medieval bastide of Caernarfon and those involved in the making of the nineteenth-century company town of Merthyr Tydfil. The elements of similarity between the physical forms of the two towns, despite the great differences between the historical conditions under which they were created, serve to emphasize the importance of this dimension.

Thirdly, the roles of agents of change can be classified according to the functions they perform – into owners, architects, builders, planners and so on. These agents may be corporate or individual. Furthermore, both within and between categories of agent there may be great variability in the concentration of decision-making over time and space.

URBAN LANDSCAPE MANAGEMENT

These discriminations are largely the products of attempts to understand historical and present-day urban forms. Value judgement and prescription are rare. The geographical urban morphologist has sought to understand the world, not change it. In this respect he differs from the architectural urban morphologist, for the creation of new forms is central to the architect's purpose. However, geographers have not been totally devoid of ideas that might form the basis for urban landscape management. Over more than 30 years, especially in the 1980s, there have appeared sporadic discussions of how the geographer's understanding of places might contribute towards this end. These discussions are strongly rooted in the morphogenetic tradition. In particular they consider the relationship between morphogenesis and the way in which societies develop self-awareness (Conzen, 1966, 1975). The key elements in this relationship merit reiteration.

All societies inhabit environments created in part by previous generations. Sometimes a society respects the creations of its predecessors; sometimes it consciously rejects them. No society can detach itself completely from its past and the landscape is never a *tabula rasa*. To seek to achieve such a condition is a profligate waste of past human endeavour. Each society leaves its mark on the landscape, creating forms that reflect the aspirations and problems of its day. These forms are part of the inheritance of future societies, which they in their turn variously alter, add to, preserve or erase. In this way an urban landscape, whether that of a large area, like a conurbation, or a small locality, like a single street, acquires its own *genius loci*. This is the product not only of the present occupants but also of their predecessors. Far from being just a reflection of the requirements of the society currently occupying it, the urban landscape is a cumulative, albeit incomplete, record of the succession of booms, slumps and innovation adoptions within a particular locale (Whitehand 1987). Urban landscapes are thus a means by which both individuals and societies can set their own needs and aspirations within a historical and geographical context.

This perspective brings up back to Conzen's justification for urban morphology. For Conzen, the historical unfolding of the built environment not only is fundamentally important in itself but also becomes the starting-point in the search for a theoretical basis for the management of urban landscapes in the future (Conzen, 1966, 1975). The past provides object-lessons for planning. In this view, the idea of the urban landscape as the 'objectivation of the spirit of a society' is fundamental. This concept can be traced back to studies on the philosophy of culture by German philosophers in the 1930s but first appeared in geography in the work of Schwind (1951). The spirit of a society is objectivated in the historico-geographical character of the urban landscape and becomes the *genius loci*. In Conzen's view the apperception of this expressiveness is an important environmental experience for the individual even when it is enjoyed unconsciously. It enables individuals and groups to take root in an area. They acquire a sense of the historical dimension of human existence. This stimulates comparison and encourages a less time-bound and more integrated approach to contemporary problems. Landscapes with a high degree of expressiveness of past societies exert a particularly strong educative and regenerative influence (Conzen, 1975, p. 101). The Conzenian urban landscape is a stage on which successive societies work out their lives, each society learning from, and working to some extent within the bounds set by, what was provided by the landscape experiments of its predecessors. Viewed in this way urban landscapes represent accumulated experience. A responsible society acts as the custodian of the urban landscape for future generations.

Although this approach has scarcely begun to be translated into a fully-fledged theory, it provides the basis for the case studies and value judgements in later chapters of this volume. Preoccupied as most societies are with current practical problems rather than long-term values, it is easy for such an approach to be overlooked. The problem becomes especially acute in societies ever more technically capable of producing substantial change, particularly in phases of economic buoyancy. Thus, in the economic boom of the 1950s and 1960s Great Britain turned its back on its *genius loci*. Mesmerized by the capabilities of technical innovation and carried forward by the momentum of rapid economic growth, Great Britain, like most Western countries, allowed long-term social and cultural needs to take second place to short-term material goals. The 1980s, in contrast, provided more fertile ground for the management of change in a way that was sympathetic to the *genius loci*. It would probably be unrealistic, however, to expect Conzen's ideas on urban landscape management to be widely appreciated, and their widespread adoption in planning practice may seem an almost Utopian prospect. Nevertheless, the dissemination of these ideas may at least help to promote greater understanding of the historico-geographical context of urban development. And, more optimistically, where they reach the right minds, such ideas may sharpen the thinking behind actual planning decisions.

RESEARCH QUESTIONS

In this light a number of interrelated questions merit study. They provide the framework for the ensuing investigations. Some questions spring directly or indirectly from the literature already referred to; others are the cutting edge of essentially new lines of investigation. They concern the agents of change at work in the development of the urban landscape, attitudes towards the identities of urban landscapes, the relationship between planning and outcome, and the ways in which these matters vary both within and between urban areas on the one hand and over time on the other.

First, in focusing on the people and organizations responsible for creating the urban landscape it is possible to draw upon a large literature, ranging from biographies of individuals (Hobhouse, 1971) to sociological studies of particular professions (Kaye, 1960). Many of the questions of central concern here, however, require purpose-designed investigations. Our questions about the agents of change may be divided into five groups.

1 Who or what is responsible for initiating urban landscape change? Traditionally, in geography, explanations have been couched in terms of physical, social and economic forces, but in the discipline of history explanations have tended to be more individualistic. How important are the various characteristics of organizations and individuals in determining their influence on the urban landscape, and are their motives consistent with an economic rationale for urban development?

2 How important relative to one another are the roles of the various kinds of

agent of change, such as property owners, architects and builders, and what are the relationships between them?

3 How important is the distinction between the creation of bespoke forms for the use of particular individuals or organizations on the one hand and the creation of forms as a speculative venture on the other?

4 How concentrated is the decision-making involved in urban development, and how important is the public domain as a seat of such decision-making in comparison to the private domain? Related to this, what justification is there for laying stress on the roles played by influential individuals?

5 What is the relationship between the location of urban landscape change and the location of the relevant decision-makers, and to what extent does this relationship have a bearing on the nature of the forms created? It would seem plausible that this nexus generally, and more specifically the degree of involvement of non-local individuals and organizations, is an important factor in determining the locational pattern of the adoption of fashions in development and design.

Secondly, in the light of Conzen's argument concerning the major importance of historical urban landscapes as cultural assets, what are the attitudes of different individuals and organizations to the identities of urban landscapes? What variations are there in the consciousness of historical legacies? Do local people and bodies show greater sensitivity to the landscape than those from elsewhere? To what extent is planning practice consistent with Conzen's standpoint?

Thirdly, three categories of questions about the relationship between planning and outcome merit consideration. They are particularly pertinent to a development-control system that contains a major discretionary element, such as that currently used in Great Britain.

1 What are the priorities of planning authorities as shown by their practice as distinct from their stated intentions? How are these priorities arrived at, and to what extent are they consistently applied?

2 To what extent is the urban landscape a *by-product* of development rather than a planning objective?

3 How important is the interaction between developer and planning authority? How significant is the initial contact between these two parties and to what extent can the interaction between them be seen as a progression towards an improved end-product?

Finally, in considering all these questions a number of sources of variation need to be borne in mind. First, in view of the differences in the factors that have been shown to operate in the development of institutional and public areas, residential areas and commercial cores (Whitehand, 1987), it seems probable that answers to some questions will vary substantially by type of area. For example, the addition of new buildings to spacious sites, such as those occupied by many institutions, is less likely to be constrained by the interests of occupiers of neighbouring sites than would the addition of similarly sized buildings to an already densely built-up residential area. Secondly, it seems probable that there will be variations according to the size, functional type and location of the urban area. For example, an old-established administrative centre is likely to possess a wider range of professions and trades than a suburban town, and its urban landscape will almost certainly contain a more diverse historical legacy. Thirdly, there have been major historical changes in the ownership, development and management of urban areas; an unequivocal answer for one period may be demonstrably false for another. Last, but by no means least, there are large geographical differences, especially national differences, that will have a bearing on the answers to the questions that have been posed.

To what extent can these variables be accommodated within the compass of the present study? In assessing this it is important to bear in mind the nature of the relationship, temporal and spatial, between people and landscape. The inherently local scale at which most people relate to the urban landscape, the small size of the units to which decision-making relates (often individual plots of land), and the short time periods, relative to the life-spans of towns and cities, over which most changes take place necessitate a concern with the micro-scale: the minutiae of urban landscape development are crucial. A further, more practical consideration is the availability of studies that can be drawn upon. These are broadly of two types. First, there are broad conspectuses of particular aspects of urban development, such as by Edwards (1981) and Cherry (1988). Secondly, there are numerous local studies. These range from local histories, of which that by Thompson (1974) is a notable example, to detailed analyses of more-specific aspects of local development, such as those by Trowell (1983) and Short et al. (1986). The local studies rarely reference one another and are seldom comparable. Seldom does either type of study provide direct answers to our questions. However, both provide useful reference points in the design of specific lines of investigation and in making judgements about the wider implications of those investigations.

It is apparent, therefore, that if firm statements are to be made about particular localities and if these statements are to be linked in an intellectually satisfying manner to wider conspectuses, limits must be placed on the extent of coverage, both historical and geographical. Thus, except for the purposes of providing an essential context, no attempt will be made to extend the compass of our study beyond Great Britain during the industrial era. Within that compass the search for answers to our central questions will primarily take the form of a number of specific investigations at the micro-scale. Punter (1989) has argued cogently for the greater use of such a case-study approach. The main problem is establishing the representativeness of the cases studied. The great advantage is the closeness that is achieved to the events under examination. Much depends on the ability to bring to bear a variety of types of evidence and to integrate detailed studies and wider perspectives. The case studies described here will be set within a national context mainly by drawing upon more general conspectuses already published. In practice, an important consideration is the availability of primary sources for detailed case studies. This varies considerably by locality and to an even greater extent by period, thereby placing major constraints on the nature of the geographical and historical comparisons that are possible. An appreciation of the character and limitations of some of these sources is essential before substantive issues can be properly addressed.

SOURCES

Apart from drawing upon a variety of published research by other authors to provide a broader context for particular case studies, this volume makes use of five main sources. These are building applications, planning applications, interviews, correspondence and minutes of meetings of public and institutional bodies. Some general aspects of the first two of these, especially building applications, require consideration before the light they shed on particular questions and localities can be properly assessed.

Building applications, submitted to local authorities in connection with the administration of local building regulations, are one of the most important sources of information about the building of British towns and cities. From various dates in the nineteenth century local authorities have required the submission of building applications for new buildings and alterations to existing buildings (Aspinall and Whitehand, 1980). Although the procedures vary both between authorities, and within individual authorities over time, for each application submitted a brief entry is normally made in a register (since 1947 some authorities have incorporated this information within their register or card index of planning applications). This entry usually indicates the date on which the application was received, the number and type of buildings involved, the name of the street in which the building or buildings are, or are to be, located, the name of the 'depositor' (often the architect), the name of the building owner, the accession number of the application, and whether the application has been approved (figure 1.1, top). The application itself usually includes a completed application form, bearing more information than is in the register. It normally provides the address of the depositor and often that of the building owner. The accompanying drawings include block and ground plans, and elevations and sections – at least in the case of new buildings and major external alterations – and in most cases bear the name and address of the owner and architect (and sometimes of the shopfitter). The drawings reproduced in figure 1.1 represent only a small fraction of the material deposited with the local authority in connection with a single building application. Other material may accompany the application form and the deposited drawings, and

Figure 1.1 Part of one folio of the register of building applications for Northampton (top) and extracts from a deposited plan. The scale of reproduction is in all cases approximately one-quarter of the original. The elevations shown are of both the proposed new building (on the right) and, unusually, the existing premises (on the left). The original drawings are in colour and in the case of those of the proposed new building include sections, elevations and plans of all floors.

COUNTY BOROUGH OF NORTHAMPTON.

Register of Deposited Plans *for Buildings and Estates.*

Date of Deposit 1935	No. of Plan	Name of Person making Deposit	Name of Builder	Name of Owner	Description of Property	Situation of Property	Report of Borough Surveyor on Deposited Plan	Recommendation of Committee	Decision of Council	Date of Service of Notice of Approval or Disapproval
16th May	4350	C. Groucock		Armany Ottomini with law work	Light Games	Towcester Road	And subject to on building bine at back to a General Interest. CONSENT WILL BE &c. IN DUE COURSE	APPROVED	APPROVED	4 JUN 1955
16th Aug	4361	J. S. Beckett jun.		Great Universal Robert Road Stores Ltd	Stores	Nos 35 to 39 Abington Street	Subject to an easement in accordance with the bye-laws	APPROVED	APPROVED	4 JUN 1955

MESSRS GREAT UNIVERSAL STORES LTD.

PROPOSED NEW STORE OR SITE AT

Nos 35, 37, 37A, 39 & 39A ABINGTON STREET, NORTHAMPTON.

SCALE: EIGHT FEET EQUALS ONE INCH

JOHN R. BRANSON & SON ARCHITECTS, 3, ST. JAMES ST, BY, BML.

SURVEY OF PREMISES Nos 35 TO 39A ABINGTON STREET, NORTHAMPTON.

SCALE: EIGHT FEET EQUALS ONE INCH

this may provide further useful information. For example, correspondence between the local authority and other parties filed with the application may enable the names and addresses of the builders, and any consultants and specialized contractors involved, to be ascertained. Post-war applications relating to larger buildings are likely to be accompanied by drawings, prepared by specialist firms, that show considerable structural detail. Separate building inspectors' books or other information filed with the application may reveal the dates of the commencement and completion of construction.

From the 1930s onward several British economists and economic historians used registers of building applications to compile data on variations over time in amounts of housebuilding activity. Among their more recent uses has been their employment in a study of the size structure of the building industry (Aspinall, 1977). There is major scope for their use in the present study in exploring the characteristics of the building industry and of property development and management that underlie the creation of the physical forms of urban areas. Also, the building plans, sections and elevations filed as part of building application provide an invaluable source for the investigation of building types and architectural styles.

Unfortunately, there are a number of limitations on the use of building applications and their registers in geographical research. First, since street numbers are frequently not given, the precise location of a building in a street may not be ascertainable without careful inspection of the plan in conjunction with information from other sources. Secondly, the date of the implementation of the project specified in the application, as distinct from the date of its approval, is not always available and in some instances information is lacking as to whether an approved project was actually implemented. Thirdly, entries in the registers are frequently made chronologically according to the date of receipt of the application and consequently in the case of enquiries about specific buildings, unless their age is known, searches for the requisite entries are likely to be time consuming. This remains a problem even where entries within individual volumes of a register are indexed by street or where separate registers exist for different parts of an urban area, which is sometimes the case with larger towns and cities. Fourthly, there are considerable variations in the accuracy and consistency of the descriptions of building applications in the registers and on the envelopes in which such applications are usually filed, and in some circumstances inaccurate results will be obtained unless the applications themselves are examined. Fifthly, care is needed in deciding on the status of the parties listed in the register as the depositor and owner (sometimes listed under 'by whom' and 'for whom' columns). For example, only in speculative housebuilding projects is the owner normally the builder; for non-residential work the name of the builder is usually only available from the register in the few cases in which an additional column for such names is provided, though it may be possible to ascertain it from correspondence accompanying the application. Finally, the researcher has to contend with the fragile condition of many of the older drawings.

To these limitations should be added problems of access. The degree to which building applications have survived is variable. Some older records have been transferred to local archives. Few areas have complete records for as far back as the middle of the nineteenth century (Aspinall and Whitehand, 1980). Knowledge of records for the period before 1947 is frequently scanty even among local authority staff directly concerned with building control, and the standard of maintenance of older records is often poor.

Unlike the records of building applications, those of planning applications are largely extant, but they cover a much shorter time span. Only since the passing of the Town and Country Planning Act of 1947 have local authorities taken on major responsibilities for planning. Planning applications are similar to building applications in the basic information that they provide about the parties to the proposed development. The file held by the local authority on each planning application submitted generally contains less information about the actual building process and those engaged in it than does the corresponding building-application file. But, unlike building-application files, planning-application files normally reveal, subject to certain qualifications (Larkham, 1986b, p. 4), the ownership of the land to which the application relates, and they contain considerable information about the processing of the application. This includes representations by people who might be affected by the proposed development, statements by consultees, planning officers' reports to their planning committee and a decision notice containing conditions of approval or reasons for refusal.

Thus, the choice between building applications and planning applications as sources of information for a particular investigation will depend on the purpose and time-span of the study. For information concerning the character of a development relative to that of its surroundings, planning applications are preferable, whereas for information on the building industry, for example on the identities and locations of firms undertaking work on particular sites, building applications are a more complete source. Frequently, however, neither source is adequate on its own. As far as information about decision-making is concerned, planning-application files by their very nature present a partial view, recording principally a local authority perspective on a development-control process that is both discretionary and political. At least where value judgements are under consideration, this source needs to be supplemented by sources that reflect other perspectives.

These, then, are major sources to be used in seeking answers to the questions that form the framework of this study. Much of the discussion of the answer that the information from these and a variety of other sources provides will be organized in relation to major functional and geographical areas within the city – the commercial core, institutional and public areas, and residential areas. The absence of a separate discussion of industrial areas reflects a lack of relevant research rather than a judgement that they are of lesser importance. Discussion begins with the area that is usually the functional heart, geographical centre and oldest part of an urban area – the commercial core.

2

Commercial Cores

BACKGROUND

Before the Second World War

Most present-day commercial cores in Great Britain were first laid out in pre-industrial times, mainly for non-commercial purposes. Even today many of their streets, and sometimes even their plots, follow medieval lines. Until the nineteenth century the large majority of central-area buildings were residential as well as commercial. Even in the late-eighteenth century most buildings in commercial cores were dwelling houses into which shop-fronts had been inserted. The shop designed exclusively for commercial purposes was, like the office and the warehouse, largely a product of the industrial era.

In the City of London, buildings designed specifically for office use were not constructed until long after specialized geographical areas, such as the financial quarter, with the Bank of England as its principal focus, had become a major feature (Thorne, 1984, p. 3). Edward I'Anson, architect and surveyor, who was a central figure in the rebuilding of the City of London in mid-Victorian times, recounted in 1872: 'When I first began to build on the new London Bridge approaches, previous to 1840, city offices as now constructed were not thought of; the houses were built as shops and dwellings, or as warehouses, and it was the same in Moorgate Street' (Thorne, 1984, p. 3). It was common even in the 1840s in the City of London for buildings to be constructed so that they could serve either as offices or as dwelling places or as both. Although the insurance companies and banks set the pace in purpose-built offices in the late 1830s, in many respects the buildings themselves involved little departure from existing residential building types (Thorne, 1984, p. 4). However, during the first decade or so of the Victorian period the external appearance of city-centre offices underwent considerable change: the Sun Insurance Office, constructed in London in 1849, expressed a corporate solidity that set it apart from domestic buildings (Duffy, 1980, pp. 260–2). Furthermore, unlike in housebuilding, architects were usually employed, though they were selected much more through networks of personal contacts than by architectural competitions, which were an important means by which the architects of public buildings were selected (Thorne, 1984, p. 5).

The City of London was almost certainly among the first of the commercial cores to begin to lose its domestic scale. But others soon followed suit. Often the change took the form of individual buildings of greater mass being constructed. Occasionally there were larger-scale redevelopments involving the laying-out of entire new streets. Grey Street in central Newcastle upon Tyne, containing the new regional offices of the Bank of England, was laid out in 1835–9 primarily as a commercial street (Allsopp, 1967, pp. 56–60). Its classical buildings were the work of a group of local architects. Within the next two decades, numerous commercial buildings designed by local architects were beginning to transform central Glasgow (Gomme and Walker, 1968, pp. 103–22).

There is considerable evidence to suggest that throughout the nineteenth century the new buildings of Great Britain's commercial cores were almost entirely designed by local architects. This was certainly true of Glasgow, which was Great Britain's second city at that time. Of the changes to the physical fabric of the main streets in central Glasgow between 1886 and 1905, 96 per cent were designed by local architects (Tate, 1983, app. I). Of the few designs by non-local architects, about two-thirds were by architects based in Edinburgh and most of the remainder were by London architects. The predominance of Glasgow architects reflected the fact that the organizations that were commissioning designs were nearly all based in Glasgow. Of the 8 per cent that had their chief office in a city other than Glasgow (nearly all of them banks and insurance companies), about one-half commissioned architects from their own city and the other half chose Glasgow architects. Responsibility for the initiation of new buildings in the main streets of central Glasgow was dispersed among a wide range of firms (figure 2.1).* Between 1886 and 1905 only six owners were responsible for more than one new building, five initiating two each and one, the Caledonian Railway Company, initiating three. Building design was more concentrated, with two prolific Glasgow partnerships accounting for the designs of nearly one-quarter of the buildings erected (figure 2.1).

The most extensive body of systematic information on the building owners and designers responsible for the development of a Victorian commercial core is for the woollen textile town of Huddersfield in West Yorkshire (Thompson, 1987). One aspect upon which this sheds light is the variations in the concentration of building ownership over the period 1871–1929. It provides no support for the view that within individual commercial cores there was an increasing concentration of ownership associated with the acquisition of sites by national organizations. The main influx of national organizations into such ownership occurred after the First World War and the tendency towards plot

---

* Here and throughout 'firm' is used very broadly (unless it is clearly used in its normal sense) to include individuals and organizations engaged in the development process but not strictly in a formal business capacity.

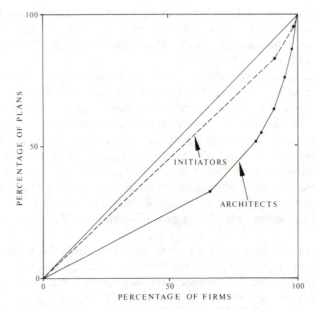

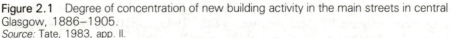

Figure 2.1 Degree of concentration of new building activity in the main streets in central Glasgow, 1886–1905.
Source: Tate, 1983, app. II.

amalgamation that it brought was counterbalanced by opposing forces. It is true that within some street blocks certain owners (in this case long-lease holders as distinct from freeholders) assembled larger units of ownership, but these units sometimes became fragmented when at a later date the property was resold (figure 2.2).

Throughout the Victorian era the design of changes to the physical fabric of central Huddersfield was predominantly the responsibility of local individuals and organizations. During the mid-Victorian building boom the work of non-local architects was confined to a few ornate, prestigious structures (figure 2.3, left). Small-scale developments, perhaps comprising a warehouse or two or three relatively unornamented shops built speculatively, tended to be designed locally. Their designers were persons in the building trade rather than professional architects. Up to the end of the nineteenth century, shop-front replacements, often associated with a change of occupier, were all designed locally.

The first instance of an owner-occupier from outside Huddersfield employing a non-local architect for a development in the commercial core was in 1899. In that year the Prudential Assurance Company, already a major national company, commissioned Alfred Waterhouse, the nationally renowned architect employed earlier to design its offices in central London and Glasgow (Barnard, 1948, p. 72; Tate, 1983, p. xv), to design its local office in Huddersfield's main retailing street. The style and materials were similar to those employed in the London building, the terracotta cladding contrasting with the predominantly local stone of existing nearby buildings.

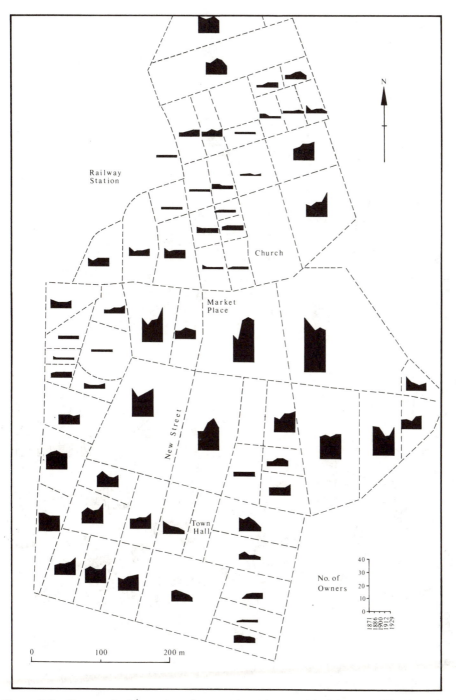

Figure 2.2 Changes in the number of owners in each street block in central Huddersfield, 1871–1929.
Source: Thompson, 1987, table 4.1 and map 4.1.

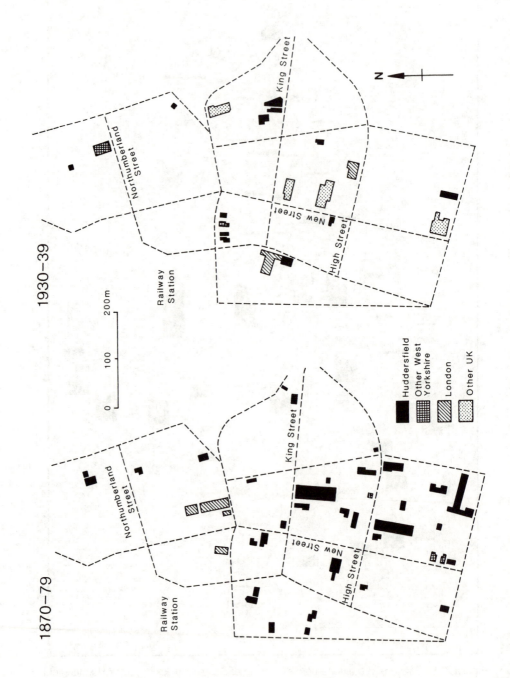

1930–39

1870–79

Railway
Station

Northumberland
Street

New Street

High Street

King Street

N

0   100   200m

Huddersfield
Other West
Yorkshire
London
Other UK

The intrusion of outside influences into central Huddersfield was much more evident in the inter-war period (figure 2.3, right), with national firms, such as F. W. Woolworth & Co., Marks and Spencer and Montague Burton, erecting buildings in their own house style, employing non-local architects and using materials alien to the area. In addition to these new buildings there were shop-front replacements, which became widespread after the First World War as occupiers increasingly adopted the view that the shop-front was crucial in projecting a shop's image. Whereas before the First World War shop-fronts in central Huddersfield had largely been designed by Huddersfield companies, now non-local designs predominated. Initially associated with the establishment of branches of firms based outside Huddersfield, the practice of employing non-local designers was quickly adopted by Huddersfield firms. Between 1918 and 1925 non-local designers introduced 'islands' into the shop-window display area and increased the height of podia. After an average time-lag of some ten years, these changes were adopted by local designers. Simultaneously, specialist 'shopfitters' rose to importance.

The post-war period

For the post-war period there is a sounder basis upon which to reconstruct the main physical changes in commercial cores and the activities of those responsible for them. The major changes in the basis for central-area development and in particular the changes that underlay the unprecedented growth in speculative building in commercial cores in the second half of the 1950s have been described by Whitehouse (1964, pp. 1–125). The main underlying change was financial. A credit squeeze in 1955, just when commercial building was reviving from the aftermath of the Second World War, created financial problems additional to those caused by the inadequacy, for the sizes of the ventures that were beginning to be undertaken, of the types of funding arrangements that had been employed in the 1930s. This situation hastened major developments in the links between property companies and those organizations still able to provide funds on a large scale, most notably the life assurance companies (Whitehouse, 1964, pp. 46–95). During the inter-war period, insurance companies had been significant developers of property in their own right, largely by building premises with accommodation in excess of their own needs and letting the surplus. This activity was in addition to their roles as mortgagees and shareholders. Now their property-development role was greatly expanded both as speculative developers in their own right and more particularly as providers of various forms of funding for development agencies.

There is some evidence to suggest that in the post-war period the significance of speculative building tended to increase relative to that for owner-occupation,

---

Figure 2.3 Provenance of architects of buildings erected in central Huddersfield in 1870–9 and 1930–9.
Source: Thompson, 1987, maps 5.1 and 5.7.

at least by comparison with the first half of this century. In his study of nine
town and city centres in West Yorkshire between 1945 and 1968, Bateman
(1971, p. 26) revealed that the median proportion of private-sector redevelopment (by total floor space) that was speculative was two-thirds. In the case of
office development in the City of London, Barras (1979b, pp. 50–3) found that
during the 1970s a similar proportion of schemes with over 10,000 m^2 of gross
floor space were speculative: this compared with about one-half in the 1950s
and 1960s. However, by the end of the 1970s users were again tending to
increase their share of development. In central Edinburgh about one-half of the
office floor space constructed between 1959 and 1978 was speculative
(McNamara, 1985, table 9.6). How far these figures for West Yorkshire, the City
of London and central Edinburgh may be taken as representative of British
commercial cores is not clear. Information on the number of private-sector
redevelopments (including major reconstructions) in the much smaller central
area of Newcastle under Lyme suggests a rise in the speculative proportion
from one-quarter in the period 1955–64 to one-third in the period 1965–74
(Ross, 1979).

Speculative redevelopment in the post-war period was heavily influenced by
a handful of companies operating on a national scale. It is probable that six
development companies accounted for well over one-half of the major shopping
schemes (those with over 4645 m^2 of gross floor space) – the large majority in
commercial cores – undertaken in Great Britain between 1965 and 1978
(Hillier Parker Research, 1979, p. 33), and Barras (1979b, p. 55, app. 2) has
shown that six development companies accounted for about one-half of the
major office redevelopments (those with over 10,000 m^2 of gross floor space) in
the City of London between 1959 and 1979. The predominance of national
firms in redevelopment generally was already apparent in the study of West
Yorkshire town and city centres by Bateman (1971), in which he revealed that
the median proportion of private-sector redevelopment (by total floor space)
undertaken by national firms was two-thirds.

There would seem to be few central areas in British towns and cities in which
the public sector undertook more than a small share of redevelopment
(Bateman, 1971; Ross, 1979). As far as shopping schemes are concerned,
between 1965 and 1978 the two largest development companies (Town and
City Properties and Ravenseft Properties) were each responsible for nearly
twice as many of the major schemes (those with over 4645 m^2 of gross floor
space) as all local authorities together (Hillier Parker Research, 1979, p. 33),
although it should be noted that in this count joint ventures between a local
authority and a developer were recorded under the name of the developer. In
the large majority of cases local authorities lacked staff with the requisite skills
(Department of the Environment, 1975, pp. 43–5).

Redevelopments for owner-occupation were, like speculative redevelopments, undertaken predominantly by national firms. In central Liverpool in the
1970s major national stores dominated retail redevelopment, apart from one
major shopping scheme (City of Liverpool, 1980, p. 16), and in the commercial
core of Newcastle under Lyme (Ross, 1979) redevelopments for owner-

occupation were also largely undertaken by national firms. The domination of redevelopment in traditional central-area shopping streets by a score or so of major chain-stores is a familiar feature, and when this is coupled with the fact that a high proportion of speculative redevelopments were carried out by a small number of companies, it is apparent that the bulk of commercial-core redevelopment in Great Britain was undertaken by just a few dozen organizations.

The interests engaged in central-area property development are more numerous, however, than such a simple account of developers might suggest. Allowance must be made for the part played by other interests, notably those of land- and property-owners and financial concerns. Information on land ownership is difficult to assemble for England and Wales. The amounts of central-area land owned by local authorities vary widely, from total ownership in central Huddersfield – although here the existence of long leases seriously limits the scope for the local authority to exercise a major influence on the built environment in the near future (Bateman, 1971, pp. 34–5) – to cases in which local authority ownership is largely confined to the sites of certain public buildings, though intermediate positions such as in Birmingham, where approximately one-third of the central area is owned by the local authority (City of Birmingham, 1980, plan 3.5), are probably more normal. On the whole, however, the direct involvement of local authorities in commercial-core redevelopment has not been in proportion to their ownership of land in these areas. For example, in the City of London, the Corporation owned at least part of the site of about one-third of the office redevelopments with over 10,000 m^2 of gross floor space that took place between 1959 and 1979 but was involved in redevelopment itself in only one case (Barras, 1979b, p. 61).

Determining the amounts of central-area land held by private owners is particularly difficult but it is evident that the ownership of such land became increasingly concentrated in the hands of major national concerns. Financial companies constituted the largest single category of landowner in the City of London, judged by the number of sites they owned among those that were developed between 1959 and 1979 (Barras, 1979b, pp. 107–13). The increasing proportion of buildings (as distinct from land) owned by major national concerns is revealed by an examination of the names of owners specified in applications to undertake redevelopments or other major changes to the physical fabric of commercial cores. Data for the commercial cores of Boston, Lincolnshire (Pain, 1980, p. 32), and Newcastle under Lyme (Ross, 1979) show a marked rise in the proportion of non-local owners in the 1950s and 1960s, although there was apparently comparatively little further change in the 1970s.

The main trend in central-area ownership has been the increasing ownership of land and property in such areas by insurance companies and pension funds (Ambrose and Colenutt, 1975, p. 52; Barras, 1979a, p. 43). For example, between 1964 and 1979 insurance companies increased the proportion of their holdings that were in land, property and ground rents from less than one-tenth to over one-fifth (Central Statistical Office, 1964–81), most of their property holdings being freeholds in city centres (Department of the Environment, 1975,

p. 23; Massey and Catalano, 1978, p. 114). In central Edinburgh the amount of land owned by insurance companies increased rapidly in the 1960s and 1970s (figure 2.4). At the same time financial institutions increased their share of the ownership of new office buildings in the City of London, either by undertaking redevelopments themselves or by purchasing sites and completed properties from development companies (Barras, 1979a, p. 34), the Co-operative, Norwich Union, Pearl, Prudential and Standard Life being among the insurance companies known to be active (Barras, 1979b, p. 73). On a national scale, between 1965 and 1978 the Norwich Union acted as a developer in ten shopping schemes with over 4645 m^2 of gross floor space, almost all in small- or medium-sized town centres (Hillier Parker Research, 1979, pp. 3–32). By 1978 financial institutions owned about one-third of the equity of Town and City Properties and Hammerson (Barras, 1979b, p. 74), two of the three main developers of shopping schemes (Hillier Parker Research, 1979, p. 23). Overall, their importance increased relative to that of the property companies, whose role was increasingly one of acting as the development agents of insurance companies and pension funds, at least as far as major schemes on prime sites were concerned (Barras, 1979a, pp. 37–8). Thus, the growth in the funds of insurance companies and pension schemes and the consistently better returns from property than from other investments (Department of the Environment, 1975, p. 23; Economist Intelligence Unit, 1977, p. 7) were major factors underlying the scale of central-area redevelopment.

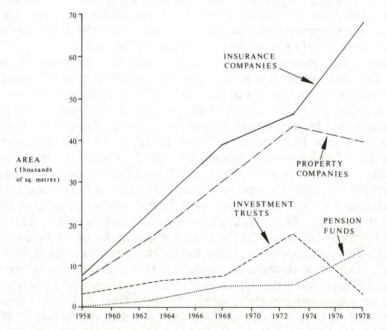

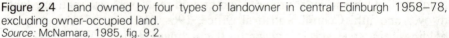

Figure 2.4   Land owned by four types of landowner in central Edinburgh 1958–78, excluding owner-occupied land.
Source: McNamara, 1985, fig. 9.2.

While the interests that owners, users, investors and, to some extent, developers have in property tend to be long term, there are other agents responsible for physical changes to the landscapes of commercial cores whose interests tend to be primarily confined to the changes themselves. Probably the most important of these for the visual environment are architects, shopfitters and, to a lesser extent, construction companies. The evidence for the extent of the areas over which these firms operated, though disparate, suggests the need to take account not only of variations according to type of activity and size of commercial core but also, in many cases, of marked changes over time. For example, a study of Boston, Lincolnshire, has shown that architects submitting plans for commercial-core changes were largely from Boston itself between the First World War and the 1940s, after which they were divided about equally between those with a local and those with a non-local provenance (Pain, 1980, p. 21). Shopfitters, in contrast, were virtually all non-local from the inception of shopfitting as a separate trade in the 1920s (Pain, 1980, pp. 29–30). At the top of the urban hierarchy, in the City of London, construction work became increasingly concentrated in the 1970s in five companies – Trollope and Colls, Higgs and Hill, Wimpey, Laing, and McAlpine (Barras, 1979b, p. 66). But as far as the development process was concerned the role of the construction companies had diminished, at least by comparison with the 1950s and 1960s. By the 1970s they had been replaced by financial institutions, with their growing demand for property as an investment, as the main partners of property companies (Barras, 1979b, pp. 51–3).

At the same time as these changes in private enterprise were occurring, there were changes in the planning policies and activities of central government and local authorities. The precise lines of the cause and effect relation between 'planning' and private enterprise are difficult to disentangle. But there is little doubt that one of the effects of the Town and Country Planning Acts was to add further to the scale of the already large changes stemming from the increasing size of the organizations interested in property: the combining of changes to the road system with redevelopment was certainly facilitated. Nevertheless, the impression, though it is difficult to quantify, is of planners responding to the agents and processes already mentioned more than acting as a positive, directive force (Department of the Environment, 1975, p. 40). Formal comprehensive plans for central areas tended to be slow to emerge and in many cases they were largely a recognition of existing patterns and trends. There would seem to be substance in the view of Ambrose and Colenutt (1975, pp. 178–9) that land-use planning was largely treated as a matter of designating areas in terms of land-use categories essentially to accommodate observed trends in population and employment. And Barras (1979b, p. 95) may not have exaggerated when he suggested that the main effect of central- and local-government planning policy on office development in the City of London was to reinforce underlying market trends. The high proportion of new shopping centres located in existing commercial cores in the 1970s would certainly seem to be attributable, in part, to local- and central-government planning policies, although as with other redevelopments the concern of developers and chain-stores to protect their existing property interests in central areas was almost certainly also a factor (Bennison and Davies, 1980, p. 23). Clearly there is scope for a more positive role for local authorities where they own the freehold of large parts of commercial cores (Department of the Environment, 1975, p. 37), although it is most improbable that there will be a sizeable increase in the amount of redevelopment undertaken directly by local authorities while central government restraints on their expenditure continue.

CASE STUDIES: HISTORY

This sketch of the principal agents and activities underlying the development of commercial cores has provided the setting for a much closer examination of the development of two particular town centres. This examination will address a number of issues that have so far only been touched upon and which demand detailed case studies.

   A major question that requires much closer scrutiny concerns the extent to which owners, their sources of funds, and those they engaged to design and erect their buildings were of local provenance. Can a clear shift from local to non-local design and control within the twentieth century be demonstrated and if so what effect did it have on the nature of the buildings constructed? It seems inescapable, for instance, that boardroom decisions taken in the metropolis against a background of national-scale operations would have produced different results from those taken by local individuals with a field of vision ending abruptly at the edge of their town centre's sphere of influence.

   These considerations are bound up with the consideration of the purposes for which commercial-core buildings were created, including not only what they were intended to function as, for example as a shop or an office, but also the types of return that the owners envisaged them providing, for example, an income from rent and a capital gain and or profit from the occupation of the premises by their own businesses. This leads to related questions concerning differences between bespoke and speculative building in commercial cores. Marriott (1967, pp. 28–9) suggests that bespoke buildings were substantially more costly per unit area than speculative buildings, and Bowley (1966, p. 390), referring to the British building industry in general, expresses the view that 'fashions in speculative markets tended to follow those in the bespoke market at a distance'. Again, looking at the British building industry in general, evidence suggests that bespoke building held up better in economic slumps than speculative building (Whitehand, 1981a), but whether this was true of building in commercial cores and if so whether it had morphological implications of comparable significance to those that have been noted at the urban fringe (Whitehand, 1972) are matters that remain largely unexplored.

Study towns and sources

To enable these and related questions to be considered it is desirable to examine commercial cores in their entirety, to make comparisons between different types of commercial core and, in view of the longevity of buildings (Whitehand, 1978, pp. 84–5; Luffrum, 1980), to examine them over a lengthy time span. Each of these desiderata increases the size of the task of collecting the requisite information, which is a sizeable one for even a small town centre over a time span of only a few decades. Consequently, the decision to study two medium-sized town centres from the First World War until 1980 was a compromise. Exemplars of two major types of British town were sought – a free-standing administrative, commercial and industrial town with a long history and a metropolitan suburban town. In view of the different social and economic histories of these two types of town it was reasonable to suppose that differences would exist between them in regard to the agents of change involved in the development of their commercial cores – for example, in the extent to which owners and architects were local and in the timing of the introduction of metropolitan firms – and that between them they would include some of the major types of commercial building. Practical considerations, notably the length and quality of the available records, to a considerable extent influenced the choice of specific towns.

Northampton, situated in the East Midlands about 100 km north-west of the centre of London, was selected as exemplifying historic English county towns with important administrative, commercial and industrial functions. In terms of its social and economic characteristics it is in many respects a typical English town (Moser and Scott, 1961, pp. 134–5), although its recent population growth, associated with its designation as a New Town in 1968, has been above average. Watford, situated 25 km north-west of the centre of London, was selected as an example of a suburban town, judged by its social and economic characteristics (Moser and Scott, 1961, pp. 120–1). Northampton's population rose from 92,000 in 1921 to 157,000 in 1981 and that of Watford from 48,000 to 74,000 over the same period, although these census figures are for the administrative areas of the two towns and understate the population catchments of their commercial cores, especially in the case of the more recent figure for Watford, which in the post-war period became part of an almost continuously built-up zone surrounding the metropolis. Watford was much the faster growing of the two towns in the inter-war period and by the Second World War the population of the catchment area of its commercial core was probably similar to that of central Northampton.

For the purposes of the study each commercial core was defined according to the extent of central commercial land use in 1980. In both towns outlying office buildings, and arterial shopping ribbons that extended out from the centre and comprised local rather than central-area shops, were excluded from the definition of the commercial core. Attention was confined at this stage to new buildings that were, to use the terminology of Conzen (1969, p. 128), plot dominants – the principal building, normally occupying the street frontage, on each site. Information about each new building, ranging in size from a single-fronted shop to a multi-functional complex occupying a whole street block, was extracted from building applications housed in the building control sections of the two boroughs. Since the dates when buildings were completed could not always be ascertained from the information filed with the building applications, for the sake of consistency the year of erection of buildings was deemed to be that in which the application was received by the local authority, although many buildings were known to have been completed in the next year, or even later. For a few buildings either there was no record that a building application had been received or the application was missing or lacked the necessary information. In some cases it was possible to obtain the missing information from the applicant but in others less complete information was obtained, or inferred, from a variety of other sources, notably Goad fire insurance plans for Northampton, Kelly's directories, and photographs in the reference section of Watford Central Library and the local history section of Northampton Central Library. In the rare cases in which the year when a building was constructed had, as a last resort, to be inferred from Kelly's directories alone, the year prior to that in which the change of entry occurred in the directory was assumed to be the date when the building was erected. Practically all the necessary information about buildings was eventually compiled, but a few names and addresses of owners and architects remained untraced. For this reason the number of buildings upon which the discussion is based differs slightly according to the aspect being considered.

The eve of the First World War

Before examining chronologically the buildings constructed in the two town centres between the First World War and 1980 it is appropriate briefly to consider each centre as a physical entity just before this period.

Immediately before the First World War, Watford was a town of inconspicuous buildings. The main exceptions in the town centre, nearly all of them recent constructions, were the Palace Theatre, the Palace Roller Skating Rink, the Central Hall Picture House, the Library, St Mary's Church and a small number of late-Victorian and Edwardian shop-front buildings. Most of the buildings were built predominantly of brick, traditionally the main building material in the area (Whitehand, 1967b), though a sizeable number had a rendering of stucco or roughcast.

Northampton had a much grander endowment of buildings, consistent with its role as a major central place within the east Midlands. In addition to All Saints' Church, there was the imposing Corn Exchange, the County Hall, Guildhall, Library, Museum and Grand Hotel and the Northamptonshire Union Bank, to mention but a few of the centrally located buildings. Most of these and many of the lesser buildings in the central area were either faced with or constructed of stone – a common, though by no means universal, building material in the area for many centuries (Clifton-Taylor, 1972, p. 121).

In their plans both town centres retained a considerable legacy from the medieval period. Plot widths in both centres were predominantly of 10 m or less, Conzen's 'standard' burgage width (Conzen, 1960, pp. 33–4), although buildings with special functions, such as inns, often occupied wider plots. Building densities were lower in central Watford, largely reflecting lower building coverages. Building heights too were on average a little lower in central Watford, although, as in central Northampton, the large majority of buildings were of two or three storeys. The commercial core of Watford comprised a single, long, medieval street, joined at right angles by short stretches of five other streets (figure 2.5). That of Northampton, in contrast, comprised a multiplicity of streets, largely reflecting a complex series of adjustments in its town plan in medieval times (Lee, 1953).

At the time of the First World War Northampton was clearly above Watford in the urban hierarchy, and further back in time the gap between the two towns was even greater, for Northampton was a major medieval town when Watford consisted of little more than an elongated street market. It was only Watford's growth as a suburban centre from the late-nineteenth century that created a town with a sphere of influence that in population size approached that of Northampton.

Northampton's higher position in the urban hierarchy was reflected in the fact that over 50 retail and service chains were already established in its commercial core in 1914 (Kelly's Directories, 1914). This was about double the number established in central Watford (Kelly & Co., 1917), although, as in central Watford, only a small minority of these were in buildings designed for them. The majority of premises in both centres were built well before multiple-shop retailing came into existence, many being pre-Victorian. Even in the 20 years before the First World War the large majority of buildings constructed in both centres were initiated by local companies and (to judge from the frequency with which owners are described in building applications as 'Mr', 'Mrs', 'Dr' or 'Esquire', or simply accorded a surname and initials) by local individuals – in the case of central Watford mostly by individuals, for Watford lacked Northampton's diversity of local firms and organizations. These buildings were largely designed by local architects, the few exceptions mostly having been designed for occupation by retail and service chains. Those built in central Northampton were on average more grandiose, sometimes being heavily ornamented as became centrally-located commercial buildings in an important Edwardian provincial town. Watford, still little more than an overgrown market town, did not justify quite such heavy capital investment, although the stylistic features of the period were clearly present, if in more muted form.

The First World War and recovery

The different patterns and styles of new building in the two centres at the end of the First World War and in the early years following it were influenced by a number of national and local factors. Particularly important nationally was the fact that, apart from a short-lived post-war boom, there was a generally depressed level of economic activity (Jones, 1935), accompanied by reduced real incomes (Prest, 1948), a slight decline in employment in the distributive trades (Jefferys, 1954, p. 50) and a low level of construction for retailing as for most other purposes (Richardson and Aldcroft, 1968, p. 62). Locally important

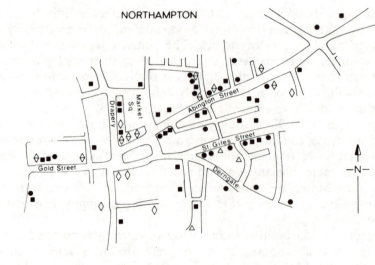

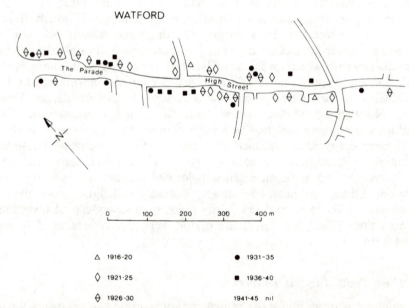

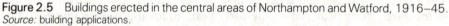

Figure 2.5   Buildings erected in the central areas of Northampton and Watford, 1916–45.
Source: building applications.

factors were central Northampton's initial advantage over central Watford in population catchment, and the already established pattern within London's suburban ring of capitalizing on rapid population growth by constructing speculative shopping parades. Also important was the fact that within or near the commercial core of Watford some large, mostly residential, plots were owned by private individuals. These were more easily acquired for redevelopment within or extensions to the commercial core than were the inner fringe belt of institutional, public-utility and industrial sites, and the areas of high-density terrace housing, that enclosed the commercial core of Northampton.

The booms in the construction of speculative shopping parades with offices above that occurred in central Watford in 1920–4 and 1926–8 (figure 2.6) can be attributed in part to local factors. It was in some respects almost as if the war had never happened, for similar structures had been erected immediately before the war – indeed a few shops were put up even during the war. As had previously been the case, these speculative developments were initiated overwhelmingly by local individuals, more than one generation in a family sometimes being involved. These included a novelist (A. B. Cox), to whom property in the town had passed by inheritance (Jones, 1971), a veterinary surgeon (F. T. Trewin), a printer (D. Greenhill), an army officer (P. Fisher) and a butcher (F. E. Fisher, brother of P. Fisher). The third of these, D. Greenhill, had, it would seem, acquired much of his property for development with the proceeds of his business activities (Leech and Cook, 1951) and the last two, P. and F. E. Fisher, had probably acquired much of theirs using the proceeds of the butchery and other activities of their father (F. Fisher), who had been a prominent local figure before the First World War and had himself been active in property development in the town (*West Herts and Watford Observer*, 1917). D. Greenhill also became a prominent figure in the town, but the positions there of several other developers remain obscure. During the period 1920–8, nine individuals were responsible for developments involving two or more shops and P. Fisher and F. E. Fisher between them undertook four separate developments within the period 1923–7.

Whereas in the years before and during the First World War Watford architects had predominated, now plans were shared about equally with architects from outside the town (figure 2.6). One local architect (W. Grace) was responsible for five developments. Although each of these had a distinctive style, there were strong stylistic resemblances to war-time and immediately pre-war buildings. Neo-Georgian styles, one of which was used in the first building constructed in central Watford after the First World War (Figure 2.7A), were to dominate new building there until the mid-1950s (figure 2.6). The style of the building shown in figure 2.7A closely resembled the style of those put up within short distances on either side just before the war (figure 2.7B, C). A further shopping parade erected close by in 1923 was also neo-Georgian, and a shop-and-office block in the vicinity arguably justifies that description (figure 2.7D). Furthermore, during 1920–3 four buildings in Edwardian styles were constructed (figure 2.7E), so there was undoubtedly an architectural-style bridge across what has traditionally been regarded as a major division between morphological periods (Conzen, 1960, pp. 7–9). In building materials too there was little change from the pre-war period, brick, occasionally with a rendering of roughcast or stucco, being almost universal, although the speculative boom

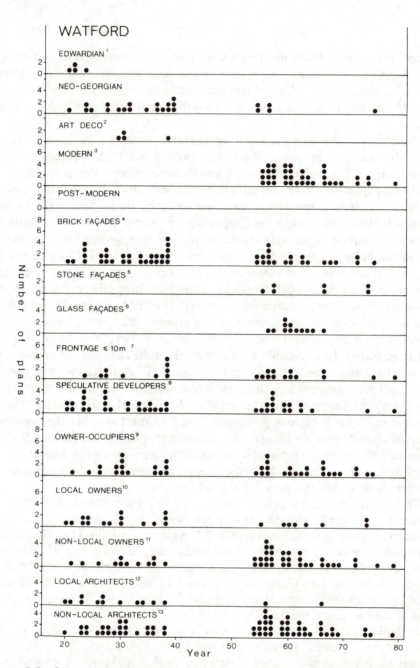

WATFORD

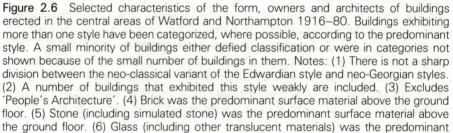

Figure 2.6 Selected characteristics of the form, owners and architects of buildings erected in the central areas of Watford and Northampton 1916–80. Buildings exhibiting more than one style have been categorized, where possible, according to the predominant style. A small minority of buildings either defied classification or were in categories not shown because of the small number of buildings in them. Notes: (1) There is not a sharp division between the neo-classical variant of the Edwardian style and neo-Georgian styles. (2) A number of buildings that exhibited this style weakly are included. (3) Excludes 'People's Architecture'. (4) Brick was the predominant surface material above the ground floor. (5) Stone (including simulated stone) was the predominant surface material above the ground floor. (6) Glass (including other translucent materials) was the predominant

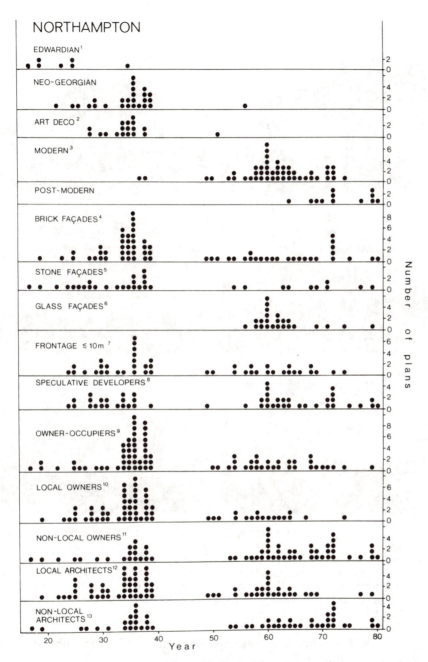

NORTHAMPTON

EDWARDIAN[1]

NEO-GEORGIAN

ART DECO[2]

MODERN[3]

POST-MODERN

BRICK FAÇADES[4]

STONE FAÇADES[5]

GLASS FAÇADES[6]

FRONTAGE ≤ 10m[7]

SPECULATIVE DEVELOPERS[8]

OWNER-OCCUPIERS[9]

LOCAL OWNERS[10]

NON-LOCAL OWNERS[11]

LOCAL ARCHITECTS[12]

NON-LOCAL ARCHITECTS[13]

Number of plans

Year

surface material above the ground floor. (7) For buildings on street corners the frontage onto the more important street has been measured. (8) Includes buildings in which the owner occupied space above the ground floor only. (9) Excludes buildings in which the owner occupied space above the ground floor only. (10) Owner whose address was within the town. (11) Owner whose address was outside the town. (12) Architect whose address was within the town. Builders submitting plans are excluded, as is a case in which the design was shared with a non-local architect. (13) Architect whose address was outside the town. One case in which a builder submitted a plan is excluded, but a case in which the design was shared with a local architect is included.
Source: building applications.

Figure 2.7 Buildings erected in central Watford, 1910–28 (photographs by the author, 1982/83). (A) Designed in 1920 by S. C. Addison, Eastbourne for J. Mitchener Esq. (B) Designed in 1910 by A. Burst, London for J. Rodwell, Watford. (C) Designed in 1910 by C. P. Ayres, Watford for Barclays Bank, London. (D) Designed in 1923 by S. Dawe, Rickmansworth for F. E. Fisher, King's Langley. (E) Designed in 1921 by W. Grace, Watford for F. T. Trewin, Watford. (F) Designed in 1928 by Moore-Smith & Colbeck, London for A. B. Cox, Watford.

ended in 1927–8 with four developments, three of them substantial, in neo-Tudor style (figure 2.7F).

Although in central Watford the speculative shopping parades of the 1920s exhibited considerable continuity with immediately pre-war and war-time developments in terms of architectural styles and building materials and the provenance of owners and architects, the scale of development was larger. Whereas previously buildings had frequently been replaced within plots of 10 m or less in width, now there was a tendency either for more than one plot to be included in a redevelopment or for larger plots not previously in commercial use to be taken in. The result was a greater interspersing of traditional-scale frontages, each with an independently designed building, with stretches in which a frontage equivalent to that of several traditional plots was occupied by a building designed as a single entity.

Building activity during the last years of the First World War and the ten years following had a quite different character in central Northampton. Scarcely a speculative shop was erected there in that period. In so far as any stimulus was given to new building it stemmed largely from the activities of organizations whose headquarters were outside the town. The Post Office moved to a major purpose-built structure in 1917, the Co-operative Wholesale Society erected a spacious new warehouse in 1919 (figure 2.8A) as part of a large increase in capital expenditure nationally (Redfern, 1938, p. 225) and the YWCA erected a memorial hall in the same year as part of its drive to provide facilities for the increasing number of women in the labour force (N. Watkins, YWCA, personal communication). The next development did not take place until 1922, when Lloyds Bank constructed an imposing building (figure 2.8B) on the large corner-site of the George Hotel. Again, this should be viewed as part of a national development scheme by Lloyds rather than as an outcome of local events (Winton, 1982, pp. 18–21). In the following year the construction of a billiard hall maintained the exclusively non-retail aspect of post-war building.

Figure 2.8 Buildings erected in central Northampton, 1919–28 (photographs by the author, 1982/83). (A) Designed in 1919 by the Co-operative Wholesale Society, London for itself. (B) Designed in 1922 by F. W. Dorman, Northampton for Lloyds Bank, London. (C) Designed in 1924 by C. Dorman & Son, Northampton for H. C. Hudson, Northampton. (D) Designed in 1925 by F. W. Dorman, Northampton for the Pearl Assurance Co., London. (E) Designed in 1926 by Campbell, Jones Sons, Smithers & Brown, London and J. Brown, Northampton for the Westminster Bank, London. (F) Designed in 1928 by F. H. Allen, Northampton for A. P. Hawtin & Sons, Northampton.

The lack of retail building in central Northampton at this time should be seen in the context of the small amounts of such building nationally (Richardson and Aldcroft, 1968, p. 62). However, when the first post-war buildings for retailing were eventually erected in central Northampton in 1924 and 1925, they were only single shop-front buildings on sites marginal to the retail core (figure 2.5), whereas by this time a national recovery in retail building was in full swing, albeit more actively in the suburbs than in existing commercial cores. The construction of other buildings in central Northampton in the mid-1920s, by the Northampton Electric Light and Power Co., the Pearl Assurance Co. and the Westminster Bank, followed the earlier post-war trend in Northampton for public services and financial organizations to be responsible for nearly all new building in the town centre, although now the sites redeveloped tended to be less peripheral than previously.

In central Northampton, despite the fact of ownership in several cases by national firms and organizations, the buildings erected during this time, unlike those erected then in central Watford, were predominantly designed by local architects (figure 2.6). And there, as in central Watford, neither stylistically nor in terms of the building materials used did the First World War mark a clear divide. The majority of the new buildings continued to be constructed of stone, or at least had a stone cladding (figure 2.6), and exhibited both the classicism and the eclecticism associated with the Edwardian period. Two of the new buildings there, both of which could have passed as 20 years older than they were, had a distinct resemblance to one another (figure 2.8C, D). However, different owners, one local and the other from London, were involved. Although the local architects employed shared the same surname (Dorman), the fact that they occupied separate premises and that no family connection is mentioned in the obituary of one of them (*Northampton Independent*, 1956) suggests that they were unrelated.

While these stylistic time-lags are of great interest, in assessing the period of recovery after the First World War the differences in the functional types of buildings that were erected in the two commercial cores merit special attention. The domination of new building in central Northampton at this time by functions other than retailing may reflect in part the greater resilience of bespoke building for public and private institutions at a time when shop building, a more-risky venture, was experiencing difficulties in raising capital, not least from within the retail trade. In the 1920s, property companies were still in their infancy (Whitehouse, 1964, p. 4) and most retailers constructing premises for their own occupation relied for capital on private sources and the reinvestment of profits (Jefferys, 1954, pp. 143–4). Retailing in central Northampton in the 1920s was primarily controlled by privately-owned companies and organizations; the appeal for funds on the open market, which contributed to the building boom in the 1930s, had as yet been made by only a small number of national chains.

If this is a plausible scenario for Northampton, why were developments so different in Watford? Part of the explanation would seem to lie in differences in landownership. Much of central Watford was still in the hands of individuals, rather than limited liability companies or corporate organizations. Although the circumstances of some of these individuals remain obscure, a strong inference may be drawn from the cases of five of them about whom there is information, that, perhaps not untypically of the Home Counties at the time, the funds applied to the construction of speculative shopping parades came from activities not primarily connected with either retailing or the development of town-centre property (*West Herts and Watford Observer*, 1917; Kelly & Co., 1929; Leech and Cook, 1951; Jones, 1971). This, combined with the less constraining morphological inheritance in central Watford and the much more rapid population growth within its vicinity, must go at least some way towards explaining the boom in shop building there at a time when almost no such development was undertaken in central Northampton. Conversely, Watford lacked both the strong local institutions and, because of its lower rank as a central place, the attractiveness to national organizations necessary to generate the bespoke developments that characterized building in central Northampton at this time.

From the late 1920s to the Second World War

Although the late 1920s are not conventionally regarded as constituting a dividing line between morphological periods, there is a case for treating them as such in both centres, though for partly different reasons. In central Watford, after eight years dominated by speculative shop developments, save for the purpose-built structures by Montague Burton, Lilley & Skinner and a local brewery, the next three years from 1929 to 1931 were characterized by a variety of new buildings, each partly, if not entirely, for owner-occupation. Five of these were for major national concerns (including the Westminster Bank, Timothy Whites, and the Post Office), but six were for local concerns (including the department store of J. Cawdell & Co., the offices of the municipally-owned Watford Gas Company, and the municipal market). The bespoke developments of 1929 for the Plaza Cinema and of 1930 for J. Cawdell & Co. departed from the neo-Georgian and neo-Tudor styles that dominated the mid- and late-1920s in central Watford. Instead, Art Deco was used – the only examples of this style in central Watford except for its use in the refashioning of the Central Hall Picture House and in muted form in the construction of Timothy Whites' shop of 1930 and the Watford Electricity Company offices of 1938. J. Cawdell & Co. (figure 2.9A) employed the same architect, Moore-Smith & Colbeck, that only two years earlier had designed a conservative, neo-Tudor speculative parade of shops and offices (figure 2.7F). The Watford Gas Company and the Post Office, however, were as conservative as the speculative developers in the 1920s and staunchly maintained the neo-Georgian tradition (figure 2.10A, B). Architects from outside the town (non-local architects in figure 2.6), especially from London, were now achieving an ascendancy that they never subsequently lost.

After a pause in building activity in 1932, corresponding to a short but marked national decline in the amount of retail building (Richardson and

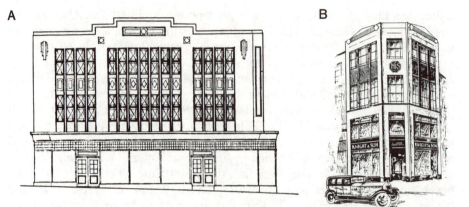

Figure 2.9   (A) Front elevation of the department store of J. Cawdell & Co., Watford, from a building application by Moore-Smith & Colbeck, London, 1930. (B) Print of the shop of Knight & Son, Northampton in the 1930s (from Northampton Central Library, Local History section). The building was designed for A. & L. Knight, Northampton, by Home & Knight, London, in 1927.

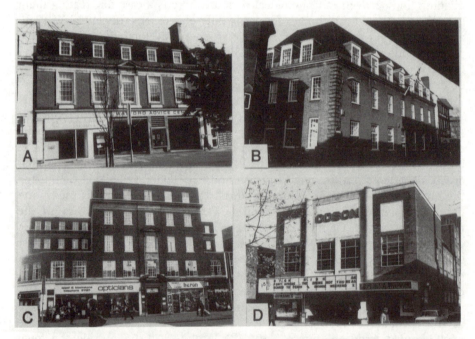

Figure 2.10   Buildings erected in central Watford in the 1930s (photographs by the author, 1982/83). (A) Designed in 1930 by S. Dawe, Rickmansworth for Watford Gas Co., Watford. (B) Designed in 1931 by H. M. Office of Works, London for the Post Office. (C) Designed in 1935 by the Prudential Assurance Co., London for itself. (D) Designed in 1936 by J. Owen Bond, Norwich for Gaumont Super Cinemas.

Aldcroft, 1968, p. 332), redevelopment in central Watford continued intermittently throughout the 1930s, but showed little evidence of the relatively high levels of commercial building activity that occurred nationally at this time. Some of the buildings erected, however, were sizeable and the use of company architects, a practice in which Boots the Chemists had been a forerunner before the First World War, increased. Speculative building ventures by individuals were being succeeded by those by companies and trusts. Indicative of the trend was the formation by D. Greenhill, one of the individuals who had undertaken a development in the 1920s, of a development company, Watford Ideal Homes. In 1934, employing its associate company, David Scott (Builders), it constructed at the north end of the main street the largest shopping parade yet. It was only now in central Watford that it was becoming common for speculative developments to be initiated by organizations rather than individuals. In 1935 the Prudential Assurance Co. erected a major five-storey neo-Georgian building, designed by its own architects' department and containing offices on the upper floors, partly for its own use, and shops to let on the ground floor (figure 2.10C) – a type of development that was becoming familiar in provincial towns. In the remaining four years of the 1930s, ten further buildings were erected in central Watford, considerably less than one-half of the number erected in central Northampton. They were a mixture of speculative and bespoke buildings, mostly brick built, in neo-Georgian style, and mainly designed by architects from outside the town, predominantly from London. Except for Marks and Spencer, Gaumont Super Cinemas (figure 2.10D) and the International Tea Company, the commercial chains were not active in constructing new buildings there at the end of the 1930s.

In central Northampton in the second half of the 1920s the implementation of a sequence of about 60 plans for new buildings was begun that by 1939 had substantially altered the town centre, in particular the main shopping streets of Gold Street, Abington Street and Drapery, and the functionally more mixed St Giles Street (figure 2.5). The only year during that period when no plans were implemented was 1932, a year in which a national decline in non-residential building occurred, and in 1936 no fewer than 13 buildings were constructed. Apart from the accelerated activity in comparison with the years of the First World War and the first half of the 1920s, a number of new features distinguish this period. First, the focus of activity shifted from the edges of the commercial core to the main shopping streets. Secondly, as well as local firms and organizations and national retail and service chains, for the first time in Northampton national property companies were involved. Thirdly, in many cases the construction of new buildings was linked to street-widening schemes. Fourthly, Art Deco and neo-Georgian styles replaced Edwardian styles, the neo-Georgian styles being associated initially with increasing use of brick, although the use of stone as a cladding material revived in the late 1930s (figure 2.6). Finally, architects from outside the town were now taking a large number of commissions, though still substantially fewer than local architects.

In central Northampton, the change from Edwardian to inter-war architectural styles was highlighted in adjacent buildings constructed by the

Westminster Bank and A. & L. Knight (figures 2.8E and 2.9B) – the first built
in 1926 and the second, one of a minority of cases in central Northampton in
which an owner-occupier redeveloped *in situ*, in 1927. The Westminster Bank
building was designed jointly by Campbell, Jones Sons, Smithers & Brown of
London and J. Brown of Northampton, and was unambiguously Edwardian in
style. A. & L. Knight's building was designed by Home & Knight of London
and, with the exception of the use by the Co-operative Wholesale Society of its
own architects for its warehouse immediately after the war, was the first
inter-war building in central Northampton on which a London firm of
architects was exclusively employed – indeed architects from anywhere outside
Northampton have rarely been engaged by Northampton owners at any time.
It not only provided a local preview of the modern movement but showed the
unmistakable hallmarks, though not the flamboyant excesses, of Art Deco.
Although small, it was highly conspicuous in a commercial core that was still
architecturally in the Edwardian period. As if to emphasize the point, in 1928
the local firm of A. P. Hawtin & Sons erected, just round the corner and
overlooking Market Square, a fine, four-storey office building, whose neo-
Georgian style, to the design of local architect F. H. Allen, gave it the aura of
a building constructed before the First World War (figure 2.8F). But this was a
final celebration of an era whose architectural hallmarks had passed out of
fashion a decade earlier. In the same year the most prolific initiator of new
buildings in central Northampton in the inter-war period, the local firm of A. R.
& W. Cleaver, adopted Art Deco for a new building just off Abington Street,
designed by local architects L. Carter & Coles. Thereafter Art Deco, together
with neo-Georgian, the main style at this time in central Watford, characterized
additions to the townscape of central Northampton until the Second World
War, although some less readily categorized styles were also employed.

Outside influence in central Northampton was by this time considerable.
Whereas hitherto the retail chains had mainly moved into existing premises,
now they began to undertake developments themselves. This was part of a
greater emphasis nationally on sales promotion, which included giving greater
attention to the location of branches, shop layout, and window display (Jefferys,
1954, p. 89). Success in competitive image projection on the high streets
required capital investment on an unprecedented scale, both to acquire what
were now expensive sites and to undertake large-scale rebuilding. This capital
was being increasingly provided by the conversion of successful privately-owned
businesses into public companies (Jefferys, 1954, p. 143), a process that had
begun before the First World War. Because of the size and number of properties
developed by the larger chain-stores in the inter-war period, the ability to raise
funds on the open market became almost indispensable (Jefferys, 1954,
pp. 143–4). Property itself now became a major consideration for the chain-
stores, and the majority of those with branches in Northampton or Watford, or
in both towns, that had not created their own estates departments before the
First World War now did so. Not only did the amount of work often justify the
employing of company architects, but an increasing concern to project a
company image was an added incentive to do so.

The manoeuvring for position that took place in the main shopping streets of Northampton is illustrated by the activities of Montague Burton, the tailors, who, as in Watford, were the first chain-store after the First World War to have their own premises constructed. Nationally, they were one of the most rapidly growing of all the multiple-shop retailers in the inter-war years (Council of the Stock Exchange, 1940, p. 1049; Jefferys 1954, pp. 296–300). Having occupied what had previously been a grocer's shop strategically placed between Marks and Spencer's Bazaar and Home and Colonial Stores in Drapery in the early 1920s (Kelly's Directories, 1920, 1924), they initiated in 1929 their own development of a larger and even more strategic site in Gold Street, which was at the time the town's main shopping street. This site included the premises of an existing outfitters (Kelly's Directories, 1928). As in their more modest development in Watford in 1921, they used a firm from their home city of Leeds to design their new building. Only six years later, when the retail centre of gravity was shifting from Gold Street to Abington Street, a site became available in connection with a scheme for street widening at what was to become the key street junction in the town centre, where Abington Street meets Wood Hill and Market Square. This site, which included the premises of a gentlemen's outfitters (Kelly's Directories, 1931), was also acquired and a further development was initiated, this time designed by the company's own architect (figure 2.11A).

These activities suggest a considerable degree of accommodation by Montague Burton to changing local circumstances, and this seems to have extended to the choice of building materials. Despite the predominance of stone façades in developments in central Northampton in the 1920s, most new buildings erected there between the construction of the first and second Burton buildings had been brick, albeit often with stone dressings. A letter, dated 23 January 1936, from the Estates Manager of Montague Burton to Northampton's Town Clerk (building application no. A486) reveals that the use of 'fireclay with terra cotta' had originally been proposed for the second Burton building but a change to an artificial stone resembling Portland stone had been made 'to satisfy public opinion'. While this is not in itself conclusive evidence that local opinion was a significant influence on the choice of building materials, it is consistent with the fact that stone became comparatively common as a façade material in buildings erected in the subsequent four years up to the beginning of the Second World War, though it did not quite regain its predominance over brick (figure 2.6).

From the standpoint of Montague Burton such matters were merely the local aspect of a major entry into property ownership and management that was going on in major towns and cities the length and breadth of the country and that left variants of the firm's house style firmly imprinted on urban landscapes as far apart as Truro and Aberdeen (Redmayne, 1950, pp. 374–480). The important place that property and its management now occupied in the firm's activities was reflected in its changing organizational structure, especially in its development of subsidiary property companies (Council of the Stock Exchange, 1940, pp. 1049–50). But if Montague Burton's decisions to build in Northampton

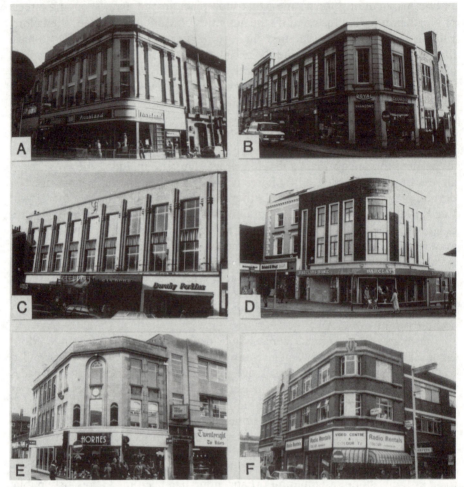

Figure 2.11 Buildings erected in central Northampton in the 1930s (photographs by the author, 1982/83). (A) Designed in 1935 by Montague Burton, Leeds for themselves. (B) Designed in 1934 by F. H. Allen, Northampton for Northampton Liberal Club. (C) Designed in 1936 by Hillier, Parker, May & Rowden, London for Sterling Estates, London. (D) Designed in 1938 by F. H. Allen, Northampton for D. A. Coldham, Northampton. (E) Designed in 1938 by F. H. Allen, Northampton for Fraser Son & Mackenzie, Northampton. (F) Designed in 1934 by W. L. Carter, Northampton for A. R. & W. Cleaver, Northampton.

must be seen as part of company policy formulated at the national level, so must they be seen in the context of decisions about property made by numerous other chain-stores.

Close on the heels of Montague Burton in redevelopment in central Northampton were F. W. Woolworth & Co. Having extended their premises in Gold Street in 1920, they opened a second shop in Abington Street in 1928, just before Montague Burton initiated their first new building in the town. The complete redevelopment of a site in central Northampton by F. W. Woolworth

& Co. did not take place until 1934, after the national slump in non-residential building in 1931–3, and it was the Gold Street store that was replaced. They were already using their own architects' department in 1920, unlike the other great variety chain-store of the time, Marks and Spencer, which, unusually among the major retail chains, has a long history of employing architects from outside the company. Although Marks and Spencer opened a bazaar in Drapery before the First World War (Kelly's Directories, 1914), they, like Montague Burton, undertook their first major central-Northampton property development in Gold Street in 1929, retaining the front portion of the existing building. Between 1934 and 1939 Great Universal Stores, Littlewoods, Associated British Cinemas, United Counties Bus Co., Northampton Co-operative Society, the Co-operative Wholesale Society, Martins Bank, and three breweries were additions to the list of retail and service chains initiating the construction of buildings for their own occupation, about one-half of them employing their own company architects, and architects from outside the town being employed by the majority of the remainder.

To these mainly outside influences in Northampton may be added those of the speculative developers. One of the most important speculative developments there was carried out by the Prudential Assurance Co. Earlier, in its new premises in Drapery, the Pearl Assurance Co. had let the space that was surplus to its requirements. In 1931 the Prudential did the same on a larger scale at the junction of Derngate and St Giles Street. In this way insurance companies invested directly in property in the inter-war period, as has already been noted in Watford. The Prudential development, however, was noteworthy in two other respects. First, it was part of one of the more extensive of several major street widenings associated with town planning schemes aimed at reducing bottle-necks in the still essentially medieval street system. Secondly, it introduced into central Northampton, through the medium of the Prudential's own architects' department, an architectural style that was to recur several times, mainly in buildings designed by the local architect F. H. Allen; this endowed parts of the southern side of St Giles Street that had been subject to street widening with an unusual degree of unity for a street that had undergone several centuries of piecemeal replacement (figure 2.11B).

If the Prudential building was not wholly speculative, in that part was owner-occupied, several subsequent developments in the 1930s were. These tended to be less flamboyant than their chain-store counterparts. Somewhat unusually for central Northampton as late as this, one was initiated by a local individual, F. W. Panther, Vice-Chairman of J. Sears & Co., the True-Form Boot Co. (Council of the Stock Exchange, 1940, p. 1816; *Northampton Independent*, 1944). But three others were initiated by London-based firms – Central Commercial Properties, B & S Property Trust, and Sterling Estates (figure 2.11C). All three were designed by the London firm of Hillier, Parker, May & Rowden (primarily known as estate agents), but the connection between the developments extended beyond matters of design. One leading personage in Hillier, Parker, May & Rowden was a major figure and major shareholder in Central Commercial Properties (which was located adjacent to the premises of

Hillier, Parker, May & Rowden in Maddox Street, London) and another had a similar position in Sterling Estates (Marriott, 1967, pp. 15–16). Furthermore, B & S Property Trust shared the same premises as Hillier, Parker, May & Rowden. The implication is that speculative development in central Northampton was more concentrated in the hands of a few than the spatial dispersion and varied architecture of the buildings, and a casual inspection of the names of the organizations responsible, might suggest. The physical effects of these developments, however, were not great, for, as in central Watford, the proliferation of speculative development by national firms did not occur until the post-war period.

Local influences in central Northampton were various in the 1930s, developments for owner-occupation being more numerous than speculative developments. Most new buildings were designed by local architects, and architectural styles were conservative, especially for speculative ventures. Indeed, the architectural styles of speculative buildings initiated by local owners employing local architects were exceeded in their conservativeness only by those of the bespoke buildings for the breweries and banks. Only a little less conservative on average were the styles of the few speculative ventures by outside firms. Next in radicalness came the styles of the local bespoke shop developments and finally, vying with one another in ostentation, those of the new premises of the national chain-stores. The latter had an especially pronounced physical impact where they replaced several pre-Victorian buildings on narrow plots, as occurred when Great Universal Stores had new premises erected in Abington Street (figure 1.1).

Yet, if the national chain-stores brought changes of scale and stylistic excesses to central Northampton, numerous smaller buildings there, mostly initiated and designed locally, had a strong moderating effect; they were often adjusted to traditional plot dimensions and reflected a slower adoption of new architectural fashions. The work of the most prolific local architect, F. H. Allen, in designing individual building replacements within the constraints of existing plot boundaries, illustrates this effect. It also shows a stylistic evolution, picking up features exhibited earlier in designs by less conservative architects; for example, echoing (figure 2.11B) the restrained neo-Georgian style of the nearby Prudential building, flirting with the modern movement in 1938 (figure 2.11D), perhaps influenced by the Knight & Son building of 1927 (figure 2.9B), and in the same year attempting a chamfered-corner building (figure 2.11E), one of a number in inter-war central Northampton associated with street-widening schemes.

These last mentioned attempts at town planning, almost the only major contribution made by the local authority to central Northampton's inter-war townscape, had earlier provided the opportunity for the local architect W. L. Carter to produce three Art Deco landmarks at road junctions. Two of them were designed for the odd-established local firm of A. R. & W. Cleaver, which, having started in the building trade in the mid-nineteenth century (*Daily Chronicle*, 1909; *Northampton and County Independent*, 1968), had become a major property owner in the town centre, and all three had chamfered corners

– a characteristic feature in inter-war central Northampton (figure 2.11F) which had local, nineteenth-century antecedents. Arguably, Carter, who had practised in Southsea and Haslemere before moving to Northampton (*Northampton Independent*, 1946b), had as great an impact on the physical form of the commercial core of Northampton as Allen, who had been articled in the town (*Northampton Independent*, 1949a) and designed more of its central-area buildings. Taken together, the influence of these two architects, combined with that of a small number of local owners with whom they were often associated – for example, A. R. & W. Cleaver, A. P. Hawtin & Sons, one of the largest building firms in Northamptonshire (*Northampton and County Independent*, 1930), and Coldham Bros, a firm with varied retailing interests – indicates the considerable impact that a few local firms could have in a flourishing provincial town even as late as the 1930s, when retail and service chains, if not yet national-scale speculative developers, were already acquiring and developing property on a large scale.

That locally-based enterprises did not flourish on a comparable scale in Watford underlines a major difference between the two centres at this time. Despite the obvious attraction of such a thriving middle-order central place as Northampton for expanding chain-stores with their own architects' departments, there was still room there in the 1930s for a variety of prosperous local firms, whether commercial concerns or architects. Watford, in contrast, had never had such a variety of local companies. Moreover, for chain-store development it tended to rank lower in the priorities of national firms than important provincial towns such as Northampton, and London firms were already undertaking a sizeable share of its architectural commissions. The fact that about three times as many buildings were constructed in Northampton's commercial core in the six years before the Second World War is at least in part a measure of the greater autonomy and maturity of its business and professional community. The effects of Watford's more rapid population growth were not to be fully felt in terms of large-scale new building in its commercial core by major firms until well after the Second World War, and then both the initiators and the architects involved were almost entirely from outside the town.

The early post-war years

The hiatus in redevelopment associated with the Second World War was even more pronounced than that associated with the First World War. Recovery was slower, reflecting not only shortages and dislocations consequent upon a prolonged war-effort, but also the imposition of post-war building restrictions, which were not abandoned until 1954, and the levying of taxes on development, which were not discontinued until 1953 (Whitehouse, 1964, pp. 13–22). When it came, the timing and form of the recovery were different in the two centres. It came first in central Northampton, in 1949, and not until 1954 in central Watford (figures 2.6 and 2.12). And whereas in central Northampton there was little concession to the neo-Georgian and Art Deco styles that had dominated the 1930s, and chamfered corners virtually disappeared from the

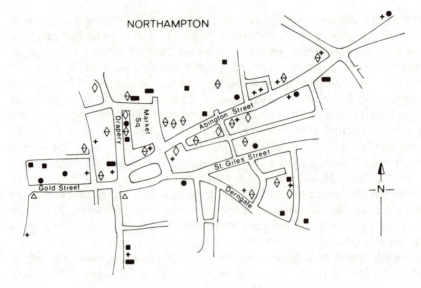

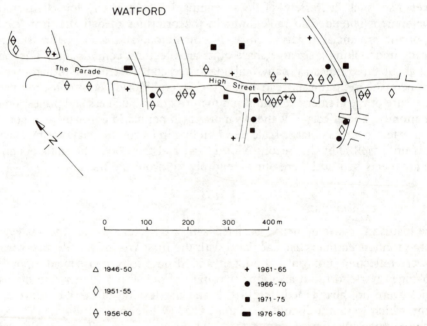

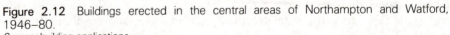

Figure 2.12 Buildings erected in the central areas of Northampton and Watford, 1946–80.
Source: building applications.

architectural vocabulary, in central Watford rebuilding took up stylistically where it had left off in 1939. This is surprising in the light of the fact that in Northampton local owners and local architects, some of the latter having designed buildings before the war, were still numerous, whereas in Watford scarcely any new buildings in the commercial core were locally owned or locally designed, and London architects had become even more dominant than they had been in the 1930s. Arguably, an important part of the explanation is to be found in the legacy left by the inter-war period. The modern style had been represented in central Northampton before the Second World War, albeit unambiguously in only two of the three buildings in which it was employed. In central Watford it had not. Furthermore, in central Watford one building erected in 1954 and two erected in 1956 involved the filling in of sites left empty when war broke out. All three were undertaken by speculative developers, who, as has already been noted, as a group tended to be conservative in their choice of architectural styles, whereas most of the early post-war buildings in central Northampton were bespoken. Indeed, these three, and a single bespoke structure also erected in 1954 (figure 2.13A), differed little (except in being even plainer) from nearby buildings erected 20 years or more earlier. In particular, Cotton, Ballard & Blow, who designed the buildings of City House Properties and JAS, seem to have been influenced by the building designed in 1934 by Ley Colbeck & Partners for Watford Ideal Homes on the opposite side of the street. This is not to say that there was no continuity in central Northampton. Brown & Henson's design for Alexandre in 1954, also on a site left vacant during the war, bore a close resemblance to their design for the adjacent building for R. Wiggins & Co., erected in 1939, and H. Bloomer & Son's building of 1953 for their fellow Birmingham firm Werff Bros (figure 2.14A) had at least a passing resemblance to the 'People's Architecture' (Esher, 1981, p. 23) of the nearby market hall, the Chronicle and Echo building and the coach station of the United Counties Bus Co., all of which were constructed in the second half of the 1930s.

In two respects, however, there were similarities between the two centres. In both commercial cores, new buildings were predominantly of brick, at least externally, and, as had been the case in both centres in the second half of the 1930s, the accommodation of new buildings to traditional plot frontages of 10 m or less was roughly as common as larger-scale redevelopment. These characteristics of materials and scale were to change in both centres as the first post-war redevelopment boom gathered momentum.

The first post-war boom

Although it may be argued that stylistically the few early post-war developments in central Northampton were modern, some of the most important features of the post-war scene in terms of both style and the nature of the development process did not emerge in either centre until the second half of the 1950s. The role of the insurance companies was crucial. In the vanguard of speculative development in the commercial cores of Northampton and Watford were the

Figure 2.13 Buildings erected in central Watford, 1954–62 (photographs by the author, 1982/83). (A) Designed in 1954 by Lewis Solomon Son & Joseph, London for Bewlay & Co., London. (B) Designed in 1957 by B. Peake, London for Norwich Union Insurance Societies, Norwich. (C) Designed in 1957 by C. Fisher, London for City House Properties. (D) Designed in 1960 by E. J. Jackson, Croxley Green for Josdor Properties, London. (E) Designed in 1962 by Cotton, Ballard & Blow, London for Central Commercial Properties, London. (F) Designed in 1956 by Dawe, Carter & Partners, Watford for H. J. Ryman, London.

Norwich Union Insurance Societies, undertaking two developments that were entirely speculative in each centre in the period 1957–62. In Northampton they used two different architects from the town itself – A. W. Walker & Partners (figure 2.14B) and R. Bryan – and in Watford they used the London architect B. Peake (figure 2.13B). All four developments were primarily intended to be occupied by shops. At the same time the Norwich Union also erected a much more prominent building – part of which it occupied itself – dwarfing the still mainly traditional buildings in Northampton's Market Square. But more

Figure 2.14 Buildings erected in central Northampton, 1953–63 (photographs by the author, 1982/83). (A) Designed in 1953 by H. Bloomer & Son, Birmingham for Werff Bros, Birmingham. (B) Designed in 1959 by A. W. Walker & Partners, Northampton for Norwich Union Insurance Societies, Norwich. (C) Designed in 1960 by Lacoste & Partners for Provincial Shop Proprietors, London. (D) Designed in 1963 by A. W. Walker & Partners, Northampton for Darby Properties, Northampton. (E) Designed in 1962 by Gray, Birch & James, London for J. Sainsbury, London. (F) Designed in 1960 by L. Cooke, Northampton for the New Peacock, Barnsley.

significant was the hidden hand of the insurance companies in various forms of financial arrangement with property development companies, notably sale-and-leaseback arrangements but also increased mortgage and equity participation (Whitehouse, 1964, pp. 46–113), for which building applications provide few clues. Between 1956 and 1964 the number of property companies submitting plans for redevelopments in the two centres burgeoned. In central Watford in that period, City House Properties (figure 2.13C), JAS, Saladon Trust, Mappin Properties (Watford), Commercial & Suburban Properties, Josdor Properties (figure 2.13D), Main Street Properties, Property Management and Development, Central Commercial Properties (figure 2.13E) and Ravenseft Properties were all engaged in developments. In central Northampton, City & Town Buildings, Provincial Shop Proprietors (figure 2.14C), Newilton, Covenant Securities, Darby Properties (figure 2.14D) and C. P. Choularton & Sons Partners were active during the same period. There is little doubt that many of these development agencies, probably most of them, were heavily dependent on financial backing by insurance companies (Whitehouse, 1964).

Few property companies undertook more than a single development in the two centres combined and few employed in-house architects. However, occasionally, standing relationships reflected other business links, as for example in the use of architects Cotton, Ballard & Blow by Central Commercial Properties in central Watford in 1962: Cotton, Ballard & Blow were an offshoot of J. Cotton & Partners, surveyors and estate agents, and Central Commercial Properties had been taken over by an amalgamation of Chesham House and City of Birmingham Real Property, the latter being owned by J. Cotton (Whitehouse, 1964, pp. 31–2).

The change to the modern style in central Watford occurred rapidly in 1955 and 1956 (figure 2.6). Curiously, as in central Northampton in the mid-1920s, one of the last buildings in the old style and one of the first in the new style were juxtaposed (figure 2.13A, F), although in this case it was the local architect (Dawe, Carter & Partners) that was responsible for the new style. As with earlier fashions, the owner-occupiers tended to adopt the modern style first, although in the ensuing, mainly speculative, boom the modern style was almost universally adopted. In central Northampton, where a vanguard of owner-occupiers had introduced the modern style before the Second World War, its post-war spread began earlier (figure 2.6), mainly through the agency of owner-occupiers. In terms of impact on the visual environment, however, the critical years for change in both centres were the late 1950s. It was then that glass became the most important façade material. In central Northampton it was particularly dominant, but it was not until the early 1960s that its effect was widespread there, the peak of the building boom occurring a few years later than in central Watford.

In both centres the modern style was used by local firms and non-local firms alike, although in the redevelopment of central Watford few local firms were active. Speculative developers adopted the new fashion almost as rapidly as owners building for their own occupation. The first predominantly glass-fronted building in central Northampton in the post-war period retained a central parapet excrescence characteristic of the 1930s, despite the fact that the building itself, occupying several traditional plots, was too long in relation to the width of the street for it to be possible to appreciate from the ground the symmetry that this embellishment was meant to emphasize. The failure of this feature to reappear in subsequent buildings, combined with the tendency to emphasize the horizontal dimension, added to the alien appearance of the new buildings that stemmed from their glass fronts and long frontages (figure 2.14E). Traditional plot boundaries, which had hitherto acted as a significant constraint on the dimensions of façades, were becoming highly vulnerable. During the 1960s, only 11 new buildings out of 29 in central Northampton and only 5 out of 18 in central Watford were within plots that were 10 m or less in width. However, the elongated character of the burgages, which still acted as a major morphological frame, facilitated their lengthways development for shop-lined pedestrian ways. The New Peacock took advantage of this in 1959–60 when it commissioned the local architect L. Cooke to design a pedestrian way in central Northampton linking Market Square and Abington Street (figure 2.14F). Watford Borough Council had exploited the length of the burgages in a similar way for the construction of its covered market in 1931.

Morphologically and in terms of the development processes at work, the striking feature of the first post-war building boom, especially in the light of our examination of earlier periods, was the similarity of developments in the two centres. In the matter of timing, however, notably the earlier onset of the boom in central Watford, there was a significant difference. In accounting for this difference three factors deserve mention. First, strategically placed in London's rapidly developing suburban ring, Watford was an obvious proving ground for property development companies, most of which were operating on a national scale for the first time. Even though population growth within the borough boundaries was tailing off, elsewhere within the sphere of influence of the commercial-core population growth was still rapid. Secondly, the existence of large plots on the edge of the commercial core eased the problems of site assembly for large developments. Thirdly, capital investment by chain-stores had been less than in central Northampton throughout the 1930s and several retail chains now sought to provide themselves with accommodation in Watford commensurate with the town's recently increased status in the urban hierarchy.

Nationally the main force of the boom that had rapidly gathered momentum in the late 1950s was spent by 1965 (Department of the Environment et al., 1972, part 1, p. 62). Indeed this was a quiet year for new building in both central Northampton, where only two buildings were constructed, and central Watford, where none were built. In retrospect this may be seen as a time when stock was taken of the major changes of materials and scale that had occurred in the late 1950s and the first half of the 1960s. Nationally there was a change of mood that was to influence the character of subsequent developments (Harvey, 1972, p. 39). However, as these subsequent developments are brought into focus it is apparent that they differed markedly in the two towns. Thus the rather similar changes that the two centres underwent during the first post-war boom seem aberrant in the light of developments before and after.

The post-modern period

The period between the first post-war boom and 1980 is perhaps noteworthy above all for a reaction against the scale and the forms of commercial-core redevelopment that had been characteristic of the 1960s. The reaction against the predominantly glass-fronted buildings, mainly constructed between the mid-1950s and the mid-1960s, was especially pronounced in central Northampton, and it is notable that it was there that they had been particularly dominant (figure 2.6). But the change that occurred, mainly from the late 1960s onward, was much more than a matter of a change in materials. As early as 1964, the peak year of the boom in commercial building nationally – in terms of the value of new orders obtained by contractors (Department of the Environment et al., 1972, part 1, p. 62) – there were signs that the bandwagon of modern architecture would not roll unchecked. A building was designed for Midland Bank close to the heart of Northampton's central area in an architectural style that was conspicuously different from the modern style that had dominated new building in that area since the Second World War. Although it had many classical features (figure 2.15A), it was certainly not a neo-Georgian style of the type that had been characteristic of new buildings in central Northampton in the 1930s or of the sort that had continued to be used in central Watford as recently as the mid-1950s. It was the first suggestion in central Northampton of an architectural style that, when later manifested in a variety of less restrained forms, was termed 'post-modern' (Jencks, 1975). It was a style incorporating earlier, often classical, architectural forms but using modern materials, sometimes with little or no attempt at their concealment – by, for example, employing traditional materials as cladding. It was thus a development out of the modern movement but at the same time a reaction against it. That the classicism in this case should have been so marked and the total appearance so at variance with the modern style is less surprising when the house style of Midland Bank is examined over a long perod. Earlier in the century, especially in the years immediately after the First World War, Midland Bank had peppered the country with neo-classical bank buildings, and the architect who designed the one in Watford in 1907 (for what was then London City & Midland Bank) was T. B. Whinney of London, the founder of Whinney Son & Austen Hall (Whinney Mackay Lewis Partnership, personal communication), who were responsible for Midland Bank's post-modern building in Northampton.

As in earlier periods in central Northampton, it was the owner-occupiers who took up the new style, although slowly at first. In 1968, after a further eight modern buildings had been erected, the Skipton Building Society unequivocally rejected the modern style for its offices in Drapery, as did Tesco Stores for their shop in Gold Street in 1970. But it was Barclays Bank in 1969 (figure 2.15B) that demonstrated clearly that post-modern architecture involved more than an incorporation into modernist architecture of styles from earlier periods. Only in 1972, when a second boom in commercial building was in full swing nationally (Department of the Environment et al., 1980 p. 6), did speculative developers adopt the post-modern style in central Northampton – for example, Grosvenor Estate Commercial Developments did so for the first stage of their shopping centre, Grosvenor Centre (figure 2.15C), and the Prudential for its adjoining shopping parade. These developments contrasted sharply with nearby modern-style buildings, though they revealed more concern with the concealment of their large size than with the articulation of a new style. Later, four of the six buildings erected during the comparative lull in rebuilding in the mid- and late-1970s were in a post-modern style (figure 2.15D, E), and one of the two

Figure 2.15   Buildings erected in central Northampton, 1964–79 (photographs by the author, 1982/83). (A) Designed in 1964 by Whinney Son & A. Hall, London for Midland Bank, London. (B) Designed in 1969 by Bryan & Pennock, Northampton for Barclays Bank, London. (C) Designed in 1972 by Stone, Toms & Partners, London for Grosvenor Estate Commercial Developments, London. (D) Designed in 1979 by Newman, Levinson & Partners, London for the Eagle Star Insurance Co., London. (E) Designed in 1979 by R. Bryan Son & Pennock, Northampton for Penwise Properties, Leicester. (F) Designed in 1975 by Douglas Feast Partnership, London for Pinstone Securities and Caran Securities, London.

exceptions was in a neo-Victorian style (figure 2.15F). The modern style had almost ceased to be used in central Northampton. Stylistic pluralism and diversity of cladding materials, with brick, stone, glass and tile predominating within individual buildings, were the order of the day.

Different circumstances prevailed in central Watford. Quite abruptly after 1964 the speculative developers, with the notable exception of the local authority, largely withdrew from the scene. The stage seemed set for the introduction of post-modern architecture, with owner-occupiers in the van-guard. But here it was primarily the chain-stores (Littlewoods, Boots the Chemists, F. W. Woolworth & Co., Wm Perring & Co., and J. Sainsbury), rather than the banks, that were rebuilding, and all of them, like most of the comparatively few other firms undertaking developments in central Watford at the time, continued to employ the modern style (figure 2.16A). Up to the end of the study period, only the Eastern Electricity Board building departed from this style with its ultra-plain neo-Georgian façade. Watford Borough Council's plain shopping centre (Charter Place), expanding from the elongated burgage tails that had earlier been occupied by the covered market, was unquestionably in a modern style (figure 2.16B), as was the adjacent YMCA office block, which bore much the same relation to it as the office block of Frincan Holdings did to the Grosvenor Centre in Northampton. Glass façades had largely disap-peared, as they had in central Northampton, but the expression was still essentially modern.

The major stylistic differences between the buildings erected in the two centres between the late 1960s and 1980 relate in part at least to the different types of firms involved. However, unlike in much earlier periods, when a tendency for local firms to be more conservative was apparent, the provenance of the firms responsible for the new buildings does not appear to have been a major factor. Both centres were dominated in this period by non-local firms (both owners and architects), a situation that had prevailed in central Watford throughout the post-war period. Furthermore, the three local architects who designed new buildings in central Northampton from 1968 onward all adopted the post-modern style. Some importance would seem to attach, however, to the fact that rebuilding in central Northampton outside the Grosvenor Centre was mainly for offices whereas in central Watford it was dominated by chain-stores. The classical variant of the post-modern style which set the most recent trend in central Northampton was scarcely more than one remove from the existing styles favoured by the financial institutions that adopted the style first. In contrast, the recent house styles of the chain-stores that were primarily responsible for the new buildings in central Watford would have required major changes if the new style were to have been adopted. The fact that in this period

Figure 2.16   Buildings erected in central Watford, 1969–74 (photographs by the author, 1982/83). (A) Designed in 1969 by F. W. Woolworth & Co., London for themselves. (B) Designed in 1974 by Ley Colbeck & Partners, London for Watford Borough Council.

chain-store building predominated in central Watford and that office building was by far the most important type of development in central Northampton reflected partly the fact that more office buildings in Watford were sufficiently detached from the town centre to fall outside the defined study area and partly the redressing of imbalances inherited from previous periods.

Developments in previous periods have a bearing on differences between the two centres in the 1970s in another way. Since post-modern architecture was in part a reaction to earlier, especially modern-style, architecture, account should be taken of the somewhat different stylistic effect in the two centres of the buildings erected previously. Buildings in the modern style constructed in the 1950s and 1960s in central Watford had been more interspersed early on with those in neo-Georgian style, and were of somewhat smaller size on average than those in central Northampton and were more varied in their façade materials. Added to this there were major differences in the assemblages of architectural styles that had survived from much earlier periods and, given the different histories of the two towns, inevitably there were important differences in the evolving communities of which these styles were in part a reflection. Watford's legacy of fine architecture from earlier centuries was minor by comparison with that of Northampton, where the long, glass fronts of modern buildings frequently stood out starkly against neighbouring eighteenth- and nineteenth-century façades. It would have been surprising in these circumstances if a mood of reaction in the local community had not developed in Northampton. There is little doubt that at least one local pressure group, the Northampton Civic Society, founded in 1966, exerted a significant educative influence. With a membership rising to a peak of about 450, it was particularly active in the late 1960s and the 1970s, judging by its publications (for example, Northampton Civic Society, 1975) and accounts of its activities in the local press. Such activity in Watford appears to have been on a relatively minor scale.

These latest developments in the two study centres should, furthermore, be seen in the light of the conservation movement. Arguably, in its antecedents and aims post-modernism stands in relation to new structures, to which attention has largely been confined here, as the conservation movement stands in relation to the existing fabric. Both are in part a reaction to large, monolithic structures out of scale with existing building forms and frequently presenting a slab-like aspect out of keeping with the heterogeneity inevitably associated with piecemeal building replacement on individual plots, especially burgages. Despite the strengths of these interrelated movements, however, and the by no means small legacy that post-modernism had already left in central Northampton by 1980, the economics of development continued to favour the redevelopment of more than one contiguous plot, and in the commercial cores of Northampton and Watford the incidence of piecemeal building replacement on individual burgage-size plots remained as low as in the first post-war building boom. A partial solution to the problem that was employed in central Northampton – one that suggests that in historic towns conservation and post-modernism are merely different facets of the same concern – was the subdivision of façades, sometimes independently of a building's internal divisions, in order to give an external impression of traditional-scale frontages. The units of redevelopment, and sometimes of occupation, therefore appear, at least at a casual glance, smaller than is actually the case. This device was employed in 1979 in the frontage of Grosvenor Centre on to Market Square (figure 2.17A) and in shops in Drapery in 1980 (figure 2.17B). These attempts

Figure 2.17   Buildings erected in central Northampton, 1979–80 (photographs by the author, 1982/83). (A) Designed in 1979 by Stone, Toms & Partners, London for Grosvenor Estate Commercial Developments, London. (B) Designed in 1980 by C. Featherstone Practice, Northampton for the Proprietary & Reversionary Investment Corporation, London.

to recapture the appearance of an urban landscape created by a process of piecemeal replacement on a pre-Victorian scale had no evident precursor in earlier periods in either town; indeed such devices would seem to have been essentially new to Great Britain in the 1970s.

Conclusions

In the course of this chronological account considerable attention has been given to individual developments and the owners and architects responsible for them. Attention has also been drawn to the way in which individual developments in combination endowed historical periods with particular characteristics. What are the main conclusions that can be drawn from this chronological treatment?

   First, the importance of the historical legacies with which Northampton and Watford entered the study period can hardly be overemphasized (cf. Freeman, 1988). Northampton, apart from having a substantially larger sphere of influence, reflected for example in a much larger representation of national retail and service chains, was more richly endowed than Watford with local firms and organizations, which had dominated the process of physical change to the commercial core. Watford in contrast was already showing marked evidence of the influence of London firms in the initiation and design of such changes. Furthermore, the large, mostly residential, plots close to the commercial core of Watford provided greater freedom for the extension of the commercial core, in the form of sizeable speculative shopping parades, than was available in Northampton, whose commercial core was more tightly hedged round both by a much more developed inner fringe belt of institutional, public-utility and industrial sites and by relatively high-density terrace housing. Similarly, within the commercial cores physical changes were heavily influenced by existing morphological frames, which acted as a moderating influence on attempts to enlarge the scale of redevelopment. Changes in the town plans of both centres were, except in the late 1960s and the 1970s, overwhelmingly adaptive rather than augmentative, to use the terms employed by Conzen (1960, p. 95). Although redevelopments frequently involved plot amalgamations, burgage lineaments survived widely. However, redevelopments on frontages of 10 m or less were most numerous in both centres between the mid-1930s and the late 1950s (discounting the years of the Second World War and those immediately following it). They were particularly rare afterwards, as the retail and service chains and the property companies operating on a national scale increased their hold on property. This resulted in long, uniform façades that among the successions of small, independently-designed buildings that had previously characterized both centres had an alien appearance. Not surprisingly, from the mid-1960s in Northampton there was evidence of a reaction against this, especially in the late 1970s when attempts were made to re-create traditional frontages by designing long-fronted buildings in such a way that they gave the appearance of consisting of more than one building.

Secondly, although in broad terms the time-span studied here is divided into rather different social and economic periods by the two world wars and these have traditionally been treated as distinct morphological periods, an important finding to emerge from the study is the degree to which the styles that characterized one morphological period continued to be reproduced in the early years of the next. Thus Edwardian styles continued to be employed well into the 1920s in both centres. The virtual termination of their use coincided with an increase in the number of designs by non-local architects. After the Second World War the modern style, which had previously been represented strongly in only two buildings in these centres, both in central Northampton, rapidly supplanted neo-Georgian and Art Deco styles in central Northampton, but in central Watford neo-Georgian styles, which had been adopted for several buildings before the First World War, continued to be used side-by-side with employments of the modern style until 1956. In both cases, unlike after the First World War, local architects were as quick as non-local architects to adopt the new style, although by this time in Watford their central-area commissions were diminishing rapidly in number. By the time of the last major stylistic change before the end of the study period, the advent of post-modern architecture, even in central Northampton buildings were almost entirely being designed by non-local architects. Surprisingly, this last change of style, though begun in central Northampton in the 1960s and completed there by the mid-1970s, still lacked any clear manifestations in central Watford at the end of the study period. In the case of all the periods of major stylistic change, if the banks and breweries in the inter-war period are excepted, owner-occupiers tended to adopt the new styles more rapidly than speculative developers. A similar conclusion has been drawn by Vilagrasa (1990) in his comparison of the commercial cores of Worcester, in the English Midlands, and Lleida, in north-east Spain, though studies of other towns suggest that it would be premature to conclude that this tendency was widespread (Larkham and Freeman, 1988).

Thirdly, the frequently noted tendency for building activity to fluctuate markedly was evident in both centres, but it would be hard to argue from the data that this was appreciably more a feature of speculative building than of building for owner-occupation. Speculative developments by individuals, as distinct from organizations, were numerous in central Watford in the early 1920s, reflecting it would seem their access to relatively secure private sources of capital during a period that was for the most part characterized by economic uncertainty nationally. In contrast, by this time in central Northampton developments by individuals had become a rarity. There, if it had not been for the activities of public and private institutions, such as the Post Office and the YWCA, building would have fallen almost to nil in the period during and immediately following the First World War. The tendency for institutions to sustain building activity during a commercial recession was also apparent in central Watford in the early 1930s, but taking the study period as a whole the number of buildings erected for institutions was too small to justify conclusions about the incidence of this category of building.

Fourthly, variations in the time series of different types of building cannot readily be disentangled from the major changes in the way in which redevelopments were accomplished. The first major change was the large-scale entry of retail chains, many of them public companies, into property develop- ment in the 1930s. Having in the first three decades of the century mainly moved into existing premises, by the fourth decade they were purchasing additional sites on a large scale, undertaking the redevelopment of these and moving into the new buildings from their converted premises. The redevelop- ment of sites that they already occupied was much less common. The second major change was the growing involvement of property companies and insurance companies in the speculative development and ownership of property; slowly in the 1930s, but rapidly from the late 1950s onward.

Fifthly, the fact that these last-mentioned changes were common to both commercial cores, albeit with differences in detail in their phasing, should not obscure the fact that from the First World War until comparatively recently Watford's commercial core was predominantly built by speculative developers, whereas Northampton's was predominantly built by owner-occupiers. Only after the early 1960s were both of these positions reversed, as the virtually complete integration of both centres within the national property market and the national-scale organization of commerce occurred. These differences were intimately bound up with long-term differences in the roles of the two towns. For example, in the early years after the First World War Watford was embedded in a rapidly growing suburban ring in which for most urban settlements the rapid provision of speculative shopping parades was a natural corollary of speculative housebuilding. At the same time Northampton was responding more to national-scale decision-making relating to a wider spectrum of social and economic provision for a larger tributary area, including for some purposes a whole county, most of which was undertaken by owner-occupiers.

Sixthly, alongside of these macro-scale factors we must view the activities of the individual firms, the linkages between them, and their shares of the market. In understanding building styles, standing relationships between owners and architects are an important factor to take account of, although owners with their own house styles frequently had their own company architects. Some linkages between firms are not apparent from building applications and ostensibly independent developments sometimes fit into a pattern of formal or informal links between firms, including those between different owners.

Finally, the extent of outside influence increased almost continuously over the time span studied. It was channelled primarily by the retail and service chains during the inter-war years but during the period after the mid-1950s the speculative developers were an even more important medium. The influence of local architects diminished even more than the number of buildings that they designed, since on average their buildings were smaller than those designed by non-local architects. Yet, in spite of these growing national-scale influences, there remains the need to understand the operation of processes at the local scale. The early introduction and long life of neo-Georgian styles in central Watford, the brief but vigorous manifestation there of the neo-Tudor style at the end of the 1920s and the beginning of the 1930s and the popularity of the chamfered-corner style in central Northampton in the 1930s are cases in point.

CASE STUDIES: ANALYSIS

This chronological account has been essentially descriptive, and often qualitative rather than quantitative in character. There are a number of questions for which only tentative answers have been provided and still others that have been scarcely touched upon. To pursue these further, a more analytical approach is necessary. The questions at issue relate especially to the individuals and organizations responsible for the changes that have been described.

First, what changes were there in the numbers and types of firms involved (owners, architects, consultants, builders and civil engineering contractors, and specialized contractors) – in particular to what extent was development activity concentrated in the hands of proportionately fewer firms over time – and how did the timing of the activities of firms vary between the two centres? Secondly, what variations were there between the two centres in the extent and intra-centre location of the activities of firms from different localities? Thirdly, what relationships (especially locational ones) existed between those responsible for initiating and preparing plans for changes and those responsible for implementing them?

To answer these questions in quantitative terms the data set was greatly expanded to include, over and above the new buildings already considered, structural alterations and additions (both extensions to existing buildings and free-standing auxiliary buildings). Together these involved 497 implemented plans in the case of central Northampton and 462 such plans in that of central Watford. Although structural alterations on their own were comparatively rare, additions to existing buildings greatly outnumbered new buildings: in central Watford in the ratio 4.3:1 and in central Northampton in the ratio 3.7:1. Despite the fact that individually many of these additions were small, in total they represent major increases in floorspace, albeit often concealed from the street.

The locations of the firms used in the analysis were taken to be at the postal addresses of their head-offices, unless there was information in the building application suggesting that work on the plan was the responsibility of a local or regional office. London was defined as the London postal area, which remained almost unchanged during the study period.

Initiators of change

Arguably the most important firms in property development and management are those initiating plans, normally referred to in building applications as the building owners. However, some of those recorded as owners in the applications were in fact lessees, and in a substantial minority of cases the true owner of the building could not be established without recourse to other sources. Thus the term 'initiator' rather than 'owner' is generally used in the discussion of the results that follows, although for most of the major additions to floor space and structural alterations, and for almost all of the new buildings, the initiator was in fact the building owner. In the few cases in which the names of the building owner and the lessee were both recorded the building owner was treated as the initiator unless there was strong presumptive evidence that it was the lessee that was the prime instigator of the changes.

The view that nationally decision-making became concentrated in the hands of proportionately fewer initiators in the post-war period is consistent with the data for the commercial cores of Northampton and Watford. The number of firms initiating plans for new buildings, additions or structural alterations in both centres rose from five in 1920–39 and four in 1940–59 to ten in 1960–79. Despite this fact, however, there is no evidence of a trend towards the concentration of decision-making in proportionately fewer hands in the two centres considered individually comparable to that at the national level. Care is, of course, needed in assessing the figures that might be taken as a measure of this, and it should be borne in mind that the size of the sites to which plans for major changes to the physical fabric referred tended to increase in both centres, at least after the Second World War, most noticeably in the case of the plans for the redevelopments that brought into existence a shopping precinct in each centre in the 1970s. Nevertheless, in Watford the proportion of plans from firms initiating three or more plans remained steady over the three periods 1920–39, 1940–59 and 1960–79 at about one-third (figure 2.18a). More surprisingly, in Northampton this proportion was actually substantially lower in 1960–79 (22

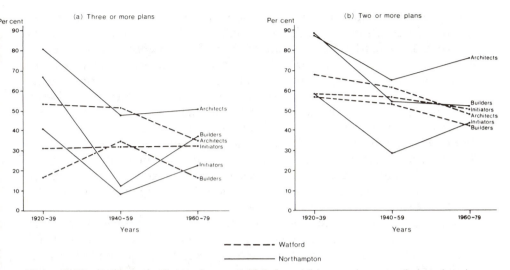

Figure 2.18 Percentage of plans for new buildings, additions and structural alterations in the commercial cores of Northampton and Watford involving firms undertaking (a) three or more plans (b) two or more plans.
Source: building applications.

per cent) than it was in 1920–39 (41 per cent). The corresponding percentages of plans from firms initiating two or more plans reveal similar temporal trends (figure 2.18b).

The paradox of a concentration of decision-making in proportionately fewer hands nationally but no such tendency, or even a reverse tendency, within individual centres is resolved when it is realized that none of the firms that amassed large amounts of property nationally – notably the insurance companies, pension funds, banks, chain-stores and development companies – individually initiated plans for more than a few properties within our study centres and that this may well be true of the majority of commercial cores. The national firms that have been most active, such as the Prudential and the Norwich Union, occupied fewer sites and implemented fewer plans in central Northampton in 1960–79 than the most active local owners (such as A. R. & W. Cleaver and P. Phipps & Co.) had done during 1920–39. Although fewer local owners had survived into the inter-war period in Watford, there too in terms of both the number of sites occupied and the number of plans implemented in the commercial core the larger local owners did not differ greatly from their national successors of 1960–79.

If the Co-operative Societies and the Gas and Electricity Boards are excluded, over the 1920–79 period 24 firms or organizations initiated new buildings, additions or structural alterations in both centres (Whitehand and Whitehand, 1983, app. I), but the timing of the activities of these firms and organizations was quite different in each case. In central Northampton they were divided almost equally between 1920–49, with 29 plans of this type implemented, and 1950–79, with 30 such plans implemented, whereas in central Watford only 12 such plans were implemented during the period 1920–49, compared with no less than 57 during the period 1950–79 (figure 2.19). This discrepancy is much greater than would have been expected from the difference between the two centres in the timing of *all* new buildings, additions and structural alterations. Moreover, if the dates of the *first* plans initiated by the 24 firms or organizations in the two centres are examined, the Northampton one was earlier in 17 cases, with in one case plans being initiated in the same year in the two centres. Central Northampton's larger population catchment, at least until the Second World War, and its much more mature and diversified economic structure may well be factors underlying this difference in the timing of investment in the two centres. This difference should also be seen in the context of the greater variety and number of local firms investing in central Northampton throughout the 1920–79 period.

It is possible to divide the initiators of new buildings into owner-occupiers and speculative developers, although the distinction is not always clear-cut and the two types of initiator operated in close proximity to one another in both centres (figure 2.20). Despite the marked increase in the post-war period in the proportion of new buildings initiated by speculative developers in central Northampton, the proportion of new buildings undertaken there in that period by retail and service chains rose – as it did in the case of central Watford. Of

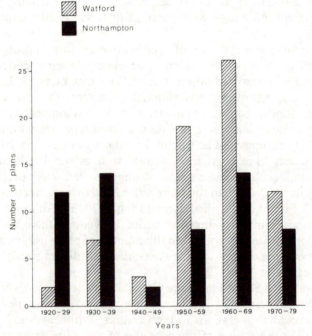

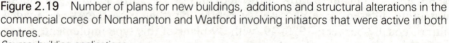

Figure 2.19   Number of plans for new buildings, additions and structural alterations in the commercial cores of Northampton and Watford involving initiators that were active in both centres.
Source: building applications.

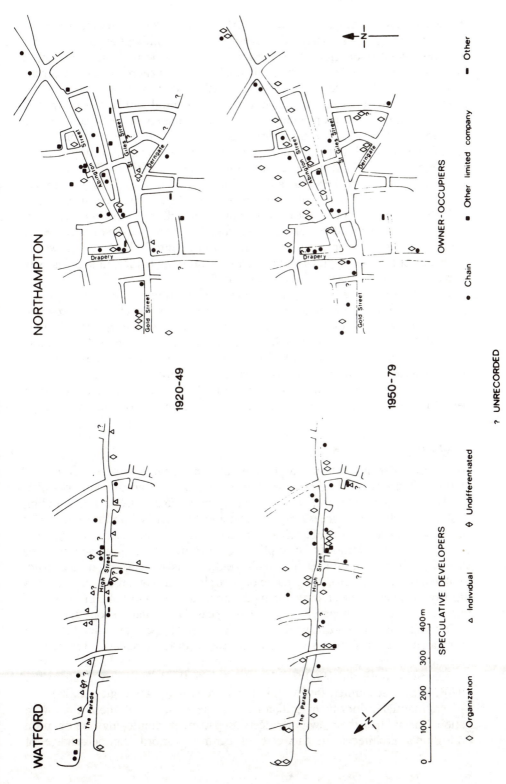

Figure 2.20 New buildings in the commercial cores of Northampton and Watford classified by type of initiator.
Source: building applications.

the speculative developments the proportion undertaken by organizations, as opposed to individuals, increased markedly. Of new buildings as a whole – that is both speculative developments and those for owner-occupation – the decline in the proportion undertaken by individuals occurred more rapidly in central Northampton. The proportion of individuals initiating new buildings was already a tiny minority in the inter-war period in central Northampton whereas in central Watford the proportion was still approximately one-half, although in assessing this difference it is necessary to bear in mind possible variations in the precision with which initiators' names are recorded in the building applications. After the Second World War the initiation of a new building by an individual was a rarity and there were no cases in either centre in the 1970s. The longer survival in central Watford of initiation by individuals may seem inconsistent with the earlier decline of local ownership there referred to previously, since the large majority of individual initiators were local. The paradox is resolved by noting that a greater proportion of ownership in central Northampton was in the hands of local companies and other local corporate bodies, in keeping with that town's more developed local economic base.

Although there was little or no intra-centre variation between the locations of speculative developments and those of the sites developed for owner-occupation, the locations of new buildings of initiators from inside the study towns differed from those of new buildings of initiators from outside (local and non-local initiators in figure 2.21). In both town centres, initiators from outside the town established in the inter-war period a strong foothold on key sites in the retail core, the periphery being dominated by local initiators. In the post-war period non-local initiators dominated both town centres, core and periphery.

Architects

As far as the constructional aspects of physical change are concerned, an architect is normally the first adviser to be engaged by an initiator of a plan involving structural work. He is usually identifiable from the building application. He is not necessarily a professionally-qualified architect and may occasionally be a member of a related profession (for example, a surveyor). Only in the case of a minority of applications for new buildings, additions or structural alterations (almost invariably applications where only minor structural works are involved), is the name of an architect not recorded. In rare cases this would appear to be an omission by the applicant but more often it is evident that the builder has prepared the plans or occasionally that a shopfitter or the initiator has undertaken this work. The percentage of plans for which the name of an architect (or similar specialist) was not recorded tended to diminish in both centres over the study period, although this was not apparent in central Northampton until the 1960s, and in central Watford there was a rise in the 1970s, largely accounted for by shopfitters preparing plans (figure 2.22a).

A substantial minority of initiators, but the majority of those that were national firms, had their own architects' department, employing one or more professional architects. In the case of central Watford the percentage of

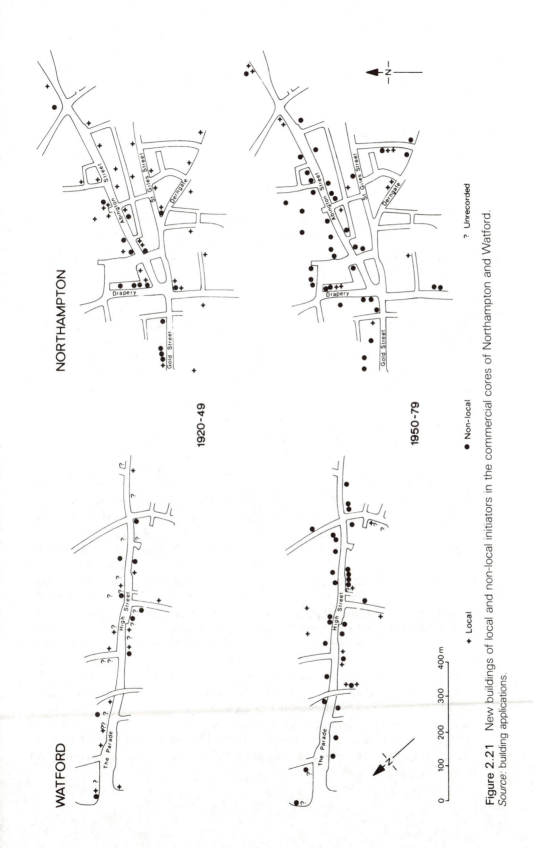

Figure 2.21 New buildings of local and non-local initiators in the commercial cores of Northampton and Watford.
Source: building applications.

WATFORD

NORTHAMPTON

1920-49

1950-79

+ Local   ● Non-local   ? Unrecorded

0   100   200   300   400 m

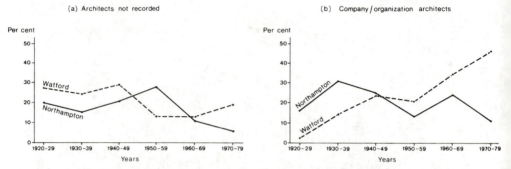

Figure 2.22   (a) Percentage of plans for new buildings, additions and structural alterations in the commercial cores of Northampton and Watford for which architects were not recorded; (b) Plans by company/organization architects for new buildings, additions and structural alterations in the commercial cores of Northampton and Watford as a percentage of all architect-designed plans of this type.
Source: building applications.

architect-designed plans (including the minority prepared by members of allied professions) that were prepared by company/organization architects increased fairly steadily from 2 per cent to 46 per cent between 1920–9 and 1970–9 (figure 2.22b), reflecting to a large extent Watford's climb up the urban hierarchy. Over the same period in central Northampton the trend was quite different, the percentages fluctuating between 31 per cent and 11 per cent, with the highest percentage being reached in 1930–9, reflecting the boom in the town at that time in activity by retail and service chains.

There was a tendency for plans to emanate from a wider spread of architects over time. This was more pronounced than the corresponding trend for initiators (figure 2.18). Again, this would appear to be contrary to views held about national trends (Marriott, 1967, pp. 27–9). In central Northampton four-fifths of the architect-designed plans implemented between 1920 and 1939 were from firms (private practices and companies) responsible for three or more plans, and four firms (F. H. Allen, Brown & Henson, Carter & Coles, and H. J. Ingman, to give them their late-1930s names) accounted for nearly one-half of the architect-designed plans implemented, a situation comparable to that existing in central Watford in the two decades before the First World War. By the post-war period the proportion of architect-designed plans implemented in central Northampton that were from firms responsible for three or more plans had declined to about one-half. In central Watford the proportion of architect-designed plans accounted for by firms responsible for three or more plans had already declined to just over one-half in the inter-war period, and by 1960–79 it had declined further still to just over one-third. This tendency for work to be spread among an increasing number of architects was related to the increasing number of initiators from outside the two study towns. The hegemony of a small number of local architects was considerably eroded and the share of the market that they lost was captured by a wide range of firms operating on virtually a national scale.

Over the 1920–79 period 16 firms of architects (nine of them company architects' departments) were responsible for new buildings, additions or structural alterations in both centres (Whitehand and Whitehand, 1983, app. I). The activities of these essentially national firms were more concentrated in the 1930–9 period in central Northampton (figure 2.23) than would have been expected from the distribution between the two centres of *all* design activity there in the study period. This was largely a reflection of the investment priorities of the retail and service chains, influenced no doubt by Northampton's more assured market at the time.

Differences between local and non-local architects are also apparent in the intra-centre distribution of the works that they designed. In the case of new buildings, the areas within the centres where local architects were involved and those where non-local architects were involved were to some extent transposed between 1920–49 and 1950–79 (figure 2.24). This partly reflected changes in the types of locations that attracted initiators from outside the towns. In the 1920–49 period the main shopping streets were dominated in Northampton, though much less so in Watford, by the national chain-stores with their own architects, local architects on the whole being engaged on peripheral buidings, used for a variety of purposes and often locally-owned. In the 1950–79 period, while the design of new buildings in central Watford was dominated almost entirely by architects from outside the town, especially those from London, in central Northampton the main points of activity for outside architects were the large office blocks located on the periphery, with Northampton architects undertaking about one-half of the mainly comparatively small building replacements in or close to the main shopping streets.

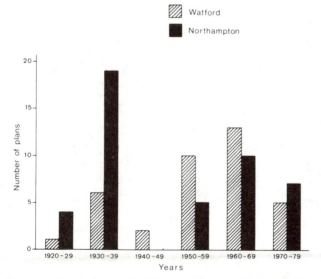

Figure 2.23 Number of plans for new buildings, additions and structural alterations in the commercial cores of Northampton and Watford prepared by architects that were active in both centres.
Source: building applications.

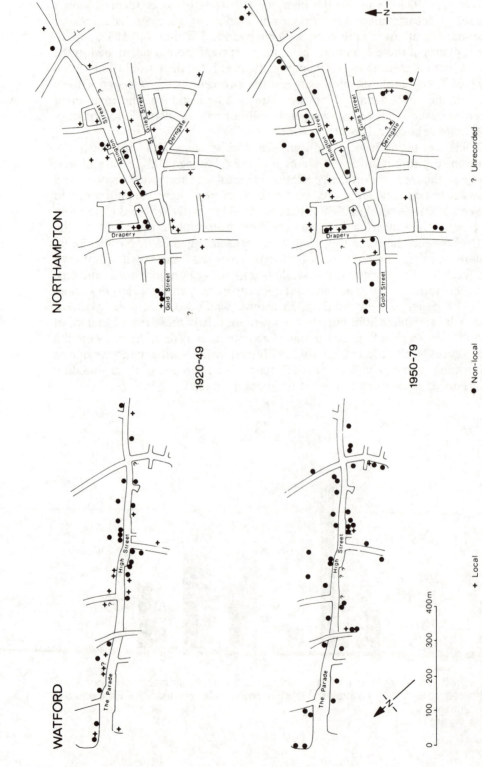

Figure 2.24 New buildings by local and non-local architects in the commercial cores of Northampton and Watford.
Source: building applications.

Consultants, builders and specialized contractors

After the architects in the chain of decision-making tend to come the consultants, the builders and civil engineering contractors, and the specialized contractors, although not all these professions and trades are necessarily involved in every plan.

In both centres until the post-war period, consultants, mostly describing themselves as 'consulting engineers', were employed in connection with only a small minority of the plans for new buildings, additions and structural alterations. Even in 1950–9 the proportion was less than 10 per cent. However, as the complexity of the development task increased and the regulations surrounding it multiplied, consultants played increasingly prominent roles. The number employed rose steeply in both centres, especially in central Northampton, where 71 per cent of such plans in 1970–9 involved consultants (figure 2.25a).

The frequency distribution of consultants by number of plans implemented in 1960–79 yields further evidence that the dispersion of activities among a large number of firms is by no means incompatible with the existence of large firms operating on a national scale. In each centre only about one-quarter of the plans for new buildings, additions or structural alterations were accounted for by firms undertaking three or more plans, a smaller proportion than in the case of architects, particularly in central Northampton, but one not dissimilar to the proportion initiated by firms that initiated three or more plans. Yet as many as nine consultants were involved in both centres during this period, and these nine accounted for 23 per cent of the plans on which consultants were engaged in the two centres: the comparable figure for the seven architects involved in both centres during this period was only 9 per cent and for the ten initiators 13 per cent. This reflects the national scale of the spheres of influence of many consultants. The initiators in this respect occupied an intermediate position

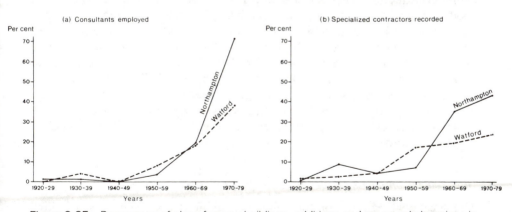

Figure 2.25 Percentage of plans for new buildings, additions and structural alterations in the commercial cores of Northampton and Watford (a) on which consultants were employed (b) on which specialized contractors were recorded.
Source: building applications.

between the consultants and the architects, many of the most prolific of the architects still being local firms, particularly in central Northampton.

The tendency for development activity within the two centres, considered individually, to be spread among proportionately more firms over time is also detectable among the builders and civil engineering contractors (the 'builders' in figure 2.18), although owing to the small number of such firms for which information was available for central Northampton for the period 1940–59 and for central Watford for the period 1920–39 this apparent tendency among builders and civil engineering contractors must be viewed with caution. The fact that only five such firms were engaged in both centres between 1960 and 1979, and that these firms accounted for only 8 per cent of the plans in connection with which such firms are recorded as having been employed in the two centres taken together, reflected the relative rarity with which the majority of builders and civil engineering contractors undertook work at long distances from their home towns.

Contracts with specialized contractors are scarcely recorded in the plans before the 1930s, although clearly the basic trades, such as joinery and plumbing, have had a long history. The boom in specialized contracting from the 1950s onward (figure 2.25b) was, with the exception of shopfitting, predominantly associated with structural engineering, and the producing and supplying of the materials associated with it, and with the implementing of fire precautions. In detail, however, the variety of specializations was large, over 50 in the case of central Northampton alone, even if some similar activities are amalgamated. About one in five plans for developments in central Watford between 1970 and 1979 and about two in five over the same period for central Northampton involved specialized contractors, numerous separate firms being recorded in the case of major developments. Unlike the firms already considered, many of the specialized contractors provided quite different goods or services, one specializing in pipe insulation, for example, having little in common with another specializing in concrete beams. Since so many different goods and services were involved, some being recorded only once in our data set, it is not surprising that for both centres about two thirds of the specialized contractors recorded were involved in only a single plan over the whole period 1920–79, the proportion for the period 1960–79 being about the same for central Northampton and nearly four-fifths for central Watford. Despite the national spheres of influence of many specialized contractors, even during the very active 1960–79 period only five such firms were involved in both commercial cores and they accounted for only 8 per cent of the specialized contracts recorded.

Inter-centre comparisons over time in the provenance of firms

The locational patterns of the initiators, architects, and builders and civil engineering contractors associated with plans for new buildings, extensions or structural alterations in the study areas changed markedly between 1920 and 1979 (figure 2.26). In the 1920s roughly three out of ten of the initiators of

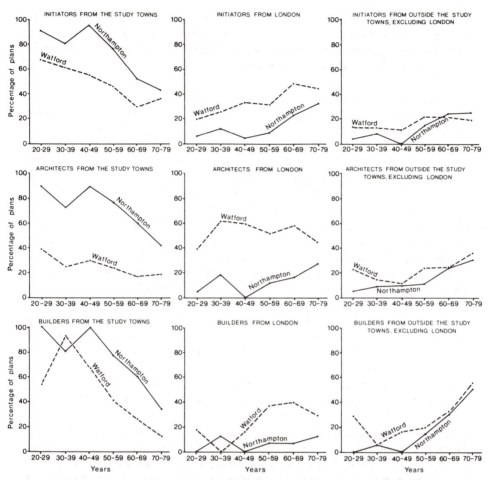

Figure 2.26 Percentage of plans for new buildings, additions and structural alterations in the commercial cores of Northampton and Watford involving initiators, architects, and 'builders' (builders and civil engineering contractors) from various locations.
Source: building applications.

plans for work in central Watford were located outside the town, the number rising to about seven out of ten in the 1960s and 1970s. Central Northampton experienced a similar increase in the number of initiators of work there from outside the town but there it occurred later: in the 1920s about one in every ten initiators came from outside the town (a figure that had been attained in central Watford some 20 years earlier), the number rising to about six out of ten by the 1970s. In central Watford the 'outsiders' were predominantly from London, but in central Northampton they were divided roughly equally between London and other localities.

These trends were associated with a generally decreasing proportion of architect-designed plans by architects from the study towns (figure 2.26), with central Northampton again lagging behind central Watford. In central Watford,

London architects rapidly supplanted local ones after the First World War, and during each decade between 1920 and 1979 between about four and six out of every ten architect-designed plans emanated from London architects. In central Northampton the impact of London architects was delayed, with their share of such plans rising to 18 per cent between 1930 and 1939 but not exceeding that level until 1970–9, when it rose to 27 per cent. The percentage of architect-designed plans by non-local, non-London architects generally increased in both cases (reaching about one-third of the plans by 1970–9), although during the inter-war period in central Watford there was a temporary decline in this percentage associated with a decline in the number of plans by architects located in Rickmansworth, a small town in the immediate vicinity. Most of these broad trends were also exhibited in the case of the plans of company/organization architects (figure 2.27), although in Watford there were comparatively few local companies/organizations possessing their own architects' department, reflecting that town's less vigorous development of local multiples.

The most striking feature in the case of the builders and civil engineering contractors (referred to collectively as 'builders' in figure 2.26) was the rapid post-war decline in the proportion of plans from firms located in the study towns. In broad terms, however, whereas in the case of initiators and architects local firms were mainly supplanted by London firms, in the case of builders and civil engineering contractors it was the share of work undertaken by non-local, non-London firms that increased the most. By 1970–9 in both central Watford and central Northampton over one-half of the plans recording the involvement of particular builders or civil engineering contractors were being implemented by builders and civil engineering contractors from outside the two study towns, excluding London.

The large majority of the consultants and specialized contractors operating in the commercial cores of Northampton and Watford were from the outset located outside the study towns. In combination with the locational changes among the traditional types of firms, this resulted in major shifts in the location

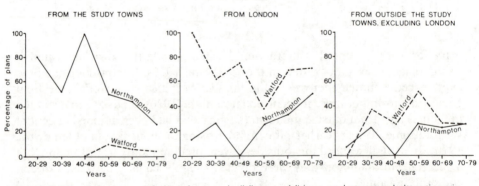

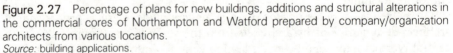

Figure 2.27 Percentage of plans for new buildings, additions and structural alterations in the commercial cores of Northampton and Watford prepared by company/organization architects from various locations.
Source: building applications.

of decision-makers in the post-war period. By the 1970s the decisions of the majority of firms of all types active in the two centres were emanating from offices in other localities. More importantly in many cases, these decisions were

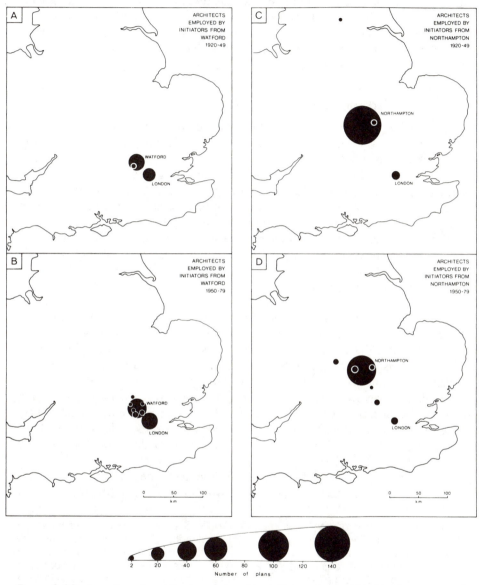

Figure 2.28 Location of architects employed by initiators from within Northampton and Watford for new buildings, additions and structural alterations in the commercial cores of those two towns. In diagram B the symbol for Watford includes an architect from the adjoining settlement of Croxley Green. In diagrams C and D the symbol for Northampton includes architects from villages in the immediate vicinity (Moulton, Quinton, and Milton Malson).

Source: building applications.

being taken against a background of business and professional relationships at a sub-national, national or even international scale, rather than in the context of a local nexus in which community relationships and business matters were intermixed. Much of this fundamental change was related to developments nationally, both in the professions and in company activities. But insight into it, especially at the local level at which it bore directly on change in the urban landscape, can be obtained by charting the links in the chains of decision-making that ultimately led to changes in the physical fabric.

Relationships between initiators and architects

The first link, that between initiator and architect, is unfortunately poorly documented in the building applications and accompanying correspondence, since the architect tends to act as the agent of the initiator, dealing with most communications with the local authority, including the submission of the building application itself. However, an important aspect is the final choice of architect and the architect's location in relation to that of the initiator, and on these matters the building applications provide a good record.

The locations of the architects engaged on plans for new buildings, extensions or structural alterations in the commercial cores of the two study towns were closely related to those of the initiators who engaged them, and major differences of distribution can be recognized between the architects employed by initiators from inside the study towns and those employed by initiators from outside those towns. It was rare before 1960 for an initiator from Northampton to engage an architect from outside the town and even between that date and 1979 there were only 14 cases in which this occurred (figure 2.28).Initiators from Watford relied almost exclusively on architects from either that town or the Greater London area, the plans from London architects emanating mainly from two firms – one (Ley Colbeck & Partners) also having a Watford office, at least from the mid-1930s – a preponderance that largely reflected the strong links those two firms had with two local department stores (Clements & Co. and J. Cawdell & Co) and a local development company (Watford Ideal Homes).

The architects employed by initiators from outside the study towns also had a strong tendency to be from the same town as the initiator (figures 2.29 and

---

Figure 2.29   Location of architects employed by initiators from outside Northampton and Watford for new buildings, additions and structural alterations in the commercial cores of those two towns. In diagrams A, B, C and D, in those cases in which the architect and the initiator are located in different towns an arrow-head indicates the location of the architect and the tail of the arrow the location of the initiator, except where the architect is located in the town in which the constructional work was undertaken (see diagrams E and F). In the interests of legibility three short-distance links in the vicinity of London (two of them between London initiators and architects in nearby 'suburban' towns) have been omitted from diagram D. In diagram B the symbol for Northampton includes an architect from the nearby village of Great Houghton. In diagram D the symbol for Watford includes an architect from the adjoining settlement of Croxley Green.
Source: building applications.

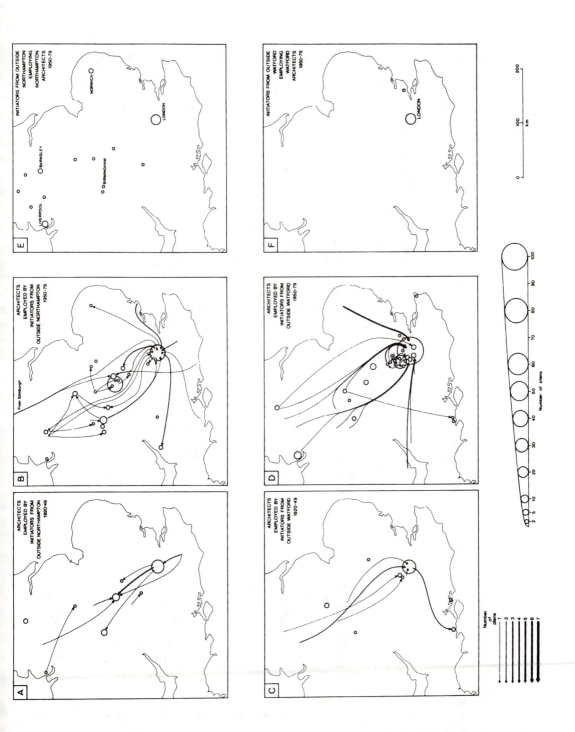

A ARCHITECTS EMPLOYED BY INITIATORS FROM OUTSIDE NORTHAMPTON 1920-49

B ARCHITECTS EMPLOYED BY INITIATORS FROM OUTSIDE NORTHAMPTON 1950-79

From Edinburgh

E INITIATORS FROM OUTSIDE NORTHAMPTON EMPLOYING NORTHAMPTON ARCHITECTS 1950-79

LIVERPOOL
BARNSLEY
NORWICH
BIRMINGHAM
LONDON

C ARCHITECTS EMPLOYED BY INITIATORS FROM OUTSIDE WATFORD 1920-49

D ARCHITECTS EMPLOYED BY INITIATORS FROM OUTSIDE WATFORD 1950-79

F INITIATORS FROM OUTSIDE WATFORD EMPLOYING WATFORD ARCHITECTS 1950-79

LONDON

Number of plans
1
2
3
4
5
6
7

Number of plans
2 5 10   20   30   40   50   60   70   80   90   100

0   100   200
km

2.30), especially in the case of Watford where in both the 1920–49 and 1950–79 periods about seven out of ten architect-designed plans for work in the commercial core were by architects from the same town as the non-local initiator, three-quarters of these being from London (figure 2.29C,D). The position was not dissimilar in Northampton in the 1920–49 period (figure 2.30), although there only 61 per cent of the cases in which the architect came from the same town as the non-local initiator involved a London initiator (figure 2.29A). For Northampton in the 1950–79 period there is evidence of an increasing proportion of non-local initiators from a wide variety of localities, stretching from London to Yorkshire, using Northampton architects for work in the commercial core, and to a lesser extent architects from other localities, and a decreasing use of architects from the same locality as the initiator (figures 2.29B, E and 2.30). This last fact is linked to a relative decline in Northampton in activity by the retail and service chains, most of which had their own architects' departments, which were almost all located in the same town, if not at the same address, as the head-office or regional office initiating the plan. In contrast, the use of company/organization architects for work in central Watford increased in the 1950–79 period both absolutely and relatively, reflecting increased investment by the retail and service chains, which were adjusting to Watford's improved standing in the urban hierarchy. Watford's own architects, however, remained virtually unused by initiators from outside south-east England (figure 2.29F), being completely overshadowed by London architects (figure 2.29D).

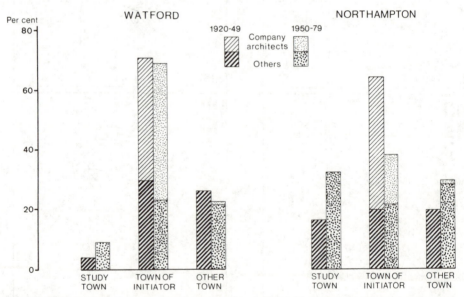

Figure 2.30 Location of architects employed by initiators from outside Northampton and Watford for new buildings, additions, and structural alterations in the commercial cores of those two towns.
Source: building applications.

The locations of consultants, builders and specialized contractors

After the initiator has engaged an architect, subsequent links are sufficiently varied in type and in direction of influence to make the notion of a single chain of decision-making inappropriate. While it is abundantly clear that the location of an initiator has a major bearing on the location of the architect selected, subsequent links are not necessarily in a set sequence, and the linkages between firms can be quite various. The building application files, which of course contain only that fragment of the record of the transactions between firms that reaches the building control section of the local authority, testify to the fact that not only do builders and consulting engineers engage sub-contractors, but specialized contractors themselves refer work to consulting engineers and consulting engineers sub-contract among themselves. However, although interrelationships clearly exist among consultants, builders and civil engineering contractors, and specialized contractors, and very importantly between architects and these three types of firms, the chain through which they become involved in a particular project ultimately leads back to the initiator. There is thus a logic in mapping the locations of the consultants, builders and civil engineering contractors, and specialized contractors in relation to those of the initiators (figures 2.31–2.33). In practice, such maps will bear a strong resemblance to those of the locations of these three types of agents shown in relation to the locations of the architects, because of the strong similarity, already implied by our analysis so far and to be analyzed explicitly later, between the locations of the initiators and those of the architects.

The locations of the consultants, unlike those of the architects, were weakly related to the locations of the initiators. In the case of activities in the commercial cores of both study towns, but especially in central Watford, the consultants employed were overwhelmingly from south-east England (figure 2.31). Within the London area the distribution of the consultants differed from that of the architects, for although some, like the architects, were concentrated in the centre, a far higher proportion were located in a 'suburban' ring, in places such as Croydon, Cheam, Epsom, Marlow, Wembley, Elstree, and Bromley. No consultants were employed from the study towns until the 1970s, when four firms appeared for the first time in the building applications for central Northampton (BMMK & Partners, J. Parkhouse & Partners, Pentad Designers & Draughtsman, and A. F. Stedman) and two in those for central Watford (Atkinson Bray & Partners, and Co-ordinated Building Consultants). With a further one appearing in 1980 in the records for central Northampton (Tapsell, Wade & Partners), there are clear indications, in Northampton at least, of the development of an active local group of consultants to complement the generally older established but still quite active local firms of architects. Clearly, the increased opportunities for work elsewhere in Northampton consequent upon the establishment of a New Town Development Corporation may have served as a fillip to this development. However, the patterns of linkages between the consultancy firms, the fact that nine consultants were involved in both centres and accounted for nearly one-quarter of the plans on which consultants

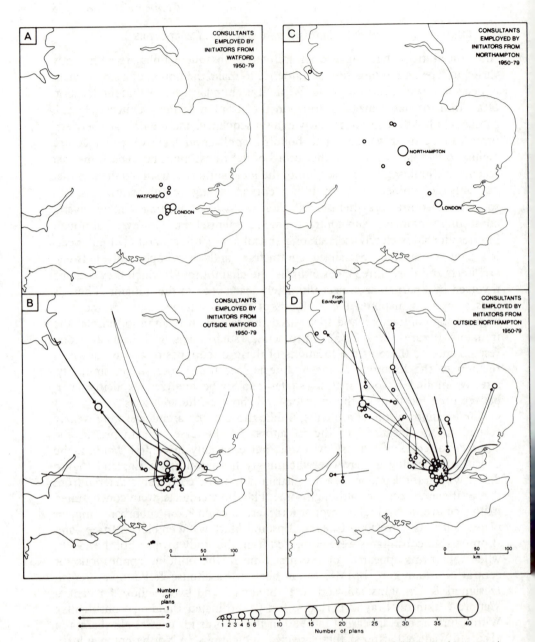

Figure 2.31 Location of consultants employed on new buildings, additions and structural alterations in the commercial cores of Northampton and Watford. In diagrams C and D, in those cases in which the consultant and the initiator are located in different towns an arrow-head indicates the location of the consultant and the tail of the arrow the location of the initiator. In the interests of legibility seven short-distance links in the vicinity of London (six of them between London initiators and consultants in nearby 'suburban' towns) in diagram B and ten short-distance links in the vicinity of London (nine of them between London initiators and consultants in nearby 'suburban' towns) in diagram D have been omitted. One Edinburgh consultant employed by an Edinburgh initiator is not shown in diagram D.
Source: building applications.

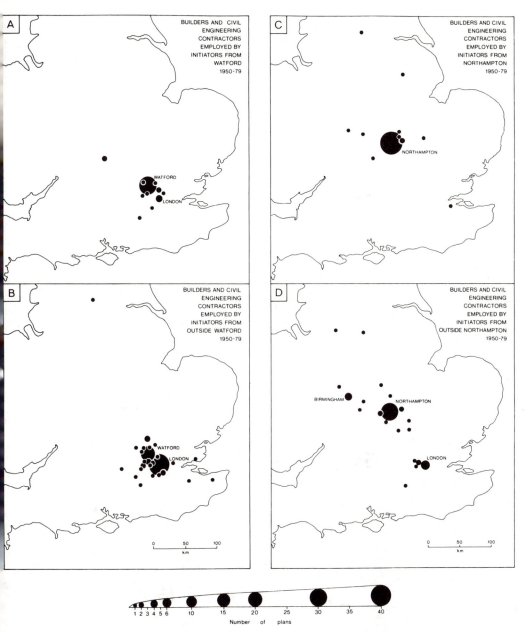

Figure 2.32 Location of builders and civil engineering contractors employed on new buildings, additions and structural alterations in the commecial cores of Northampton and Watford. In diagrams A and B the symbol for Watford includes builders from the adjoining settlements of Croxley Green and Bushey. In diagrams C and D the symbol for Northampton includes builders from villages in the immediate vicinity (Great Houghton, Pitsford, Earl's Barton, Rothersthorpe and Horton).
Source: building applications.

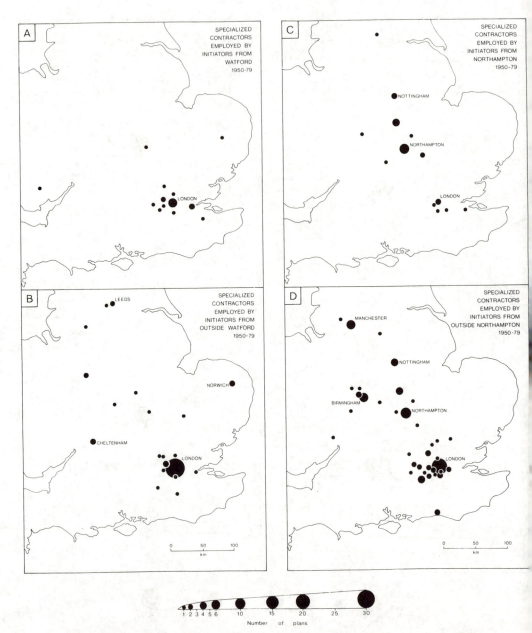

Figure 2.33 Location of specialized contractors (including shopfitters) employed on new buildings, additions and structural alterations in the commercial cores of Northampton and Watford. One firm in Penryn, Cornwall and one in Newcastle upon Tyne are not shown in diagram D.
Source: building applications.

were engaged in the two centres, and the fact that a higher proportion of consultants than of other types of firms had offices in more than one locality strongly suggest that the spheres of influence of many consultants were national.

As might be expected from the necessity for their prolonged presence on the site of the constructional work, the builders and civil engineering contractors engaged in the commercial cores of Northampton and Watford had a distribution pattern that was strongly influenced by the location of the study towns. There was a sharp decline in their numbers away from Northampton and Watford in the case of the projects of initiators from the study towns and a slightly less sharp decline in the case of the projects of initiators from other localities (figure 2.32). This 'neighbourhood effect' contrasts with the tendency in the case of all the other types of firms involved in the building process for clusters of firms to be located in (or in the case of the consultants and specialized contractors to some extent around) the major towns and cities, and is reflected in the small number of such firms (only five even in the 1960–79 period) active in both study towns.

The distribution of the specialized contractors operating in the commercial cores of the study towns reflected in part the relative diversity of their goods and services. Like most of the consultants, the specialized contractors were widely dispersed (figure 2.33) – much more so than the builders and civil engineering contractors – though they were somewhat less concentrated in the main towns and cities than the initiators and architects. In contrast to the distribution of the general builders, relatively few of the specialized contractors were located in the study towns, and the neighbourhood effect was comparatively slight. But, although the specialized contractors were far-flung, there were sizeable numbers in London and in towns around London.

Other relationships between firms

If all plans, both of initiators inside and of initiators outside the study towns, are viewed together, the dominant feature is the strong association between the locations of the architects and those of the initiators (figure 2.34). In central Northampton 85 per cent of plans in 1920–49 and 62 per cent of those in 1950–79 were prepared by architects located in the same town as the initiator. For central Watford the comparative figures were 62 per cent and 61 per cent. In that centre in the 1950–79 period, unlike the 1920–49 period there and both periods in central Northampton, the high degree of association between the locations of the initiators and those of the architects was mainly accounted for by the large number of plans initiated and designed in London rather than in the study town. Furthermore, in the case of central Watford in the 1950–79 period nearly two-thirds of the cases in which the initiators and architects were located in the same town were accounted for by company architects, whereas for the 1920–49 period there and for both the 1920–49 and 1950–79 periods in central Northampton the comparable proportion was only just over one-quarter.

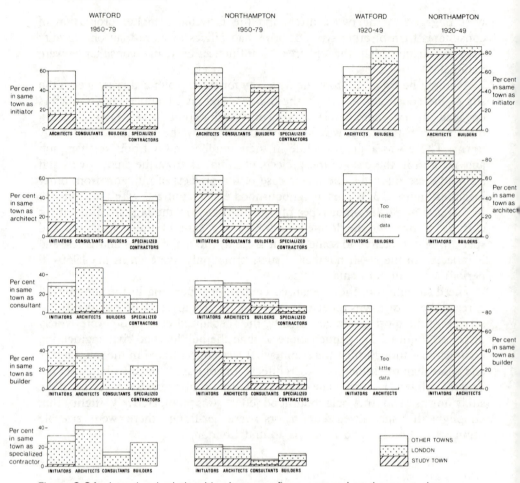

Figure 2.34   Locational relationships between firms engaged on the same plan.
Source: building applications.

Standing relationships between initiators and architects appear to have been a widespread feature in both centres. The prolific activity in central Northampton of the local firm of A. R. & W. Cleaver (20 plans initiated between 1920 and 1939) gave rise to design work that was shared among three Northampton firms of architects, two of them concurrently (W. Lawson Carter, to use its most recent of several names recorded in the building applications, and F. H. Allen). The work of E. Poole (later the Ernest Poole Trust) between 1919 and 1966 was undertaken by a succession of six different firms of architects based in Northampton or its vicinity. The large majority of national firms depended on their own architects' department, although the activities of Marks & Spencer in both centres suggest that they had standing relationships with the London firm of A. E. Batzer in the 1930s and 1940s and subsequently with the Watford firm of Munro & Partners (formerly James Munro & Sons). Whereas in Northampton standing relationships generally reinforced the tendency for initiators and architects to be located in the same town, in Watford, owing to several strong relationships between Watford-based initiators and London architects, they tended to have the opposite effect, particularly in the 1920–49 period.

Once an architect has been engaged for a specific project he exercises a major influence on the choice of other agents involved in the preparation and implementation of plans, although the extent of this influence relative to that of the initiator varies. If we examine the locations of the five main types of firms, the degree of locational relationship becomes evident (figure 2.34). The initiators and architects stand out as having had a much greater degree of locational association with the three other categories of firms than any of these three had with one another. This was partly a reflection of the influence that the initiators and architects exercised in the selection of consultants, builders and civil engineering contractors (referred to collectively as 'builders' in figure 2.34), and specialized contractors.

In Northampton in the 1950–79 period the initiators had the strongest locational relationship with each of the other types of firms (measured by the percentage of them located in the same town or city), with the architects having the next strongest such relationship and the other types of firms being comparatively weakly related. The consultants, builders (and civil engineering contractors), and specialized contractors were located in the same town in no more than 14 per cent of cases whereas the corresponding figure for the association of each of these three types of firms with the initiators and architects was never below 20 per cent. For the 1920–49 period there are insufficient data to compile a comparable graph for the consultants and specialized contractors, but the tendency for builders and civil engineering contractors to be located more in the towns of initiators than in those of architects is evident (figure 2.34), but with a much higher percentage in both than in 1950–79. However, 38 per cent of the cases in which the builder (or civil engineering contractor) was located in the same town as the initiator were accounted for by four firms (all from Northampton) performing the role of both initiator and builder (Northampton Co-operative Society, W. B. Chattell, A. R. & W. Cleaver and A. P. Hawtin & Sons) – a dual role that had almost disappeared by the 1950–79 period.

The pattern in Watford was broadly similar. There were, however, a number of differences, associated with the fact that many more firms had a common location – London. The consultants, builders (and civil engineering contractors) and specialized contractors were all more highly associated with one another locationally than they were in the case of Northampton. The particularly high concentration of architects, consultants and specialized contractors in London was also a factor in the consultants and specialized contractors being, in contrast to the position in Northampton, more highly associated locationally with the architects than with the initiators. And as before, the high proportion of cases (83 per cent) in which the builder (or civil engineering contractor) came from the same town as the initiator in the 1920–49 period must be viewed in the light of the fact that a significant proportion of these (in this case 26 per cent) were accounted for by just two firms (Harry Neal of Northwood and G. & J. Waterman of Watford) performing the dual role of initiator and builder.

Standing relationships between initiators and architects on the one hand and other types of firms on the other do not appear to have existed on a par with those between initiators and architects, although sometimes the number of occasions on which individual initiators or architects engaged particular types of firms was too small to permit inferences to be drawn with confidence. Architects employed the services of the same consultant for successive plans in less than half the cases in each centre and in most of the cases in which they did so a single initiator was involved. Initiators more often used the same consultant for successive plans, although in the majority of cases in which they did so a single architect was involved. Instances of architects using the same builder (or civil engineering contractor) more than once were almost entirely confined to cases in which a single initiator was involved, and initiators' relationships with specific builders (or civil engineering contractors) tended to be short term by comparison with their relationships with individual firms of architects. The very nature of the goods and services provided by specialized contractors meant that their connections with other types of firms were highly sporadic, with more than a single contract with the same firm being extremely rare.

Conclusions and implications

Light has been shed on the changing relationships within that part of the construction industry concerned with commercial property and on how these relationships, among others, underlay the development of the commercial cores of two towns of similar size at present but with substantially different functional histories. It is useful to summarize the findings on these aspects and to consider their implications.

There is a presumption in our account of the pattern of investment in the commercial cores of Northampton and Watford, particularly of investment by the retail and service chains that were active in both towns, that the timing of new building and of the cumulatively no less important additions to existing buildings was related to a major extent to the different social and economic structures of the towns over a long period, not least to the smaller size of central Watford's population catchment until the Second World War. This is borne out by the strong survival of the property interests of local individuals in Watford as recently as the inter-war period and the delay in that town of the main phase of investment by the retail and service chains until well into the post-war period. In inter-war Northampton, in contrast, local investment in the physical fabric of the commercial core, particularly in new buildings, was predominantly by companies and was accompanied by investment by national firms on a much greater scale than in central Watford. Since most of the retail and service chains had their own architects' department, these differences of timing were reflected in the proportion of plans for building work in the commercial core that were prepared by company architects, reaching a peak in Northampton in the 1930s but not until the 1970s in Watford.

In other respects, however, there were clear parallels, including in some cases similarities of timing, between the two centres. In both cases there was a change in the 1970s, reflecting to some extent national trends, from new building by chain-stores in the main shopping streets to comprehensive redevelopment for central shopping precincts and the construction of dispersed office blocks near the edges of the central area. Another change, partly related to this one, was that in both cases initiators from outside the town, having established a strong foothold in the core of the retail area in the inter-war period, by the 1970s dominated almost the entire commercial core – a parallel outward shift tended to occur in the areas where non-local architects were employed.

A further major similarity between the two centres was the absence of any significant tendency for there to be an increasing concentration of central-area development activity in the hands of proportionately fewer firms. If anything the trend was the reverse of this in the case of architects. A comparable study by Freeman (1987) of the county town of Aylesbury and the suburban centre of Wembley is for the most part consistent with these findings. An important factor accounting for the insignificant increase in the concentration of such activity was the tendency for firms operating on a national scale to be involved in fewer plans within the centres considered individually than the local firms that they had replaced. However, account should be taken of the fact that firms recorded under different names in the building applications, and therefore treated here as separate entities, were more likely in the post-war period to be effectively, if not formally, part of larger organizational units (cf. Freeman, 1987, p. 127). To the extent that the links thus involved were between firms undertaking different activities (for example, an initiator and an architect), their main significance here is the bearing that they have on the question of the concentration of activity as a whole, but any links between firms of the same type (for example, two initiators) clearly have a direct bearing on the interpretation of figure 2.18. There is no evidence, however, to suggest that either type of link existed on a large scale among the firms and other organizations involved in the development process in the commercial cores of Northampton and Watford during the study period, and instances that have come to light are by no means confined to the post-war period. What is a much more important consideration is the tendency for the main national owners of property to spread their interests widely over the country as a whole. This is almost inevitable in the case of the main owner-occupiers, the retail and the service chains, but it is also the case with organizations primarily interested in property as an investment. For example, the 93 town- and city-centre properties owned by Prudential Pensions (one member of the Prudential Group) at the end of 1980 were spread over no less than 56 towns and cities (Prudential Pensions, 1981).

The dominating role of initiators and architects in decision-making is confirmed by the fact that the three other main types of firms involved in the building process had closer locational associations with initiators and architects than with one another. But it is not only as the selectors of other firms that initiators and architects assume the key role but also as direct agents of change. In this respect the extent to which such firms have local roots and are imbued with a sense of place takes on a special importance. Ironically, of the types of firms that have been examined it is the initiators and architects which showed the most pronounced tendency over time to become divorced locationally from the commercial cores in which the tangible effects of their activities were to be seen. Frequently operating from the same town as one another, they became increasingly concentrated in London.

Often, either the architects were employees of the initiators or they had standing relationships with them. In contrast, the consultants, who only became numerous in the post-war period, had weaker standing relationships with the other types of firms and they were from the outset essentially adventitious, tending to have locations in south-east England and national spheres of influence. Least interconnected of all with the four other types of firms and most widely dispersed geographically were the specialized contractors. But both the consultants and the specialized contractors showed signs in the last two decades of the study period of becoming less concentrated in London, and in the case of the consultants there is evidence of the recent development of firms based in the study towns. However, it is in the nature of the roles of these firms that their sense of place is of less consequence for the urban landscape than that of initiators and architects.

The building and civil engineering contractors afford a further contrast. Although they were increasingly rarely located in the study towns, they mostly remained in their vicinity, tending to be more closely linked with initiators than with architects. But their role in shaping the visual environment became a subordinate one after the virtual disappearance of the initiator-builder in commercial cores in the latter part of the study period.

As far as the comparison between commercial cores is concerned, some important findings have been revealed about the agents of change at work in the centres of two towns that, in social and economic terms at least, are fairly typical of suburban and county towns in Great Britain. The decline of local firms in central Northampton, which is the more self-sufficient and more distant from London of the two centres, showed a marked time-lag relative to the decline of local firms in central Watford – a similar time-lag in the case of the county town of Aylesbury and the suburban centre of Wembley has been shown by Freeman (1987). And the influence of non-local firms in central Northampton was much less restricted to that of London-based concerns than was the case in central Watford. It might be thought, therefore, that central Northampton, experiencing as it did a longer survival of firms with a sense of place among those involved in changing the urban landscape, would have resisted longer the incursion of alien forms. However, the circumstances were more complex than this, since not all initiators and architects had the same degree of influence. The multiple stores and service chains usually brought in both architects from outside the towns and 'house styles' employed nationally, vying with one another in the scale and ostentation of their buildings in the case of the retail chains. On average they sought to exploit the larger and more assured market of Northampton first, investing heavily in central Watford some 20 years later as its underendowment relative to its greatly increased population catchment became evident. In this respect, therefore, it was in central Northampton that a sense of place was threatened first.

These findings afford a glimpse of the relationships that lie behind physical changes to commercial cores. The replication of many of them in a parallel study of two comparable centres by Freeman (1986, 1987, 1988) suggests that they are not confined to the localities studied here. To obtain a more complete picture a great deal more needs to be known about the initiators of change, especially the life histories of firms and organizations, their movements within and between centres, their titles to property, and how all these factors affect their interests in, and the timing of, various types of adaptation and renewal of the physical fabric. The users of property, whether owner-occupiers or lessees, can be traced through street directories, although piecing together their movements from such sources is very time consuming (P. J. Aspinall, personal communication). The assembling of information about absentee owners is more difficult. In this case the laborious combing of rate books, in so far as they provide a record of the owner rather than an intermediary, seems to offer at least a partial solution (Thompson, 1987, pp. 64–85). However, with the domination of new building in the post-war period by retail and service chains and development companies, whose activities are scattered widely rather than restricted to a particular town or city, the use of the records of individual corporate bodies has become an increasingly attractive, if not always practicable, means of tackling the problem. Direct information on the funding of physical change, however, is liable to remain particularly fragmentary.

3

Institutional and Public Areas

The commercial cores of towns and cities bear the strong impress of market forces, for the agents of change are primarily commercial organizations. Institutional and public areas, in contrast, reflect direct action by a variety of bodies – including those administered by local and central governments – whose primary purpose is not usually the making of a financial profit. The nature of the functions performed by these public and institutional bodies frequently entails the use of large areas of land. Collectively these make up much larger parts of the urban area than do commercial cores. Broaderwick's (1981) map of institutional and public areas created in Birmingham up to 1973, though not intended to be exhaustive (the sites of schools, for example, are omitted), strongly suggests the importance in the urban area of institutional and public sites, both numerically and in areal extent (figure 3.1). With the exception of a limited range of government and religious land uses, the sites of public and institutional land uses are a tiny minority of those within the commercial core. They are characteristically dispersed over more distal areas, frequently forming part of a fringe belt (Conzen, 1969, p. 125). Their distribution bears an intimate, but by no means simple, relation to periods of hiatus in the outward growth of residential areas (Whitehand, 1987, pp. 76–94). As with commercial cores, it is important to view this geographical pattern in a historical context.

HISTORICAL BACKGROUND

In Great Britain, as elsewhere, spaces for communal activities have long been a feature of urban life. In medieval times they were particularly associated with traditional games, festivals and military training, and were to a large extent located on extensive urban-fringe sites. Buildings, as distinct from spaces, for community purposes were more limited in scale: bridewells, almshouses,

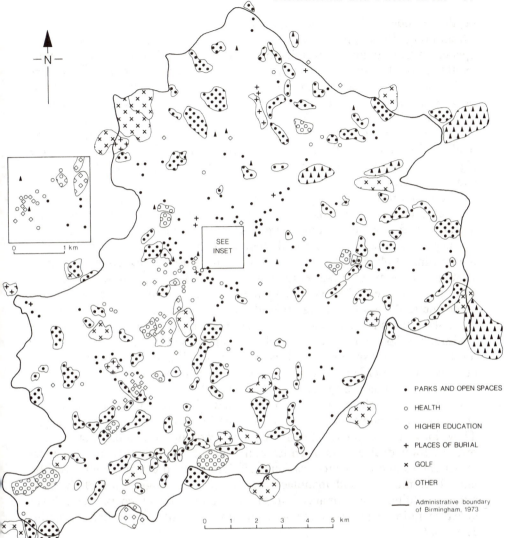

Figure 3.1 Institutional and public areas created in Birmingham up to 1973. Sites in and around the city centre are shown inset.
Source: Broaderwick, 1981, fig. 5.94.

grammar schools and town halls were mostly very small structures (Chalklin, 1980, p. 66). The largest and most numerous community buildings in medieval times were churches and the buildings of the religious orders, the latter being predominantly located at the urban fringe.

It was in the seventeenth century that secular public buildings and spaces became major features of the urban landscape. In England, public promenading became a major form of public leisure-taking, the development of promenades being associated with a rapid growth in the popularity of gardens and gardening. St James's Park in London, designed for King Charles II, was one of the grandest of the open spaces created in the seventeenth century (Rasmussen, 1960, pp. 89–91). And several of London's royal parks were opened to the public in the middle of the seventeenth century (Rasmussen, 1960, pp. 87). Commercial pleasure gardens were also developed on the edge of London – an idea that soon spread to provincial towns, some of these provincial pleasure gardens adopting the same names as their London precursors (Borsay, 1984, p. 2). Although for the bulk of the population the chief recreational retreats from increasing urban congestion were the common lands within walking distance of the urban fringe, by the middle of the eighteenth century the majority of county towns had public walks or gardens (Borsay, 1984, p. 3).

The creation of outdoor amenities for public secular use was soon followed by the erection of buildings for a variety of secular community purposes. Theatres and assembly rooms were followed at the end of the eighteenth century and in the early nineteenth century by buildings for such functions as the housing of libraries, learned institutions and museum collections (Chalklin, 1980, p. 56). Some of these ventures were financed by entrepreneurs, either to manage them themselves or to let them; others were paid for by individual landowners. A major role was played by well-to-do local townspeople who subscribed for shares to pay for a building or to the endowment of the institution or body it housed and might also subscribe annually thereafter to pay for the running expenses. Motives were varied but it is unlikely that the objectives of subscribers, as distinct from those who provided mortgage loans, were primarily financial (Chalklin, 1980, pp. 63–7).

In the nineteenth century a variety of new kinds of public buildings were erected in large numbers, and on average the individual buildings were larger. They included hospitals, lunatic asylums. workhouses, court houses and prisons. Individual donors of entire buildings played their part, but the most important source of finance was subscriptions from the increasingly wealthy landed, commercial and manufacturing classes. Although some of the new public buildings were financed from local and national taxes, the role of government in the provision of public buildings was still very limited (Chalklin, 1980, p. 67).

PARKS AND OPEN SPACES

In Great Britain the first official governmental recognition of the need for public parks came in 1839. This was contained in the Report to Parliament of the Select Committee on Public Walks. However, although public parks and open spaces were to become the most important public land use in cities in terms of areal extent, few parks accessible to the populace existed until the second half of the nineteenth century. Botanical and zoological gardens, which to some extent succeeded commercial pleasure gardens in the mid-nineteenth century, were usually associated with the formation of societies supported for the most part by individual membership subscriptions. The case for open spaces for the general public was taken up by the public health movement. It was argued that parks provided lungs with clean air. The first public park in Great Britain was given by Joseph Strutt to Derby in 1840. The first park instituted by a local authority in Great Britain was established at Birkenhead in 1843 (Broaderwick, 1981, pp. 97–8). Much of its cost was defrayed by selling some of the land for housing. A major part of the funds for the early municipal parks was raised by public subscription (Broaderwick, 1981, p. 98; Conway, 1985, pp. 234–6). The design of municipal parks became a matter of civic pride. Manchester organized a competition in 1845 for the design of its first three parks, and received over 100 designs. The nine short-listed competitors included, in addition to local designers, entrants from Cirencester, Dublin, Leeds, London and York. The first prize and the commission for the work was awarded to Joshua Major & Son of Knowstrop, near Leeds (Conway, 1985, p. 258). It would seem that for such enterprises designers were already undertaking commissions in places remote from their home areas.

Public open spaces grew slowly in number until the 1870s in London and the 1880s in Great Britain's provincial cities. There was a considerable increase in the number created during the few years just before and just after the First World War (Whitehand, 1981a). Many of these were recreation grounds, reflecting the increased popularity of organized sports. They were often of somewhat smaller areal extent than the public parks created in the nineteenth century and had few aesthetic pretensions. The playing fields added in the inter-war period were also essentially utilitarian and far removed in conception from the carefully landscaped Victorian public parks, with their lodges, refreshment rooms, fountains, lakes, and ornamental trees and shrubs. Since the First World War much of the provision of public open space has been an integral part of the design of municipal housing estates.

PLANNING

It is a short step from the creation of buildings and spaces for specific community purposes to more-concerted attempts at planning. Cities laid out to preconceived street systems have a history that goes back to the ancient world. They were a hallmark of the German colonization of eastern Europe in medieval times. As far as the public and institutional areas of cities are concerned, broadly contemporaneous with the separate parks created at the fringe of British cities in the seventeenth and eighteenth centuries was the creation, more particularly in major cities in continental Europe, of grand axial streets associated with a great variety of public buildings, monuments and open spaces. Several early examples in European capital cities were ceremonial approaches to palaces. Such developments required a strong authority, especially where they entailed major changes to existing street systems. Notable early axial streets outward from city centres were the Champs-Elysées in Paris, designed by the celebrated landscape architect André Le Notre, for Colbert, and begun in 1667 (Morris, 1979, p. 164), and the Unter den Linden in Berlin.

Perhaps even more important on the continent of Europe has been the creation of major roads and public spaces and buildings in the zones formerly occupied by city fortifications. In 1782 in Vienna, the open area beyond the Renaissance walls, in which building had been prohibited for military reasons, was converted, at the behest of the Emperor Josef II, into a recreation zone for the population of the city. And its design and maintenance became the responsibility of the municipality (Lichtenberger, 1970, p. 52). The medieval notion of common land became fused with the aesthetic principles of the Renaissance. The idea of the boulevard-ring within a former fortification zone appears to have been adopted first in France, in the seventeenth century (Morris, 1979, p. 165), but it was taken up widely in Europe in the nineteenth century. The associated zone of public buildings, promenades, parks, utilities and transport termini became a particular characteristic of major European cities.

At much the same time that old-established cities in Europe were being encircled by broad zones of public and institutional land use, the idea of a surrounding public amenity zone, or parkland belt, was being taken up in the design of certain nineteenth-century new towns. An early example, the first of many in Australasia, was in Adelaide. It was created and surveyed by Colonel William Light in 1837. Williams (1966, pp. 67–71) draws attention to the possibility that Light was influenced by both the parkland belt surrounding New Thurso, in Caithness, Scotland, created by Sir John Sinclair in 1812, and T. J. Maslen's suggestions for laying out new settlements in Australia, including his ideal town surrounded by parkland. The Australian parkland town may in its turn have influenced the twentieth-century green-belt concept.

In practice, coherent, planned schemes of public parkland or other open space in and around cities in Great Britain have largely been confined to the garden cities, municipal housing estates and post-war new towns. Early-twentieth-century proposals for a green girdle around London were probably influenced by the park systems around Chicago, Boston and other American cities (Thomas, 1963). They intended to provide a ring of grass and trees within the outward development of the urban area. The much wider green girdle proposed in 1933 by Raymond Unwin in his plan for the development of Greater London was intended to become a discontinuous park belt. The London Green Belt that was ultimately approved reflected Patrick Abercrombie's much broader purpose of restricting urban growth, encouraging agriculture and enhancing the appearance of the countryside. Large-scale belts of public and institutional space within British cities tend to mark previous standstills in residential growth associated with housebuilding slumps or topographical and other obstacles, or both (Whitehand, 1987, pp. 76–94). They have seldom been consciously contrived, although once in being they have often later received statutory protection.

AGENTS OF CHANGE: BIRMINGHAM

Who were the agents responsible for this diverse type of land use? As in the development of commercial cores, a number of roles may be played, either separately or in combination. These include the provision of land and finance, the organization and design of development, and the implementation of plans through constructional work or other physical changes on the ground. These roles may be undertaken by individuals or organizations, the latter being either public (for example, local government) or private (for example, a charity).

The composition of an organization is clearly relevant to its decision-making, as Hennock (1973) has argued in relation to municipal policy. Reflecting the heterogeneity of public and institutional land uses, the motives of decision-makers in regard to such land uses are diverse. In addition to the economic motives that are paramount in the development of commercial cores, there may be religious, political, social, personal or altruistic motives, or some combination of these . And there may, of course, be ulterior motives. For example, in the 1880s, Cardiff Corporation received from the Bute estate a 'valuable and munificent gift' of some 42 ha of land for a park. However, the land was poorly drained and would have been expensive to prepare for building. The agreement required that the Corporation spend at least £30,000 on the work necessary to convert it for recreational purposes. Thus, the Bute estate obtained a much improved environment for the residential development it was contemplating on adjacent land (Daunton, 1977, pp. 79–80). Such a motive has been far from rare. In the eighteenth and nineteenth centuries it was quite common for landowners to donate land and money for the building of churches which would increase the attractiveness of their estates for residential development.

It is informative to examine briefly for a major city some of the more important agents of change that have been influential in the development of institutional and public areas, considering first municipal agencies and then relating the roles played by these to the roles of other bodies. Birmingham, now the second city in Great Britain, is an example that has been studied in detail by Broaderwick (1981).

Despite its size, Birmingham did not become an incorporated borough until 1838. For much fo the eighteenth century its government was like that of a small town, consisting of Justices of the Peace and the Court of the Leet, which looked after such matters as markets and nuisances. A third body, the churchwardens, dealt with church and parish business. The major expenditure of the parish was on poor relief, which was controlled by the Overseers of the Poor. There were few public buildings apart from a lock-up, the workhouse and the churches. Historian and resident of the town William Hutton wrote in 1783: 'We are a body without a head. For though Birmingham has undergone an amazing alteration in extension, riches and population, yet the government is nearly the same as the Saxons left it' (Hutton, 1783, pp. 86–7). Although the Street Commissioners had been established in 1769, their powers were very limited until the early nineteenth century. Even after Birmingham became an incorporated borough, there were only four major Corporation undertakings – the police force, the prison, the asylum and the public baths – until the Improvement Act of 1851, when a number of other administrative bodies, including the Street Commissioners, were brought under the authority of the Council.

Despite these changes, the 1850s were not a period of high municipal expenditure. In part this can be accounted for by the Council's difficult financial position owing to the underestimation of the cost of providing drainage and roads under its new powers and the debts inherited from the Street Commissioners. But also important was the changing composition of the Council. There was considerable support for the growing Economy party, led by Joseph Allday, an owner of an eating-house. The party successfully opposed an attempt to bring the waterworks under municipal control in 1854, and in 1855 it prevented the Council from making an application to Parliament for powers to raise additional loans. The Finance and Public Works Committee resigned *en bloc*, allowing Allday and his associates to assume control. For several years, expenditure by the Council on new construction and the acquisition of major assets almost ceased.

The easing of these municipal retrenchments in the early 1860s can also be understood in the light of the changing composition of the Council. Indeed, knowledge of such changes provides a necessary background to understanding important aspects of the chronology of urban landscape change in Birmingham during the second half of the nineteenth century. In 1858 Allday left the Council and in 1861 the Economists were defeated. The new leader was Thomas Avery, who had retired from his scale-making business of W. & T. Avery. There was now a transition to an expansive role by the municipality. The increased activity of the Council was particularly evident during the mayoralty of Joseph Chamberlain (1873–6). The provision of gas and water was taken under municipal control, the construction of a new council building was begun and a major scheme of central redevelopment was initiated by the Corporation. In the takeover of gas and water supplies the Birmingham Corporation was by no means an innovator; there had been 49 municipal gas undertakings in England and Wales by 1870, most of them having resulted from the purchase of a private company (Hennock, 1973, p. 117). But Birmingham did become noted for the enterprise of its Council and its civic pride. Such pride is apparent in the speeches of Joseph Chamberlain: 'I have an abiding faith in municipal institutions, an abiding sense of the value and importance of local self-government, and I desire therefore to surround them by everything which can mark their importance, which can show the place they occupy in public estimation and respect and which can point to their great value to the community' (Boyd, 1914, pp. 41–2, quoted in Broaderwick, 1981, p. 81). Civic pride and religious fervour were closely associated. This perspective was in marked contrast to that which had prevailed in the 1850s.

Fluctuations in municipal policy more generally have been studied by Hennock (1973). He argues that when power rested with Birmingham's small-scale businessmen, as in the 1850s and early 1860s, the Council had little inclination towards or aptitude for large-scale activity. But when the Council was controlled by men accustomed to running major businesses, such as in the Chamberlain era, this was reflected in large-scale municipal activity. The financial acuity of councillors was of especial importance before Treasury grants became a major feature of local government finance. Hennock envisages a cycle of municipal activity. This begins with a rise in municipal expenditure associated with the heavy involvement of the local business elite in Council affairs. As a consequence rates rise and there is a reaction by ratepayers, especially small-scale property owners. The balance of power on the Council shifts from the elite to small-scale businessmen, who introduce a period of economy (Broaderwick, 1981, pp. 82–3). However, the occupation of key positions was more important than numerical dominance on the Council, for at no time between 1839 and 1912 did members of the big-business class constitute more than one quarter of the Council (Hennock, 1973, p. 53, fig. 5).

The the representation of business interests on the Council declined in the twentieth century, the decline of that of big business being disproportionately large. However, it was not until after the Second World War that the business interest as a whole ceased to play a dominant role in the Council (Morris and Newton, 1970, p. 117). This was later than in many other provincial cities. The continuing strength in Birmingham of the representation of the medium-size-business interest on the Council may be accounted for partly by the concern of builders and estate agents to retain a position on the Council during a period of increasing municipal investment in housebuilding (Morris and Newton, 1970, pp. 117–19).

In the twentieth century, local government in Birmingham and adjoining local authorities has reflected the tendency for local government in Great Britain generally to become increasingly important as a creator of institutional and public land use. At the same time local government has in the running of its affairs become influenced to a greater extent by national government and national issues. This is reflected in the strength of the affiliation of councillors to national political parties and the large measure of financial and legal subservience to central government.

The growing significance of the local authorities in Birmingham as creators of institutional and public land use is evident from figure 3.2. From a position of minor importance until the mid-1870s, by the early 1900s local government in Birmingham had become the most important provider of institutional and public sites. But besides varying over time its importance has varied considerably according to type of land use. In the case of several types of land use, by the time that local government in Birmingham was taking a dominant part in the provision of institutional and public sites, the majority of sites had already been established (figure 3.3).

In the case of parks and open spaces, apart from a few sites established before 1870, the establishment of sites, which took place rapidly, was undertaken mainly by a mixture of the local authorities, private individuals, and societies, with the local authorities providing by far the largest share. Most parks that were not actually provided by the local authorities were taken over and managed by them, often from the outset. In contrast, 44 per cent of the sites of health institutions were established by societies, most of them concerned with specialized disorders, although their role dwindled from the 1930s onwards. Local government health establishments were mainly fever and mental hospitals founded between 1870 and the First World War. Higher education was

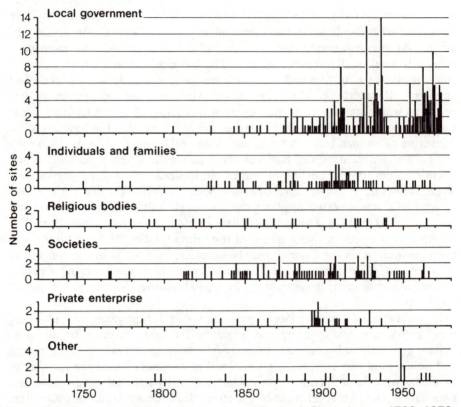

Figure 3.2   Bodies establishing institutional or public sites in Birmingham, *c*.1730–1973.
Source: Broaderwick, 1981, fig. 5.54.

different again, with one-third of the sites (19 in number) having been
established by individuals, ten of them by a single family (the Cadburys).
Responsibility for the establishment of the remainder of higher education sites
was fairly evenly divided between local government – which was a major
provider after the Second World War – societies, and religious bodies
(Broaderwick, 1981, pp. 163–6).

For institutional and public land-use development as a whole, the picture that
emerges is of a great variety of bodies and individuals exercising influence. The
City Council apart, the only single body, family or individual wielding a high
degree of direct influence was the Cadbury family. If attention is confined to the
institutional and public sites surveyed by Broaderwick, the Cadburys were
directly responsible for 18 sites (three parks or open spaces, four health
institutions, ten institutions of higher education and one golf course). No other
family or individual was responsible for more than three sites, five being
responsible for two or three each. Indeed the Cadburys are an example of a
family whose influence has extended over virtually all facets of the urban
landscape, including the residential landscape.

The interest of the Cadburys in parks and golf courses was related to the
family's wider concern with town planning. They were, for example, a

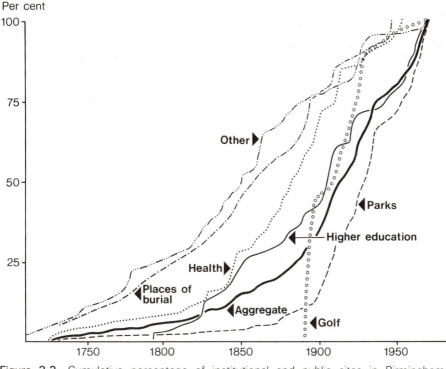

Per cent

Figure 3.3 Cumulative percentage of institutional and public sites in Birmingham, *c*.1730–1973.
Source: Broaderwick, 1981, fig. 4.9.

significant force in the establishment of the West Midlands Green Belt. Three of the four hospital sites that they provided were former family homes (Moseley Hall, Woodlands and Uffculme). The fourth and largest hospital site, that of the Queen Elizabeth Hospital, was bought and donated to the City by W. A. Cadbury, who was Chairman of the City's Health Committee. The family's concern for education was closely related to its Quaker beliefs and was manifested in both its donations of land (for example, to the University of Birmingham) and its active involvement in specific institutions, such as the Selly Oak Colleges. The high representation of institutions in the south-west quadrant of the City (Figure 3.1) reflects in part the location of the land holdings of the Cadburys.

The Cadburys as a family are exceptional in the extent of their direct, documented influence on institutional and public land use in Birmingham. Many other influences exercised by individuals and families, either in official capacities (such as through serving on committees) or through social networks, are far more difficult to establish. But such influences may be crucial. Furthermore, individuals and families may exercise significant indirect influence. The main aristocratic landowners in Birmingham, the Calthorpes (Cannadine, 1980), were apparently directly responsible for the instigation of only one site for community purposes (Calthorpe Park), but they were glad to sell, and occasionally donate, land to a number of institutions, small and large, the presence of which, they envisaged, would aid their attempts to develop their estate as a high-class residential area (Broaderwick, 1981, pp. 171–2). The words of Lord Calthorpe's agent concerning a grant of land in 1900 to the new University of Birmingham illustrate the point: 'It will open up a large area of building land which is at present not available' (Cannadine, 1977, p. 470). In this way the Calthorpes, like the Cadburys, made a significant contribution to the large amount of institutional land use in south-west Birmingham, but their role was more passive, and economics, rather than altruism, would appear to have been the main motivating force.

In Birmingham in the twentieth century there would seem to have been on balance an increase in the concentration of decision-making concerning the development of institutional and public areas as the activities of the City Council, and their responsibilities for areas once administered by separate

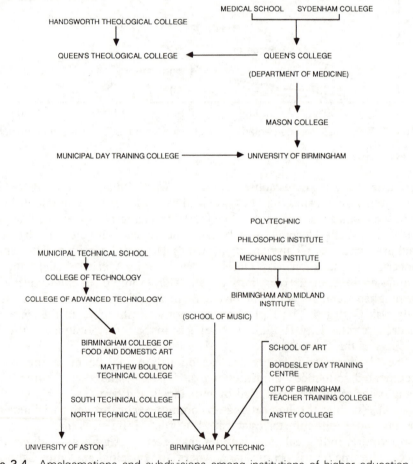

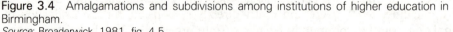

Figure 3.4 Amalgamations and subdivisions among institutions of higher education in Birmingham.
Source: Broaderwick, 1981, fig. 4.5.

authorities, increased. At the same time there was a tendency for local organizations to be subsumed by national bodies and for central government to exercise increased control over the local authorities. This was to some extent counterbalanced by the creation of new, specialized organizations, but it was compounded by the tendency for some types of institution, for example in higher education, to become parts of larger conglomerates (figure 3.4). In general, however, local initiative would appear to have survived more in the development of Birmingham's institutional and public areas than it did in the commercial cores that have been examined.

A NATIONAL CONTEXT: THE CASE OF TOWN HALLS

While Broaderwick provides an integrated account of the particular case of Birmingham and to some extent sets that city within a broader historical context, knowledge of how agents of change responsible for individual types of institutional and public land use fit into a national pattern of relationships is limited. As in the case of commercial cores, it is for the nineteenth century that the earliest extensive data on individual agents of change have been assembled. An outstanding example of the compilation of such data is that by Cunningham (1981) for British town halls between 1820 and 1914. In fact the term 'town hall' is interpreted very broadly by Cunningham to include not only the buildings referred to locally as town halls, but also varying numbers of other public buildings and monuments, such as assembly rooms, public offices, guildhalls, public halls, vestry halls, libraries, museums, municipal buildings, city chambers, law courts and exhibition halls. All these building types tend to be prominently located, frequently near the edge of the commercial core. Of all buildings they are probably the most symbolic of civic consciousness; each combining the role of showpiece with a specific or general local-community function.

Unlike commercial buildings, public buildings as important as town halls were frequently the subject of design competitions. It would seem that architectural style, especially in the nineteenth century, was a more crucial issue to town and city councils than to commercial organizations. Such competitions, though generally unpopular among architects, were a significant means by which architectural ideas were disseminated, particularly as a result of associated publicity in the professional press. Despite this, there is no evidence that in the major cities the introduction of new architectural styles in town halls was noticeably ahead of that in other building types. The continuing use of an old style in a public building was more common than the early introduction of a new one (Cunningham, 1981, pp. xiii–xiv). But, for the early introduction of 'polite' architecture in small and medium-sized towns, town halls did in many places stand out. It was sometimes a decade or more later that such places began to acquire 'polite' commercial buildings, notably purpose-built banks. For example, the town hall erected in 1862–4 in the modest Devon town of Tiverton (population about 10,000 in 1861) was very grand indeed beside the plain, mainly Georgian, traditional buildings that dominated the town centre. It was built to the design of a Bristol architect, following a competition that attracted as many as 60 designs (Cunningham, 1981, p. 68). Even the bank buildings that were being erected in Devon towns from the 1870s onward were subdued by comparison. In many country towns of Tiverton's size, or a little larger, more-modest corn exchanges and assembly rooms were erected by private enterprise at about the same time. However, for town halls that provided the full range of municipal offices, such as those that were erected in major cities like Birmingham, Leeds and Glasgow in the 1870s and 1880s, small and medium-sized towns mostly had to wait until the 1890s or later. Furthermore, although in small towns public buildings frequently stood out because of their grandeur relative to the overwhelming majority of other town buildings, for magnificence few of them could compare with their counterparts in major British cities (Cunningham, 1981, p. 69).

Developments in Birmingham exemplified the sequence of municipal building in major British cities in the nineteenth and twentieth centuries. During the 1830s, following a design competition in 1831 in which 67 designs were entered, a new town hall, in the form of a Roman temple, took shape on a cleared side within a short distance of the commercial core. Designed by the Liverpool architects J. A. Hanson and E. Welch, it was quite distinct in appearance from the town halls being built in small and medium-sized towns at the time, a sizeable proportion of which were hard to distinguish externally from small Regency mansions. Within 40 years this building, despite having been extended, was completely inadequate for the housing of the City's growing municipal functions. Accordingly, on an adjacent site a major redevelopment took place for a council building containing a variety of offices, a banqueting hall and a council chamber. It was designed by a local architect, R. Yeoville Thomason – although he had been placed second in the design competition to W. H. Lynn of Belfast. Within a few years this new council building was extended to provide more offices and an art gallery. A further major extension was constructed in 1906–19. In the 1920s an even more grandiose civic centre scheme was planned nearby. In the design competition for this, entries were received from as far afield as America, France, Sweden and Switzerland (Jones, 1940, p. 572). The winning scheme, by Maximillien Romanoff of Paris, was, however, too costly and was amended by the City Engineer in conjunction with other architects (Sutcliffe and Smith, 1974, p. 449). Only part of this plan was completed. The rigid monumentality of the design and that of a subsequent scheme approved by the Council in 1944 was already out of fashion by the 1950s (Sutcliffe and Smith, 1974, p. 450). There have been further 'master plans' in the post-war period, by the City Architects of the time. But only parts of them have taken shape on the ground, most conspicuously a new library, constructed in the early 1970s on the combined sites of the previous library and Mason College (the first site of the University of Birmingham), and, close by, a convention centre, the construction of which began in the late 1980s.

Birmingham's main civic complex contains fewer architectural unconformities than its complicated history of incremental and incomplete schemes might lead one to expect. Its council building, designed at the beginning of a period when Gothic was superseding classical as the fashionable style for municipal buildings, was essentially classical in style, like its earlier town hall. Back in fashion in the inter-war years, classical styles were also employed in the 1920s civic centre. However, a recent major development, the convention centre, though appropriately placed in space and time for the continuing of this tradition in the form of post-modern classicism, is actually closer in style to modernism. Its large expanses of glass and stone cladding contrast with nearby buildings in classical style.

Cunningham's (1981) data allow consideration of the national pattern of architectural commissions that provide part of the context for comparable scenarios of municipal building in towns and cities, large and small, country-wide. The large-scale use of non-local architects for 'town halls' (in Cunningham's broad sense) was already evident by the middle of the nineteenth century (figure 3.5), with London architects receiving some 15 per cent of all commissions. Individual donations from local wealthy people were a major source for the financing of 'town hall' building in the nineteenth century, local landlords and local industrialists being about equally represented among the donors (Cunningham, 1981, p. 80). The influence of such individuals on 'town hall' design has probably been relatively small, although from time to time their influence may have extended to the selection of architects. Where design competitions were held, commissions were not necessarily awarded to the winners, and cases of local architects being appointed after others had won the competition were by no means rare. The use of local contractors, many of them apparently having connections with local councillors, was more common than the use of local architects (Cunningham, 1981, p. 81). Despite notable cases of indecision and vacillation by town and city councils on matters of design, it would appear that, once a commission had been made, councils to a large extent deferred to the chosen architect on substantial matters relating to the construction of the building (Cunningham, 1981, p. 89).

In the course of the nineteenth century certain changes were apparent in the location of architects relative to the places for which they accepted commissions to design town halls and similar buildings. In 1820–66, architects operated primarily within regional networks, but a few provincial architects were already being commissioned to undertake projects farther afield and a few London architects were being commissioned from much farther afield (figure 3.5). In 1867–93, intra-regional networks weakened slightly but these were supplemented by a pattern of countrywide commissioning of London architects (figures 3.6 and 3.7) and the increased use of local borough surveyors, the latter having been used hardly at all before 1850. There was, however, little if any increase during the second half of the nineteenth century in the commissioning of provincial architects outside their own regions.

By the second half of the nineteenth century a handful of architects had become influential nationally. Of these, Alfred Waterhouse was exceptional. He acted as assessor in at least 15 competitions for 'town hall' designs between 1866 and 1897. These were in places as far apart as Plymouth, Belfast, Nottingham and Edinburgh. Lorenz curves relating the cumulative percentage

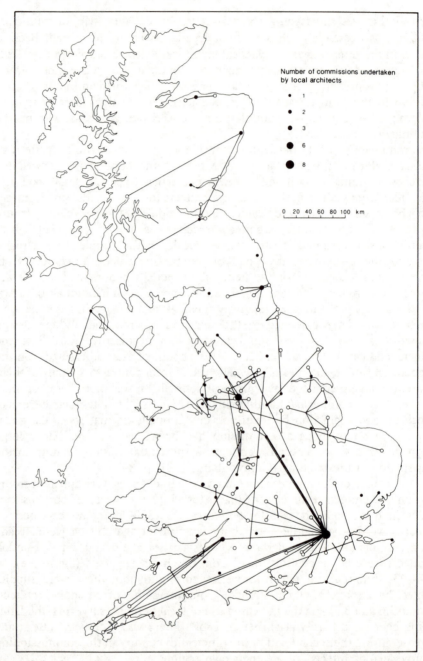

Figure 3.5　Spatial relationships between the locations of 'town halls' (including other types of public buildings) in the British Isles and the locations of their architects, 1820–66. Circles indicate town halls and are linked by lines to the locations of their architects. A solid circle indicates that the architect was local (i.e. based in the town or city in which the town hall was located). Places where more than one commission was undertaken are shown by larger circles. Minor omissions and distortions have been necessary in the interests of legibility. Joint commissions and exclusive commissions are given equal weight.
Source: Cunningham, 1981, app. III.

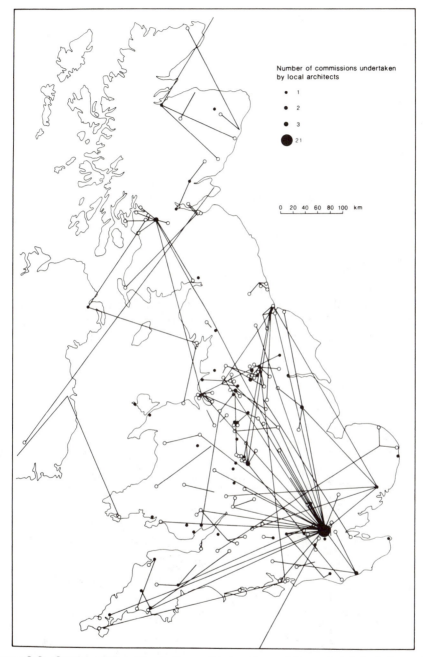

Figure 3.6 Spatial relationships between the locations of 'town halls' (including other types of public buildings) in the British Isles and the locations of their architects, 1867–93. Circles indicate town halls and are linked by lines to the locations of their architects. A solid circle indicates that the architect was local (i.e. based in the town or city in which the town hall was located). Places where more than one commission was undertaken are shown by larger circles. Minor omissions and distortions have been necessary in the interests of legibility. Joint commissions and exclusive commissions are given equal weight.
Source: Cunningham, 1981, app. III.

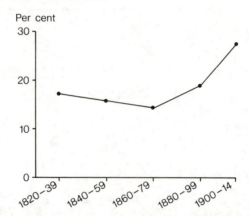

Figure 3.7   Variations in the percentage of 'town halls' (including other types of public buildings) in the British Isles that were designed by London architects, 1820–1914. Borough surveyors are excluded.
Source: Cunningham, 1981, app. III.

of competitions to the cumulative percentage of assessors suggest that between 1850 and 1914 this source of influence on 'town hall' design was highly concentrated – and that there was only a marginal change towards greater dispersal during the second half of that period (figure 3.8). Although there are

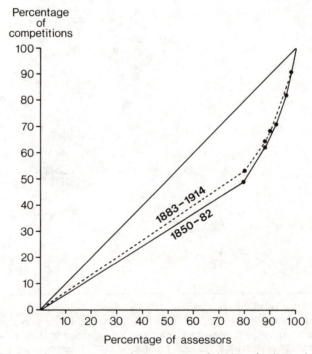

Figure 3.8   Degree of concentration of assessment of designs for 'town halls' (including other types of public buildings) in the British Isles in 1850–82 and 1883–1914.
Source: Cunningham, 1981, app. II.

no comparative data at the national scale for other types of building, it is a reasonable inference that the design of public buildings was particularly concentrated. The heavier dependence on local architects for the design of commercial buildings at this time suggests that nationally for this type of building the distribution of commissions was relatively dispersed and, as will be shown later, there is the basis for a similar inference in the case of residential buildings.

Since the types of public building included by Cunningham as 'town halls' are diverse, it is probable that the distributions of architectural commissions, both among architects and geographically, revealed by his data are not unrepresentative of all large-scale institutional and public building of that period. There is a need, however, to investigate the individual contexts and physical layouts within which particular architectural designs for institutional and public buildings have been produced and implemented. An effective way of doing this is to examine the historical development of individual major public and institutional sites. The choice of specific sites is constrained by the availability of information. A site of national importance, in London, and the site of a major provincial university will be considered.

A NATIONAL SITE

The estate of the Commissioners for the Exhibition of 1851 is located just south-west of London's Hyde Park, almost adjacent to the site of the Great Exhibition. The detailed research on its historical development by the Historic Buildings Board of the Greater London Council (GLC) provides the factual basis for an exposition of the main individuals, organizations and factors responsible for its changing physical form. It becomes possible from this information to bring into sharper focus the kind of decision-making that underlay the broader patterns so far discussed.

Comprising some 35 ha, the estate was bought by the Commissioners, partly with the surplus from the Exhibition and partly with central government funds. The purpose was to provide a site for institutions that would pursue the general aims of the Exhibition and 'extend the influence of Science and Art upon Productive Industry' (GLC, 1975, p. 49). As President of the Commission until his death in 1861, Prince Albert was responsible for framing much of the policy for the utilization of the estate.

Much of the northernmost part of what was to become the Commissioners' estate (the Gore House estate) had been previously sought by the Government as a site for a new National Gallery. Indeed it was with this purpose still in mind that the Government provided a large part of the sum that the Commissioners paid for the Gore House estate. The whole area was at the time in one of the most desirable parts of London's urban fringe, from the standpoint of housebuilding, and land values were rising. The Prince felt that it was essential that the negotiations for the land should take place in secret, and the contract was signed in May 1852 in the name of John Kelk, a builder, the sum paid being £6894 per ha (GLC, 1975, p. 54). The other major part of the estate had belonged to a Swiss nobleman, Baron de Graffenried Villars. Again Kelk was engaged to undertake the negotiations. In this case the owner's agents, the surveyors Wigg and Pownall, had prepared a plan for developing the area for residential purposes. The negotiations were complex and at one point the Commissioners found themselves placed by Kelk in a position of having a moral obligation to develop the site for residential purposes. This was not at all what the Commissioners had intended and apparently led to the replacement of Kelk by the builder Thomas Cubitt, who reopened negotiations. An eventual purchase price of about £7900 per ha was agreed, apparently in the face of competition from a South Kensington builder. The sale was concluded in March 1853 (GLC, 1975, p. 55).

Smaller landholdings were subsequently acquired, but three small properties that the Commissioners wished to acquire they failed to obtain. The site that was eventually assembled by piecemeal purchase had rather irregular boundaries. Some adjustments were therefore made with owners of adjacent land, apparently without major difficulties. These provided more satisfactory boundaries within which to build (GLC, 1975, pp. 55–8).

The earliest extant record of a possible layout of the estate is a faint sketch by the Prince, produced just after the Gore House contract was signed (GLC, 1975, p. 58). At about the time that the purchase of the Villars estate was assured a rough plan was produced by Edgar Bowring, the Commissioners' secretary. This plan showed roads in approximately the positions of three present roads on the west and south sides of the estate, a layout that by August 1853 had had a further road added by Prince to create an arrangement of main roads close to their present positions (figure 3.9A). A National Gallery was proposed for the centre of the site, surrounded by museums and colleges of art and science. Outlying sites were intended for private houses, official residences or other institutional buildings, an 'Academy of Music', and premises for learned societies. The plan and the memorandum that it accompanied were distributed quite widely for criticism. Alternative schemes were proposed by James Pennethorne, who as architect to the Office of Works had been making plans for a National Gallery in the area, C. R. Cockerell, T. L. Donaldson, and two non-architects, Henry Cole, a Commissioner and Secretary of the Science and Art Department, which had been set up under the Board of Trade, and Richard Redgrave, an artist who had been recruited to the Science and Art Department by Cole. Donaldson envisaged his National Gallery as being at an intersection of north–south and east–west axes culminating in a 'Hall of Glory' (figure 3.9B). He made no concession to the realities of piecemeal growth and change. Pennethorne's various alternatives were also symmetrical. In one scheme a National Gallery straddled the northern part of the site, separated from other major buildings by a very large formal garden (figure 3.9C). Cockerell, evidently influenced by the uncertainties that at the time surrounded the acquisition of what were to be the north–west and north–east extremities of the estate, proposed turning the site into virtually a triangle with two boulevards

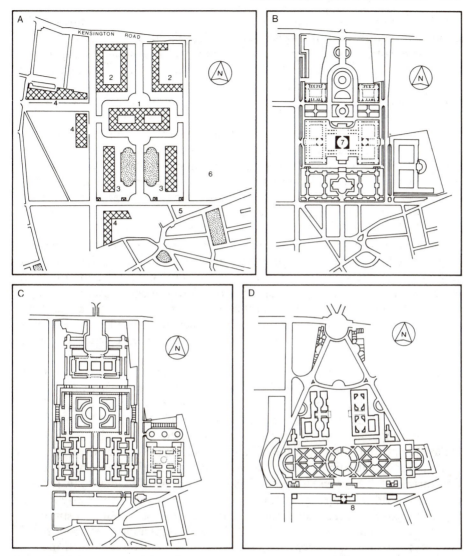

Figure 3.9 Proposed plans of the estate of the Commissioners for the Exhibition of 1851. (A) Based on a sketch of August 1853 by Prince Albert. (B) Scheme proposed by T. L. Donaldson in 1853. (C) Scheme proposed by James Pennethorne in 1853. (D) Scheme proposed by C. R. Cockerell in 1853. Key: (1) National Gallery: (2) Colleges of Art and Science; (3) Museums of Industrial Art, Patented Inventions, Trade Museums, etc.; (4) Private houses, official residences, or other institutions; (5) Possible site of hall for Academy of Music; (6) Possible site of learned societies; (7) Hall of Glory; (8) Music Hall.
Source: GLC, 1975, figs 19–22.

meeting at the north end (figure 3.9D). In contrast, Cole and Redgrave eschewed the classical layouts favoured by the architects. They recognized, furthermore, that building operations would be piecemeal and that the layout needed to retain its integrity in the course of this lengthy process. For example, a multi-purpose gallery across the northern end of the site was planned so that it might be constructed in stages (GLC, 1975, pp. 80–6).

The street plan that was eventually laid out in 1854–6, under the supervision of Thomas Cubitt, was similar to that shown on Prince Albert's plan. Resemblances between the main streets and the avenues of Napoleon III in Paris and the Unter den Linden in Berlin have been suggested. In view of the Prince's strong connection with Germany and the fact that 1855 was the year of Queen Victoria's state visit to Paris, neither of the resemblances should be surprising. The names of the two main north–south streets, Exhibition Road and Prince Albert or Albert's Road (later changed to Queen's Gate), and the main east–west road, Cromwell Road, were chosen by Prince Albert in 1855. Plane trees were later planted at the roadsides. These were protected by metal grilles set in the pavements, a device that had been noted by Cole in Paris (GLC, 1975, p. 59).

Despite the laying out of roads, the building types to be erected, and even the land use, remained uncertain within the main rectangle of the site. The effect of the Government's involvement was to retard development. Furthermore, the threat of war had led to a proposal from the Government to locate a barracks on the eastern edge of the estate, on the present site of the Victoria and Albert Museum. Adherents to the Prince's scheme devoted considerable energy to opposing this proposal. In a letter to Gladstone, then Chancellor of the Exchequer, Bowring emphasized the breach of faith that would occur if a barracks were constructed on an estate that had in large part been sold to the Commissioners in the believe that developments taking place on it would enhance the value of neighbouring property. The proposal was dropped in the summer of 1855. It was briefly revived in 1858, and Gladstone, by then out of office, was reported to be angry when it was quashed (GLC, 1975, p. 61).

Parliament's rejection, in 1856, of the project for a National Gallery on the estate raised the question whether partnership with the Government served the Commissioners' purposes. In April 1858 the Prince decided to ask the Treasury to dissolve the partnership, putting forward as a reason the five-year delay caused by governmental indecision over the location of 'national institutions'. The Treasury, under Disraeli, agreed, and the Commissioners set about raising the funds with which to repay the advance that the Government had made to them. They eventually obtained a loan from the Commissioners of Greenwich Hospital, the interest payment on this being raised by letting for housebuilding parts of the estate outside the main area intended for institutional development (GLC, 1975, pp. 61–2).

Largely because of the uncertainty over the development of the main rectangle engendered by the controversy over whether the National Gallery was to be moved to South Kensington, the first institution to build on the estate, the Science and Art Department, occupied the eastern site that was separated from the main rectangle by Exhibition Road. Cole and Redgrave had in 1854 submitted plans to the Commissioners for an enormous museum on the main rectangle. But it would seem that meeting the Department's immediate, pressing needs could not await the result of the protracted debate about the development of that area. The outcome in 1855–7, under the stringencies of a wartime economy, was a temporary structure – a large iron shed to the east of Exhibition Road – designed and erected by C. D. Young & Co., an Edinburgh firm whose London office was at the same address as the engineer Sir William Cubitt, one of the Commissioners. This was soon to become the South Kensington Museum and much later, after many adaptations, replacements and additons, including the inauguration of major extensions to the design of Aston Webb, it became the Victoria and Albert Museum (GLC, 1975, p. 98).

By early 1858, perhaps as a result of Cole's influence in particular, it had been decided that a garden, surrounded by buildings, should be a central feature of the main rectangle. However, although this provided an open centre, the large buidings permitted at the northern and southern ends of the site would limit the extent of the north–south vista. In mid-1858, following the decision to discontinue the Government's involvement in the project, a layout was proposed in which a central exhibition ground and garden for the Royal Horticultural Society would be flanked on its western and eastern frontages by a combination of public buildings and private houses. Hitherto the Prince's ideal scheme had precluded private houses from the main part of the site, although the Prince was not opposed to the combination of institutional and money-raising projects. William Jackson, building lessee on the other side of Queen's Gate was alarmed by the suggestion that private houses should be constructed on the main part of the site, and the Commissioners were accused of a breach of faith by at least one of the purchasers of Jackson's houses. The Commissioners maintained that Jackson was not entitled to lead his house purchasers to suppose that the Commissioners' site would be kept open or developed in a particular way. The Prince, however, was concerned about the objections, and in May 1859 the Commissioners decided to reserve the eastern and western margins of the Royal Horticultural Society's garden for public buildings for at least seven years. Nevertheless, in 1859 Cole's officers went so far as to estimate the financial return that parts of the main rectangle of the site would yield if privately developed (GLC, 1975, p. 60).

By the summer of 1860 any suggestion of the addition of a central north–south road was being rejected by Bowring as being inconsistent with the principle of the layout, which he envisaged as the same as that adopted in the cases of the Louvre in Paris and the great London squares. By 1861 the Royal Horticultural Society's garden was open, the South Kensington Museum had been open for several years and at the south end of the main rectangle a building for the 1862 Exhibition was under construction (figure 3.10A). But the death of the Prince at the end of the year came at a time when the prospects for future development were uncertain. In 1862 a scheme for a museum of natural history between the Royal Horticultural Society's garden and Queen's Gate was rejected by the House of Commons. And the 1862 Exhibition was less successful than had been expected. The vast quadrangle of public buildings envisaged by the Prince seemed a distance prospect (GLC, 1975, p. 64).

At the end of 1862 the suggestion of granting leases for housebuilding on the sides of the main rectangle was revived. An alternative suggestion was to dispose

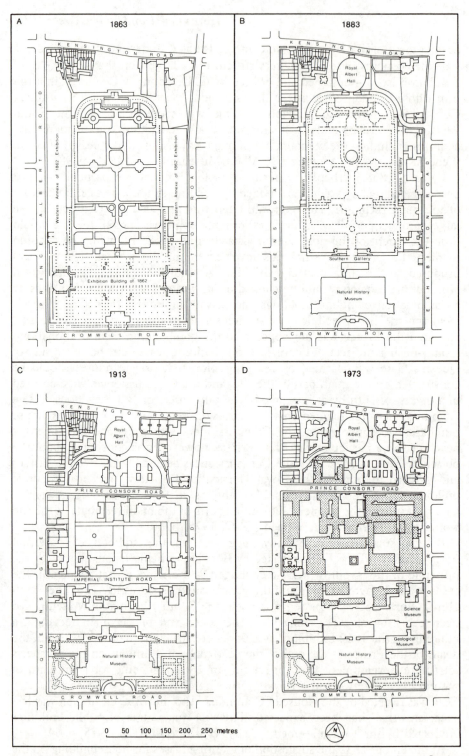

Figure 3.10 Estate of the Commissioners for the Exhibition of 1851 at four dates. On the plan of 1973 the stippled buildings are those of Imperial College.
Source: GLC, 1975, insert between pp. 54–5.

of the estate to the Government. In the event, in 1864 some 6 ha of the 1862 Exhibition site were sold to the Government at just under half the supposed market value of £37, 000 per ha on the condition that the land be used for the purposes of science and art. This sale alleviated the Commissioners' immediate financial problems. However, it did not lead to any greater activity on the Commissioners' land. During the period 1862–7 there was little change on the ground. In contrast, there was a rising tide of housebuilding in the vicinity. The national collection of portraits did in 1865 move to the south side of the Royal Horticultural Society's garden. And the suitability of the estate as an exhibition place had been enchanced by the authorization of the construction of the South Kensington railway station in 1864, just to the south of the estate. However, although in 1866 the Royal Academy of Arts was close to accepting a site of some 1.2 ha, it decided to accept instead the offer of a more accessible site at Burlington House, over 2 km to the east (GLC, 1975, pp. 64–5).

Although they were achieving little success in promoting institutional development, the Commissioners were able at this time to enhance greatly their financial position by taking advantage of the boom in housebuilding. Between 1861 and 1867, ground rents worth £23,000 were sold (GLC, 1975, p. 66). However, as housebuilding went into decline in the late 1860s and early 1870s there was an outburst of institutional and public building activity under various auspices both on and just off the estate. This lasted from 1867 to 1873. The buildings constructed included two for the Science and Art Department: the Cast Courts of the South Kensington Museum, designed by Henry Scott and his assistant J. Wild (GLC, 1975, pp. 113–15), and the Science School (now Huxley Building) in Exhibition Road, designed by Cole, Scott and Redgrave (GLC, 1975, pp. 234–7). Just north of the estate a committee appointed by the Queen was responsible for the erection of the Albert Memorial to a design by G. Gilbert Scott, funded by a combination of subscriptions and a parliamentary grant (GLC, 1975, p. 154). On the northern edge of the estate, on a site leased from the Commissoners, and with Cole as the main driving force behind its creation, the Royal Albert Hall was built to a design by Francis Fowke and funded by subscriptions (GLC, 1975, p. 177). On an adjacent site another committee was responsible for the building of the school that was to become the first home of the Royal College of Music. The Commissioners themselves were responsible for the construction of two large galleries in 1869–71 (the Eastern and Western Galleries), again to the design of Henry Scott, which were to house annual international exhibitions (figure 3.10B). These buildings were funded by the Commissioners, whose financial state had improved sufficiently for them to have made an offer in 1870 to buy back from the Government the part of the site of the 1862 Exhibition that they had sold to it, which was still lying vacant at the south end of the main rectangle (GLC, 1975, pp. 196–200). Finally, on that vacant site, the Government began work in 1873 on a great museum. This was to rehouse the natural history collection, which was to be moved out to Kensington from its increasingly congested premises in Bloomsbury. Alfred Waterhouse, who was only 36 years of age, had been appointed to execute the design for the new building prepared by the recently deceased Fowke, but eventually produced his own design, to which the Natural History Museum was constructed over a period of some seven years (GLC, 1975, pp. 201–16).

The boom in institutional and public building activity in 1867–73 created an extensive area of monumental buildings around the Royal Horticultural Society's garden. However, by the mid-1870s the Commissioners were again facing financial difficulties. The exhibitions, which ended in 1874, made a large loss, the dispossession of the Royal Horticultural Society seemed imminent, and the daily classical concerts in the Royal Albert Hall were proving costly (GLC, 1975, p. 67). With high prices being obtained for land for housebuilding, the temptation to lease parts of the main rectangle for housebuilding was considerable. By June 1874 a block of land in the north–west corner, extending nearly 200 m down Queen's Gate, had been sold for housebuilding, despite the fact that concern had been expressed in the House of Commons when it was advertised for sale. In 1875 a site immediately east of the Royal Albert Hall was similarly advertised for sale. However, criticisms of the architecture of the new housing in South Kensington were beginning to appear in architectural periodicals and although a lease to a local builder, Thomas Hussey, had been arranged, housebuilding on the main-rectangle sites was delayed. Norman Shaw was consulted and the board of management of the Commissioners recommended that future designs for private building on the estate should be prepared by a distinguished architect. Although this might involve 'some pecuniary sacrifice', the Commissioners approved the recommendation, resolving in 1877 that 'the private dwellings erected on the main square ... shall be of an artistic character' (GLC, 1975, p. 68). Unfortunately for the Commissioners, their deliberations on architectural style were overtaken by a contraction in the demand for large houses. In 1878 Hussey's solicitors told them that 'there are at the present moment acres of large mansions at South Kensington empty but finished . Two of every three builders have failed or are on the verge of it.' And the weak demand for large houses in the area, despite the fact that housebuilding in London as a whole was rising to a new peak (Spensley, 1918, p. 210), was confirmed in 1881 by the Commissioners' surveyors (GLC, 1975, p. 68).

Meanwhile, further attempts were being made to revive institutional development. In 1876, huts to house a small solar physics observatory had been built in the Royal Horticultural Society's garden. In the same year the Commissioners had suggested to the Government that they would give £100,000 and part of the site for a science museum and library on Exhibition Road. This offer was renewed in 1878 but with the site changed to one extending across the entire width of the Royal Horticultural Society's garden. The Government declined the offer, giving as a reason the need for strict economy because of the depression in trade at home and complications abroad (GLC, 1975, p. 69).

The early 1880s were a period of little institutional development on the estate. An exception was the construction in 1882–6 of the City and Guilds College between the Eastern Gallery and Exhibition Road, to a design by

Waterhouse (also a rare case in which a provincial builder was employed) (GLC, 1975, pp. 238–42). The last years of the 1880s, however, saw the beginning of changes that entailed a fundamental reorientation of the plan of the estate. In 1887–90 Imperial Institute was constructed across the centre of the southern part of the Royal Horticultural Society's garden to a design by T. E. Collcut, whose entry in the design competition was preferred to that of, among others, Aston Webb and E. Ingress Bell (GLC, 1975, pp. 220–7). Although the Commissioners granted the site at a nominal rent, subscriptions were well below the eventual cost of the building, and the Government became involved in securing the financial viability of the project. A further crucial development for the layout of the main rectangle was the construction in 1890–4 of the Royal College of Music (figure 3.11), funded by a donation from a Leeds ironmaster, Samson Fox, and designed by A. W. Blomfield (GLC, 1975, pp. 228–30). This building and Imperial Institute, together with the two new east–west roads on to which these buildings faced (Imperial Institute Road and Prince Consort Road), were an irreparable blow to the idea of a north–south open-space axis (figure 3.10C). The lost chance of north–south axial grandeur was still being lamented in 1911 by *The Builder*, which was of the opinion that 'anything more inept ... can hardly be imagined' (GLC, 1975, p. 72).

In 1889 the Commissioners publicly announced that they would 'no longer consider the grant of sites for public institutions' as being their principal function. The disposing of parts of the estate for private, non-institutional

Figure 3.11 Royal College of Music, constructed 1890–4, blocking the southward vista from the Royal Albert Hall (photograph by the author, 1987).

purposes was formally recognized as a *bona fide* means of raising income with which to further the Commissioners' purposes, which included from 1891 the endowment of scholarships (GLC, 1975, p. 70). Much of the initial filling in of residual, undeveloped, smaller sites in the main rectangle took the form of residential development, mainly flats. The fact that high-density building was now the most economic form of development was attested by the conversion of existing houses into flats. Alfred Waterhouse, already employed in connection with the laying out of Imperial Institute Road, was engaged to ensure that the new buildings in Prince Consort Road harmonized with those already existing (GLC, 1975, p. 70).

It was not until the early twentieth century, with the building of the Royal College of Science, on a site on the south side of Imperial Institute Road previously mooted for the Tate collection, and the building of the Royal School of Mines, that the major part of the first cycle of institutional and public building on the estate, as distinct from the creation on it of formal open spaces (figure 3.10C), was concluded. These last two major buildings, designed by Sir Aston Webb, in combination with the same architect's almost simultaneous transformation of the South Kensington Museum into the Victoria and Albert Museum, substantially changed an urban landscape that had for some three decades retained much of the character bestowed on it by the first major wave of institutional and public building in 1867–73.

Since the First World War, adaptations, additions and redevelopments on this site have created an intricate pattern of change, predominantly within the main lineaments of the existing morphological frame. Formed by the amalgamation of several existing institutions, Imperial College has occupied almost the whole of the central part of what was the main rectangle of the Commissioners' estate (figure 3.10D). This has been accompanied by substantial adaptation and redevelopment. Many of the dwelling houses that had proved an economically attractive form of land utilization during much of the second half of the nineteeenth century have been adapted or redeveloped for institutional purposes. Thus, despite the slow and fitful beginnings to their occupation of the area and the attractions of housebuilding on some of their potential sites, during the twentieth century institutions collectively have been ousting residential users from what was the main part of the Commissioners' estate. Similar processes of 'colonization' by institutions with growing space requirements have been widely recorded in studies of fringe belts (Whitehand, 1987, pp. 83–93).

One further twist in the train of events concerns the alignment of the layout of the main rectangle. Imperial Institute Road, the construction of which on an east–west alignment had dispelled the notion that a north-south axis of open space could survive, has itself ceased to be a public right of way. As Imperial College incorporated buildings on both sides of the road in the course of its expansion, the case for closing the road to through traffic became overwhelming.

Looking back on the Commissioners' role, we can see that their influence in creating a major area of institutional land use was considerable. It would be hard to argue that a comparable area would have been likely to have come into existence even if they had not existed. The specific institutional and public purposes for which the Commission was created denied the Commissioners much of the choice of development that would have been available to most owners at the rural–urban fringe. The Commissioners' means for achieving those purposes, especially those afforded them by their highly influential membership and, initially, their Royal leadership, were considerable. However, perhaps the most important finding of this case study is the major extent to which such a powerful body was constrained by the social, economic and cultural context within which it was working. First, the decision whether to move to the area was to a large extent in the hands of the individual institutions themselves. Secondly, the economics of development, which favoured residential, rather than institutional, use during substantial parts of the period when sites were being taken up for their initial urban development, could only be ignored at a cost. As the nineteenth century wore on the Commissioners showed themselves to be increasingly aware of this, and the granting of leases for housebuilding changed from being regarded as incompatible with their aims to being a perfectly justifiable part of estate management. Thirdly, although towards the end of the nineteenth century the Commissioners apparently showed increasing concern for architectural style, such matters and the layout of individual sites were to some extent in the hands of architects commissioned by other bodies. Finally, despite remaining substantial landlords, the Commissioners' scope for influencing further change was very limited once the initial development of the estate had been completed.

A PROVINCIAL SITE

The former estate of the Commissioners for the Exhibition of 1851 is one of the major institutional sites in Great Britain. Some of the most influential personages in the land have been involved in decisions directly affecting its development. A further perspective on institutional landscapes can be gained by switching attention to a substantial provincial institutional site, important in its local milieu, but in a number of respects more removed from the scene of national decision-making. Again, the choice of the study site was heavily influenced by the availability of records. In this case advantage was taken of an opportunity to gain access to the records of the University of Birmingham, from which a detailed reconstruction of major aspects of the decision-making concerning the development of the University's site is possible.

After small beginnings as Mason College in the last quarter of the nineteenth century, the University of Birmingham has gradually come to occupy a site somewhat larger than that of the Commissioners. Unlike the development of the Commissioners' site, the development of the site of the University of Birmingham has not previously been subjected to detailed investigation. The University's records, though poorly filed and apparently incomplete, cast light on both the manner in which individuals entered into the development process and the factors responsible for the division of that development into distinct phases.

In the early 1900s, having outgrown its buildings on the edge of the city centre, the University began to shift its activities to the city fringe at Edgbaston. There a new site had been donated by the Calthorpe family (Burstall and Burton, 1930, pp. 29–33), whose importance as landowners in south-west Birmingham has already been mentioned. Records have been found of some 24 variations on schemes that were proposed for the layout of the campus between 1900 and the end of the 1960s.

The initial schemes, monumental in conception, were prepared by the London-based architects Aston Webb and E. Ingress Bell, the former of whom had played a significant role in the development of the Commissioners' estate. They envisaged essentially a semicircle of buildings with a clocktower, a fashionable feature at the time (Pevsner, 1966, p. 170), located within it (figure 3.12). A substantial amount of building took place in accordance with these schemes between the early 1900s and the First World War, although by the end of this period the semicircle was far from complete. A subsequent major planned elaboration, never implemented, consisted of a further semicircle of buildings, which, added to existing and previously proposed buildings, would have resulted in an oval shape (figure 3.13).

The next phase of development took place in the late 1920s, following a further gift of land to the University by the Calthorpe family. Instead of the addition of a further semicircle, an avenue was proposed, leading north from the original entrance of the University on the base of the semicircle. Sir Aston Webb was now 78 years of age and, since completion of the work would take some years, this was presumably a major factor leading to the commissioning of another architect. Although Maurice Webb, son of Sir Aston, had in 1925 been consulted about the new biology department building (University of Birmingham, 1925), the local architect William Haywood was commissioned to design a layout for the expansion of the University with the avenue as its central axis

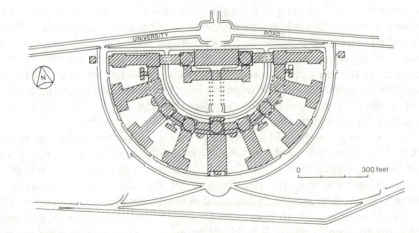

Figure 3.12   An early proposal for the layout of the University of Birmingham, by Aston Webb and E. Ingress Bell.
Source: MS map, in Estates and Buildings Department, University of Birmingham.

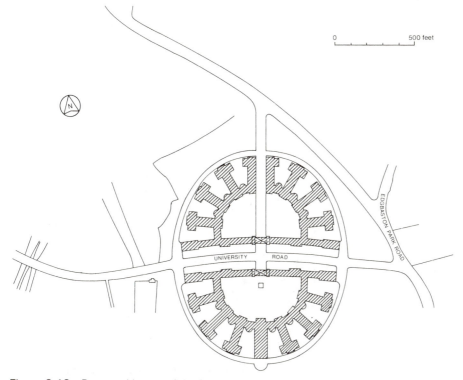

Figure 3.13   Proposed layout of the University of Birmingham, 1925.
Source: Birmingham University: suggested future developments. Unpublished plan, dated May 1925, in Estates and Buildings Department, University of Birmingham.

(University of Birmingham, 1928a). The idea of an avenue had emanated from the Calthorpes. Haywood prepared two schemes for the University Grounds Committee (University of Birmingham, 1928b). The one adopted (figure 3.14) showed the main avenue as previously approved by the Council of the University (University of Birmingham, 1928c). Tenders for the lodges and building work in connection with the entrance gates at the northern end of the 'Avenue' were invited, following recommendations by Haywood (University of Birmingham, 1929c).

The lodges were in fact the only buildings in Haywood's scheme that were constructed. Apart from these, the tree-lined avenue, and the premises of the Barber Institute of Fine Arts, constructed in 1937 on the eastern extremity of the site, the new site north of the semicircle was to remain as fields, sports fields and a gravel pit until after the Second World War. However, despite the reluctance of the University , a development that did occur was the extension of University Road across the railway and canal to a new hospital site. At the insistence of the City Council this became a public right of way, virtually bisecting the University site (University of Birmingham, 1929a, 1929b, pp. 8–9, 1930).

In the midst of the Second World War, in 1941, the University's Vice-Chancellor, Raymond Priestley, was already considering the choice of an

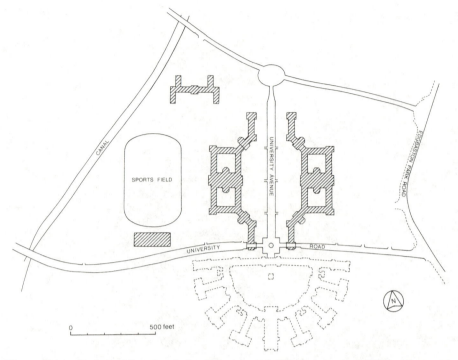

Figure 3.14 Proposed layout of the University of Birmingham by William Haywood, 1928.
Source: The Birmingham University proposed layout of grounds north of University Road, A. Unpublished plan by William Haywood, undated, in Estates and Buildings Department, University of Birmingham.

architect to take responsibility for the major physical expansion of the University that was envisaged as taking place after the war. He had evidently sought the advice of the Vice-Chancellor of the University of Reading on the qualities of Verner O. Rees, a London-based architect, and received an enthusiastic response (Franklin Sibly to Priestley, 29 September 1941. File 12).* In May 1942, Priestley presented a memorandum to the University Senate urging the preparation of detailed plans for all developments that involved building, anticipating that these would qualify as part of the public works programme that the Government was likely to launch after the war (Memorandum to Senate, 'Development at Edgbaston', 20 May 1942. File 741). In the autumn of that year the University Secretary, C. G. Burton, sought the advice of the President of the Birmingham Architectural Association on the name of an architect 'who could prepare a schedule which could be issued to Architects in connection with competitive designs' (University Secretary to Cyril Martin, 7 October 1942. File 4). Apparently acting on the advice received, the Pro-Chancellor, E. P. Beale, eventually consulted the Acting Secretary of the Royal Institute of British Architects, C. D. Spragg, on whether the University

* File numbers refer to files in the Senate Store Room, University of Birmingham.

should hold a design competition (Pro-Chancellor to Spragg, 21 April 1944. File 12). The upshot was that Spragg provided a list 'of the more outstanding architects who have had experience of University and College work'. The list excluded the names of Birmingham architects and those who had already done work at the University, on the ground that their qualifications would already be known to Beale. In his covering letter Spragg wrote: 'I think the two names I would recommend for your most serious consideration are those of Mr. Percy Thomas [at the time President of the Royal Institute of British Architects] and Mr. Verner O. Rees' (Spragg to Beale, 5 May 1944. File 12). These names, together with two others on the list and that of Robert Atkinson, a London-based architect who had previously done work at the University, appeared on the shortlist that Beale included in a subsequent letter to Spragg. The name of Haywood, then aged 67, was not mentioned. In the letter further advice was sought on how next to proceed, this being 'rather a delicate matter when dealing with men who are prominent in their profession, as it really comes to suggesting that they should submit outline plans in a sort of limited competition on the basis of details of the accommodation required which would be supplied to them' (Pro-Chancellor to Spragg, 3 August 1944. File 12). No reply to this letter has been found. Two months later, Atkinson and Rees had been interviewed at the University, and Rees, about whom the Vice-Chancellor had sought advice three years earlier, had been appointed (Atkinson to Burton, 20 September 1944; Rees to Burton, 20 September 1944; Pro-Chancellor to Spragg, 12 October 1944. File 12).

Although the University had already appointed a local heating and lighting engineer to work on the site (Hoare, Lea & Partners), it is clear that the layout and appearance of the University site in the immediate post-war years were primarily in the hands of Rees. But he felt constrained by the existing layout, and his first concern was to ascertain 'how much the layout of the future buildings is controlled by the condition that there should be a vista from the Entrance Gates' (Rees to Burton, 24 October 1944. File 12). Burton's interpretation of the conditions attaching to the transfer to the University of the land north of University Road was that 'we are under at least a moral obligation to maintain the Avenue, but it could, of course, be modified' (Burton to Rees 27 October 1944. File 12). Rees concurred with this (Rees to Burton, 31 October 1944. File 12). However, both of his initial proposed layouts departed considerably from the Haywood scheme that had been adopted in 1928. In one, Scheme A, the Avenue was to be bridged by archways about half-way along, linking the buildings on either side and converting that part of the Avenue closest to the existing buildings into a quadrangle (figure 3.15). In the other, Scheme B, a much more drastic departure, the Avenue was to bifurcate about one-third of the way from the gates to circumnavigate the proposed library, which was to be located across the existing line of the Avenue to form the northern side of a quadrangle (figure 3.16). This second scheme was practically the antithesis of the scheme accepted in 1928. According to Rees, as more-detailed information became available about the requirements of the

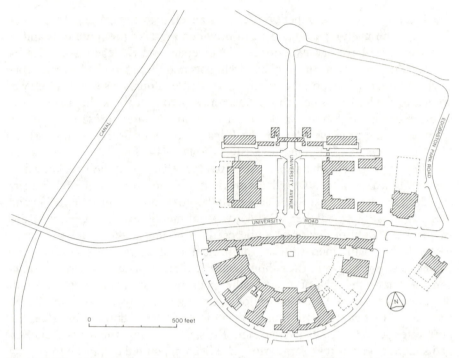

Figure 3.15   Proposed layout of the University of Birmingham Scheme A, by Verner O. Rees, 1945.
Source: University of Birmingham: lay-out of proposed new buildings, Plan A. Unpublished plan by Verner O. Rees, dated January 1945, being Plan No. H25 in Estates and Buildings Department, University of Birmingham.

different departments, his scheme to preserve the Avenue by bridging it, Scheme A, became 'less and less feasible'. He argued as follows:

> The archways suggested across the main axis of the Avenue to link together the wings of the Arts departments, and to hold the centre of the plan seem unnecessary, and the omission of any accommodation for Education results in a smaller building insufficient in importance for its position. Plan 'A' devised to secure the maintenance of the Avenue, thus becomes unbalanced, with the Library over-weighting one side. (Rees to Pro-Chancellor, 27 June 1945. File 42)

This criticism by Rees of his own scheme to preserve the Avenue appears to be the only surviving documentary record of the arguments for and against a decision that was to reorient fundamentally the layout of the site of the University. The report of the meeting of the Developments Committee on 4 July 1945 that endorsed Rees's crucial recommendation reads as follows:

> Numerous points arising on these alternatives [Schemes A and B] were dealt with in Mr. Rees' letter in which he now advocated Scheme B. This would mean a considerable shortening of University Avenue and absorbing the lower area into the building scheme. It was eventually agreed that the Calthorpe Estate be approached with a view to their consent being obtained for the

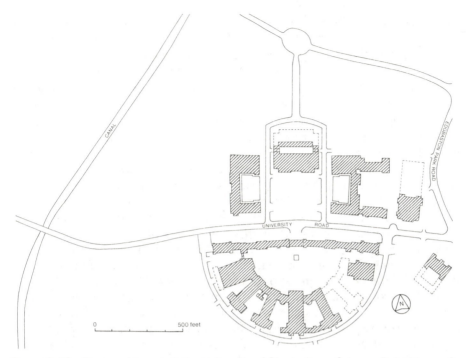

Figure 3.16 Proposed layout of the University of Birmingham, Scheme B, by Verner O. Rees, 1945.
Source: University of Birmingham: lay-out of proposed new buildings, Plan B. Unpublished plan by Verner O. Rees, dated January 1945, being Plan No. H24 in Estates and Buildings Department, University of Birmingham.

> developments on the lines suggested in Mr. Rees' report and as per attached plan. (University of Birmingham, 1945, p. 2)

There is no reason to believe that the letter from Rees referred to in the minutes of the meeeting was other than the one dated 27 June 1945 from which Rees's argument against the scheme involving the preservation of the Avenue has already been quoted. Running to six pages of typescript, it deals primarily with matters pertaining to individual buildings and contains no more of substance on the relative merits of the alternative schemes than has already been quoted.

If written arguments about the future of the Avenue that have not come to light were presented it is surprising that no reference is made to them in the extant documents. The only person present at the fateful meeting of the Developments Committee who is still alive is I. A. Shapiro. He has no recollection of those arguments being presented, which if anything reinforces the suggestion that the subject did not receive rigorous scrutiny (I. A. Shapiro, personal communication).

In this instance the morphogenetic argument would certainly have favoured a proposal consistent with the scheme adopted in 1928. The Avenue was a well-established axial feature, with maturing trees lining it on either side. The

Calthorpe family had apparently gone so far as to make it a condition of the transfer of the land to the University that the Avenue be maintained. Yet a contrary proposal was adopted with apparently little argument offered in its favour, and with no sense of the importance of the decision detectable in the surviving documentation or recalled by the one surviving person present at the meeting that approved the proposal.

The acceptance of Rees's recommendation by the Committee on such an apparently slender basis is probably indicative of the powerful position that he would have enjoyed as an architect commissioned by an organization to design a building complex for its own occupation. Quite apart from his professional authority on matters of design, he was, as a result of his discussions with the heads of various University departments, in possession of more information about the University's building requirements than any other individual. He probably had greater freedom than an architect commissioned by a speculative housebuilder, who would have been subject to the changing pressures of the market as transmitted through house sales. As to the recommendation itself, it should be viewed in the context of changing fashions. The grand avenue of the garden city, so fashionable in 1928, was passing out of favour, as Rees would have been well aware. It is hard to avoid the speculation that it was this, more than the space requirements of individual University departments or groups of departments, that was at the root of Rees's preference for abandoning the central feature of the University site. However, his presentation of the issue as primarily an insoluble 'functional' problem was reinforced by his reaction to the Calthorpes' acquiescence in this proposal:

> I am very happy to know that Sir Fitzroy Calthorpe accepts the idea of the formation of a 'University Quad' in front of the Tower.
>
> I had, as you know, spent much time and energy in thinking of every possible way of incorporating the Avenue. He will be glad to hear that the Developments Committee has decided that the Boiler House shall adjoin the Canal, South of University Road. (Rees to Burton, 13 September 1945. File 42)

There then followed a series of modifications to Scheme B. By May 1949 a roadway had been proposed for the north–west edge of the principal group of new buildings (Rees, 1949), thus making it possible for vehicles to bypass the main complex of buildings.

Much of this planning was to prove fruitless. During the early stages of the implementation of Rees's scheme there was a major split between him and the University, leading to a law suit. Thus, as with the schemes of Aston Webb and Ingress Bell and Haywood, events conspired to prevent completion of the proposals.

When the new architects for the layout of the site, Sir Hugh Casson and Neville Conder, prepared their initial report (Casson and Conder, 1957), Rees's scheme had scarcely begun to take shape, although its centrepiece, the library, was under construction (figure 3.17). Casson and Conder adopted a standpoint distinct from that of all their predecessors. On the Aston Webb buildings they commented that 'the strong half-circle encloses too harshly a north facing

Figure 3.17 University of Birmingham Library, under construction in 1957, athwart the Avenue, which previously provided the main axis of the University campus. Some of the poplar trees that lined the Avenue are still evident in both the foreground and background (photograph from University of Birmingham archives).

courtyard, while its northern range, fortunately not fully completed, sets up an unfriendly, indeed almost impassable barrier against the rest of the University site' (Casson and Conder, 1957, p. 9). The public thoroughfare running east–west through the middle of the site at the insistence of the City Council they termed 'a merciless slice through the University's heart' (Casson and Conder, 1957, p. 8). Of the demise of the Avenue they said: 'The grand axis of the north approach has, since the building of the Library, become meaningless – we believe mercifully so. It has ceased to exist as a monumental conception' (Casson and Conder, 1957, p. 8). Here then was the seal of approval on Rees's decision. But in few respects did Casson and Conder's proposals of 1957 (figure 3.18) resemble those of Rees, except where the existing morphological frame virtually compelled conformity. Emphasis was placed on a ring road, a very fashionable conception as traffic increased in the 1950s. Some of the roads in Rees's scheme were incorporated. The development of this idea was to lead ultimately to the severance of the link between the entrance to the now severely truncated Avenue and the incipient ring road (Casson Conder & Partners, 1964). Already identified by Casson and Conder in 1957 as 'meaningless', by

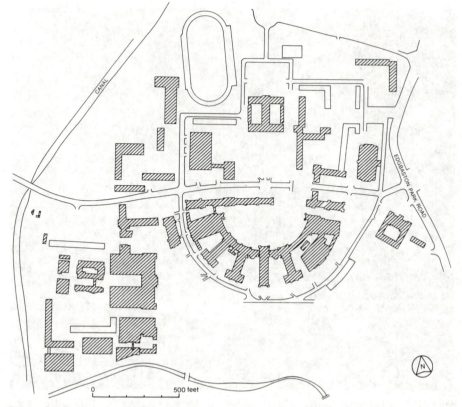

Figure 3.18   Proposed layout of the University of Birmingham, by H. Casson and N. Conder, 1957.
Source: Development of the University site. Unpublished plan by Sir Hugh Casson and Neville Conder, dated April 1957, being Plan No. H10 in Estates and Buildings Department, University of Birmingham.

the end of the 1960s the grand entrance to the University that had been conceived in the 1920s gave access only to a car park. The southern two-thirds of the two lines of stately poplars that had flanked the Avenue had been felled, save for a few survivors in the quadrangle south of the Library. The residual one-third of the Avenue terminated abruptly in a 7m drop where the ring road had been excavated across it.

In relation to previous plans, two proposals by Casson and Conder are noteworthy. First, they proposed that University Road should be closed as a through route, thus reversing the decision of 1929/30 and providing a close parallel with the history of Imperial Institute Road within Imperial College. Secondly, after consideration had been given to a variety of possibilities for filling in the gap that had been left in the original semicircle of buildings designed by Aston Webb and Ingress Bell, they proposed that the semicircle remain incomplete. This curious decision stemmed, it would seem, from Casson and Conder's criticisms of the Aston Webb and Ingress Bell buildings already noted.

Like the study of the development of the estate of the Commissioners for the Exhibition of 1851, this examination of selected aspects of the physical development of a single institution deals with a unique set of circumstances. However, again like that previous study, it yields findings that would appear to be of wider significance. First, although the timing of developments was strongly influenced by key individuals within the University and the opportunities they recognized locally and nationally for obtaining funds, the plan of the site and how it evolved were largely determined by a succession of architects. Secondly, the justifications for architects' recommendations on layouts, especially those involving reversals of recommendations by previous architects, appear to have had little substance, in so far as they were committed to paper. Although existing morphological frames acted as a powerful constraint, architects appear to have conformed to the fashions of their time, even when to do so created difficulties in relation to existing layouts. Thirdly, a strong element of cumulative causation was evident, especially in the post-war period. Rees's recommendation that the Avenue should bifurcate around the Library led to a succession of proposals each of which was plausible in the light of its predecessor but as a series led to a fundamental reorientation of the layout of the University site. In this way a scheme based on the axis of the Avenue was transformed into one in which a number of roughly quadrangular 'cells' were a principal feature. At the same time a primarily axial system of vehicular access was changed to one in which a ring road was the main feature.

CONCLUSION

Unlike commercial developments, those for public and institutional purposes are often not motivated primarily by profit. But they are heavily constrained by economic factors. Their financial basis, however, tends to be different from that of commercial developments. Funded as they are by a diversity of means, including subscriptions, donations and government grants, they are collectively less vulnerable to the economic fluctuations to which commercial developments are sensitive. Differences in funding do not mean, however, that the decision-makers involved are necessarily different. Businessmen play a role in both public bodies and private institutions. Indeed, it has been argued that in nineteenth-century Birmingham there was a positive correlation between the extent of the influence of the local business elite in municipal government and investment in municipal building projects. It should not inferred from this, however, that elite decision-making bodies, whether drawn from the local business elite or from a wider range of the elite, are able to override economic forces. Indeed, the activities of the Commissioners for the Exhibition of 1851 show how a socially elite body can be highly constrained both by its own financial state and by the vagaries of the economic climate.

Public and institutional buildings have a particularly strong symbolic significance. This is evident in the greater individuality of the architectural styles of such buildings in comparison with those of commercial buildings, many of which have been built speculatively. In the case of municipal buildings, the importance attached to architectural style has been associated with design competitions, the significance at an early date of non-local, especially London-based, architects, and the erection of monumental, though seldom avant-garde, buildings.

Local control in institutional and public areas has ostensibly remained stronger than in commercial cores, where local ownership has gradually been replaced by that of national concerns. With the major exceptions of decentral-ized and regional offices of central government, institutional and public areas have for the most part remained in local ownership and under local administration, though the influence of central government on the funding of their development has sometimes been strong.

Architects have been crucial in translating into particular architectural styles the aspirations of those initiating developments. The lengthy debates of the Leeds University Sites Committee on the relative merits of Tudor and Georgian styles (Beresford, 1975, p. 136) during the inter-war period were probably unusual. Once an architect has been commissioned his influence is usually overriding. This influence is, however, heavily subject to the fashions of the time, a fact that encouraged the hotchpotch of architectural styles and design features that exist on the large majority of institutional and public sites that have been developed over many decades. This last characteristic is compounded by the frequency with which extensive schemes are overtaken by economic and other events and are seldom implemented in their entirety.

Thus, institutional and public areas present a number of contrasts to commercial cores. These go well beyond the obvious locational differences relating to the functions these areas perform and the economics of land use. They concern also the ways in which developments are undertaken, the degree of survival of local decision-making concerning development and, sometimes related to this, the symbolic roles that physical structures and spaces perform. The next step is to switch the focus of attention to residential areas. These not only provide different insights but, by the comparisons they afford, further illuminate the development processes that occur in commercial cores and institutional and public areas.

4

Residential Areas

BACKGROUND

The Georgian and early-Victorian periods

Residential areas are much more likely than institutional and public areas to have been created predominantly for profit. While in this respect they are more like commercial cores, they differ from them in having for the most part been created *de novo* during the industrial era.

The large majority of British towns and cities underwent their first major post-medieval residential extensions in the eighteenth century. A number of different types of contributor to the process of residential development at this time may be recognized. Particularly important were landowners, developers and builders. The roles of these agents in the development process tended to overlap.

The owners of potential residential-development land consisted of a variety of organizations and individuals (Chalklin, 1974, p. 58). Of major importance among the organizations were the municipal authorities. More numerous, but generally smaller, were institutional bodies, especially organizations of a religious, educational or medical nature. Among the private individuals, in addition to the gentry, there were local traders and professional men.

Some landowners, perhaps through an agent, acted as promoters of residential development by laying out streets and plots. They then either sold plots to builders or took on the role of ground landlord, granting building leases whereby the builder and his assignees had use of the land. Most building leases were for a specified term, 99 years being quite common, after which the land and buildings were to be surrendered to the ground landlord. Other landowners conveyed potential building land to developers who acted as promoters of residential development instead of the original owners (Chalklin, 1974, pp. 57–8).

Residential developers came from a variety of occupations. First, there were those who by profession or occupation were concerned with land development or building – surveyors, architects, solicitors and various types of craftsmen involved in building, such as bricklayers, carpenters and joiners. Secondly, there were members of a variety of occupational groups not connected with land or building – merchants, well-to-do tradespeople, professional men, and manufacturers (Chalklin, 1974, pp. 58–9).

Finally, there were those who undertook or organized the actual building operations, each project usually comprising the building of one or two sizeable houses or a few working-class dwellings. These builders, or 'building undertakers', were usually individuals, although occasionally they were formal partnerships or associations of building craftsmen. They were essentially of two types. First, there were craftsmen-builders, such as bricklayers and carpenters, who carried out part of the building operation and contracted the remainder to other craftsmen. Secondly, there were those from outside the building trades who contracted craftsmen to undertake the entire work of construction. The construction of houses was in neither case a full-time occupation. For those from outside the building trades their participation in such undertakings might involve no more than a single project in a lifetime (Chalklin, 1974, pp. 167–9).

Thus, despite the burgeoning of residential development during the eighteenth century its organization remained an essentially part-time activity. Much the same was true of the financing of residential development (Chalklin, 1974, p. 60). Loan capital was provided by professional men (especially attorneys-at-law), well-to-do tradespeople, manufacturers and members of the leisured classes. It may be assumed, although there appears to be little direct evidence until the first half of the nineteenth century (Dyos, 1968, p. 664), that ground landlords were a source of capital. Despite the development of a national capital market, it was rare, even in the early nineteenth century, for residential developments in provincial towns to be funded by loans from outside the town or nearby settlements.

Unlike in the late twentieth century, only a small minority of residential property was owner-occupied. Houses were owned primarily as an investment. Many of those responsible for the erection of houses continued to retain them for many years after construction, mainly for letting (Chalklin, 1974, pp. 172–3). Craftsmen-builders as distinct from builders outside the trade, were more likely to sell on completion the houses that they built, so as to release capital with which to build further houses. The purchasers were spread widely across the occupational spectrum with individuals frequently owning up to three houses, occasionally more (Chalklin, 1974, p. 161).

This outline of the activities of the main parties involved in residential development in the early industrial era is also substantially true of the greater part of the nineteenth century. Building firms remained small. In London in the middle of the nineteenth century about one-half of all housebuilders built only one ot two houses a year (Dyos, 1968, p. 659), and most parts of England were even more dominated by small firms (Aspinall, 1982, pp. 77–8).

The late-Victorian and Edwardian periods

During the last quarter of the nineteenth century there were changes in the structure of the housebuilding industry in London. During the building boom that peaked in London in 1880–1 the number of medium-sized and large firms increased, and in the subsequent slump it was the small firms that tended to go out of business. When the next boom developed, at the end of the 1890s, less than 3 per cent of firms were building over 40 per cent of London's new houses, though small builders were still numerous, with 60 per cent of builders building six houses or fewer in a year (Dyos, 1968, pp. 659–60).

Beginning slightly earlier, there were changes too in the financing of residential development. Building societies had originally been of two basic types; either erecting houses themselves or lending money to members for their own undertakings. In each case regular subscriptions were the means of raising money from members, and the societies were dissolved when members' dwellings were paid for. During the second half of the nineteenth century, building societies changed from being temporary creations to being predominantly run on a permanent basis. Their main function became the advancing of loans to house purchasers. In north Leeds, at least, they were not involved in making loans to developers (Treen, 1982, p. 177). Indeed, it is not clear what the main sources of capital for development were in that area. Financial support from pre-development landowners was apparently unusual there. More generally, it is probable that solicitors were increasing their importance as channels for investment in housebuilding (Dyos, 1968, p. 669). But the sources of capital for housebuilding remained almost entirely local, even in the case of developments for the upper middle class (Simpson and Lloyd, 1977, p. 9).

A variety of other changes took place in the late nineteenth century that were by no means confined to London. Springett (1986) draws attention to an increasing professionalism in housebuilding in Huddersfield. Architects, surveyors and estate agents had larger roles to play. The small-scale, *ad hoc* nature of residential development characteristic of the eighteenth century and much of the nineteenth century was becoming less dominant. The opportunities afforded by rapid residential growth were creating more-sophisticated relationships and more full-time specialists.

Despite these changes, those undertaking housebuilding at the end of the nineteenth century still included many who were not primarily engaged in building for a livelihood. The study by Trowell (1983) of the suburb of Headingley in Leeds between 1838 and 1914 makes this clear. 'Entrepreneurs', comprising people of independent means, manufacturers, merchants and a miscellaneous group, were responsible for 19 per cent of the houses erected in his study area at this time. Land or estate agents, architects and surveyors accounted for a further 14 per cent. Judging by Treen's study of the nearby area of Lower Burley during much the same period, it was common for those undertaking housebuilding to construct several dwellings, live in one and let the remainder (Treen, 1982, p. 172).

A noteworthy feature of Trowell's findings was the widespread use or architects to prepare the building plans deposited with the local authority. There is no doubt that some of these architects were builders calling themselves architects. But the fact that 82 per cent of the proposed houses in approved building applications were designed by architects who at some time during the study period had a town-centre practice (Trowell, 1983, p. 106), suggests that architects, albeit broadly defined, may well have played a more widespread role in Victorian residential development than has been often assumed (Bowley, 1966, p. 348). Before Trowell's detailed studies of deposited building plans it had been widely thought that the form taken by the majority of Victorian dwellings reflected the use by local builders of readily available pattern-books. That bespoke villas and mansions should have been the work of the most eminent architects in Leeds came as no surprise. But there was a second tier of local architects who were principally engaged for the preparation of the much more numerous speculative houses. These were particularly terrace houses, and included many back-to-back houses (Trowell, 1983, p. 101). It seems likely that many, perhaps most, of the architects engaged in preparing plans for such ordinary dwellings lacked a formal training and qualifications as architects, but there would appear to be little hard evidence on this matter. Nationally, as late as 1911 only 27 per cent of those calling themselves architects were members of the Royal Institute of British Architects (Kaye, 1960, p. 175).

Before the First World War, control over housebuilding was exercised in two main ways: through by-laws and by the restrictive covenants of landowners or developers. Official control of residential development was largely confined to the regulation of building standards through by-laws. These were primarily concerned with health and safety. Their influence on building plans was by no means negligible. Forster (1972) envisages one of the effects of their periodical revisions as being to amplify fluctuations in building activity. The influence of their stipulations concerning the heights of rooms and the size of windows became a bone of contention among architects of the Arts and Crafts movement in the two or three decades preceding the First World War (Harper, 1977).

Covenants controlling residential development also sometimes had an effect on the appearance of dwellings, occasionally going so far as to specify types of windows and the form of doorways (O'Donoghue, 1983, p. 325). Their use was particularly significant in areas developed for middle-class occupation, especially where sites were leased for a limited term before reverting to the landowner. Covenants specifying maximum dwelling densities and precluding land uses incompatible with high-class residential areas were among the most common. Some landowners required plans and elevations of houses to be submitted for approval before development could take place (Jones et al., 1988, pp. 6–8).

Viewed from a late-twentieth-century standpoint, a striking feature of the period before the First World War was the fact that land developers and housebuilders tended to be different people. The laying out of streets and plots and the construction of houses were largely in different hands.

The combination of land promotion and construction by the same firm is mainly a twentieth-century phenomenon. It accompanied the acceleration in the growth of the larger building firms at the end of the nineteenth century. With it came other changes. These included the gradual separation of the architect's job from those of the developer and builder. Although not formally recognized in the code of professional practice of the Royal Institute of British Architects until 1920, the divorce of the architect's professional activities from the commercial aspects of development and building was becoming increasingly evident towards the end of the nineteenth century. Other significant changes by the First World War were the decline of leasehold tenure in new residential developments and, increasingly, the abandonment by major landowners of attempts to exercise control over the physical form of such developments.

The inter-war period

The vigorous residential development that took place during most of the period between the two world wars was quite distinct in character from that of the Victorian and Edwardian periods. A number of factors were involved. First, there was an acute housing shortage, following a slump in housebuilding covering roughly the decade 1910–19. Secondly, rent control imposed as a wartime emergency measure was not removed at the end of the war (Daunton, 1984, pp. 1–38). This had a major effect on the viability for landlords of rented dwellings and thus struck at the basis of the ownership of the majority of residential properties. Thirdly, the growth of the building societies increased the supply of mortgages both for builders and owner-occupiers. It became possible for families with limited means to find the capital to become owner-occupiers. Other sources of funds for building firms were profits from contracting work and, as the inter-war period progressed, for companies such as Wimpey, New Ideal Homesteads and Costain the proceeds from the issue of shares (Horsey, 1985, p. 4). Fourthly, the depressed state of agriculture was encouraging the sale of farms and landed estates for residential development at a time when the motor bus and the electric train were increasing the access of the urban population to large areas of the countryside. Finally, there was major social change, including the growing emancipation of women, increasing concern for the individuality of the home, and the growing importance of home ownership as a status symbol.

Town planning in the inter-war period was still 'little more than a token regulatory hand' (Cherry, 1988, p. 109). It is true that a nationwide system of supervision over development was established, based on the preparation by local authorities of town-planning schemes with which future development was intended to be in accord. But such schemes were, with notable exceptions (Massey, 1967), slow to be prepared, and when prepared the controls over residential development that they provided were in practice minimal. The assignment of maximum densities of houses within defined areas was a major aspect of the town-planning schemes but, where builders proposed densities in excess of those specified, disapprovals by local authorities were discouraged by the possible requirement on them to pay compensation for loss of development value (Horsey, 1985, pp. 9–10).

On the ground, the dividing line of the First World War was striking. The rectilinear layouts, of terraces in England and Wales and tenements in Scotland, that had dominated eighteenth- and nineteenth-century residential development became unfashionable. They gave way to more-curvilinear street systems. In most of England and Wales, even the cheapest houses were now semi-detached or, at most, in short terraces. In Scotland, the tenement was adapted to the more-curvilinear streets, and blocks of four maisonettes, resembling semi-detached houses in appearance, were constructed in large numbers.

In contrast to the period before the First World War, the construction of working-class housing by local authorities took on major importance in the inter-war period. It was evident that private enterprise, which had previously provided 95 per cent of working-class housing, was unlikely to be equal to the task of rectifying the housing shortage. The Tudor Walters Committee on building construction and the provision of dwellings for the working-class set the standards for the unprecedented boom in council housebuilding that characterized the 1920s. Its report, published in 1919, owed a great deal to one of its members, Raymond Unwin (Cherry, 1988, p. 83). Since Unwin had been a major figure in the garden-city movement and had been responsible for the use of pseudo-vernacular styles in early garden suburbs (Harper, 1977, p. 28), it was understandable that the Tudor Walters Report should have given the seal of approval to the simplified neo-Georgian cottage style and relatively low densities (not exceeding 30 dwellings per ha) that he espoused (figure 4.1A). These recommendations concerning style and density were adopted widely by local authorities.

Private housebuilding was now largely for middle-class owner-occupation. It was, furthermore, increasingly being undertaken by firms that combined the roles of developer and builder. In other words, decision-making on the layout of roads and plots was in the same hands as decision-making on the actual construction of houses. In the 1930s even small builders were operating as developer-builders, frequently obtaining capital from building societies (Horsey, 1985, p. 7). To design and sell their houses, they often used estate agents, some of whom employed trained architects.

The stylistic antecedents of the houses erected by private enterprise during the inter-war years were predominantly the pseudo-vernacular styles, notably those of Voysey, and neo-Georgian styles that became fashionable in the two decades before the First World War. A simplified pseudo-vernacular was now the dominant style for speculatively-built houses. In such houses the ornamental embellishments according to social status that had been characteristic of the nineteenth century were largely absent. A bay window, often faced with 'Tudor' timbers and stucco, or perhaps pebble-dashed or tile hung, was a characteristic feature. The semi-detached house, to a 'universal' plan, was overwhelmingly the predominant form (figure 4.1B), save among those houses intended for an upper-middle-class market (Bentley, 1987, pp. 10–14).

Figure 4.1 (A) Neo-Georgian cottage-style terrace houses in Birmingham (photograph by the author, 1990). (B)Semi-detached houses in Birmingham (photograph by the author, 1990). (C) Large, Stockbroker's Tudor, detached house, constructed speculatively in the early 1920s at Amersham (photograph, 1990). (D) Houses in Anglo-Scandinavian style in Birmingham (photograph by the author, 1990).

A notable feature of residential development in the inter-war period was the stylistic contrast between speculative housing and local authority housing. Unlike in the nineteenth century, the architectural styles of speculative houses were not, on the whole, products of the diffusion of bespoke domestic architecture down the social hierarchy (Horsey, 1985, p. 14). The styles adopted for bespoke houses designed by members of the upper ranks of the architectural hierarchy – such as neo-Georgian and the modern style – were rarely adopted on a large scale by speculative housebuilders. They were of minor importance compared with simplified pseudo-vernacular, semi-detached.

The resistance of inter-war speculative housebuilders to styles introduced by leading architects in the bespoke market reflects the well known conservatism of builders. But in this case there was a further factor. A noteworthy feature of the 1920s was the involvement, in the aftermath of the Tudor Walters Report, of architects in the design of local-authority housing (Horsey, 1985, p. 14), almost all of which was intended for people who could not afford private-sector accommodation. Thus, neo-Georgian 'cottage styles', favoured by such architects, tended to be equated with a low status in the minds of private housebuyers. For speculative builders, who were aiming at an essentially middle-class market, to have adopted such stigmatized 'council housing' styles would, at that time, have been to court disaster (Punter, 1986a, p. 52).

Despite these major changes, private housebuilding in the inter-war years was still essentially in local hands. For example, all the building firms that erected dwellings in the outer London suburb of Banstead between 1925 and 1939 were located within a radius of 10 km from the centre of the suburb (Butcher, 1974, p. 38). Just to the north-west of London, a similar domination by local firms was to be found in the dormitory town of Amersham between 1919 and 1929 (Collier, 1981, app. I). And there was still a wide variation in the number of dwellings erected by different firms. In Banstead six firms (10 per cent of whose active in the area) were responsible for one-half of the dwellings erected, but no less than 22 firms built only one or two dwellings each (Butcher, 1974, app. I). Variability in the size of firms had its correlate in the landscape. In his study of the London suburb of Bexley, Carr (1982, p. 254) found that large, homogeneous, lower-middle-class housing estates were constructed where large-scale speculative builders were able to acquire sites of sufficient size to enable them to benefit from economies of scale. Smaller plots were developed by small builders with higher-quality housing. Thus, important underlying influences on the urban landscape were the size and distribution of landownership units and the willingness of landowners to sell.

Despite the opportunities afforded by surviving building records in the possession of local authorities, there have been few studies of the architects responsible for the houses erected by private enterprise during the inter-war period. Information on the architects who designed privately-built houses erected in Amersham reveals a less localized pattern than in the case of housebuilders. Defining architects as the individuals and organizations listed as 'architects' in building applications, 50 per cent of the privately-built houses constructed in the period 1919–29 were designed by architects located in Amersham, just under 30 per cent were designed by architects located within 24 km of the centre of Amersham (largely between Amersham and London) and the remainder, just over 20 per cent, were designed by architects based in London, nearly all in the central area (Collier, 1981, p. 7). In a sense these percentages understate the importance of 'non-local' architects since during the 1920s some architects previously working entirely from London offices opened additional offices in the rapidly growing suburbs and dormitory towns, including Amersham itself (Collier, 1981, pp. 45–9, 65–6).

The geographical distribution of offices from which designs for privately-built houses emanated varied according to house size. An examination of a sample of roads in Amersham on which only large, detached houses were constructed between 1919 and 1939 reveals that a higher proportion of the architects of these houses were located in London – 38 per cent, compared with 34 per cent in Amersham and 28 per cent in other places (MacGregor, 1984, app. I). One-half of the houses in this sample were speculative, including some of the largest houses (figure 4.1C). Only a small minority of these were designed by Central London architects. The majority were designed either by building firms in the vicinity of Amersham or on their behalf by a prolific local firm of estate agents, Swannell and Sly, which employed trained architects (A. T. Sly, personal communication). Of the bespoke houses, one-half were designed by

London architects, and the majority of the remainder were designed either by Swannell and Sly or by another local firm, W. Gomm, a building firm that designed many of the houses that it constructed. Apparently, even in one of outer London's most exclusive residential areas it was common for builders to prepare their own architectural drawings. Indeed, it may have been more common than, for example, in Headingley before the First World War (cf. Trowell, 1983, p. 108). These 'architects' were not members of the Royal Institute of British Architects and their designs were not restricted to speculatively-built houses.

Clearly the description 'architect' in building applications and other local authority building records was used by or applied to many individuals who were not professionally-qualified architects and firms that did not employ professionally-qualified architects. In 1938 it was estimated by S. C. Ramsey, in a paper presented to the Royal Institute of British Architects, that only 20 per cent of plans for small private houses submitted to building societies in that year were architect designed (Burnett, 1978, pp. 252–3). He considered that ten years earlier the proportion would have been only 5–10 per cent. The low proportion of houses built by private enterprise that were designed by architects in the inter-war period is confirmed by Bowley (1966, p. 378). The fact that Ramsey's percentages are tiny compared with those of Trowell for Headingly before the First World War no doubt reflects Ramsey's much stricter definition of the term 'architect'. The comparison does not justify the conclusion that there was a dramatic decline in the role of architects between the two periods. Until the Architects (Registration) Act of 1938 was passed, anyone could use the title 'architect'. Thereafter it was restricted to those whose names were on the Register of the Architects Registration Council of the United Kingdom (Kaye, 1960, p. 156).

The evidence concerning the roles of the various agents involved in residential development up to the Second World War is fragmentary, and care should be taken in generalizing on the basis of disparate studies. Much more research is necessary, particularly systematic investigation of the building applications submitted to local authorities. Nevertheless, it has been possible to outline a pattern of development that future research seems likely to supplement and modify rather than change in its essentials. Against this background, attention will now be focussed on the post-war period, which, like the period following the First World War, saw major changes in the physical forms of residential developments and in the roles of the individuals and organizations responsible for these forms.

The post-war period

Under the new planning system introduced by the Town and Country Planning Act of 1947, planning schemes were replaced by Development Plans. These were intended to provide a framework for future land use. With minor exceptions, all development proposals were to be scrutinized in relation to such plans and became subject to the permission of the local planning authority

(LPA). The requirement that for the majority of significant additions and alterations to the urban landscape a planning application be submitted to the LPA has remained in effect throughout the post-war period. The Town and Country Planning Act of 1968 replaced Development Plans, with a two-tier arrangement: Structure Plans, which were broad statements of intent, and a variety of Local Plans, which consisted of more-specific proposals for small areas. Preparation of these new plans involved greater public participation, but these changes and others, including the recent withdrawal of Structure Plans, left intact the basic procedures of development control that followed the Act of 1947. These entail the scrutiny of the planning application by LPA officers, who are professional planners, consultation by them with other bodies, notably the Highway Authority and the relevant town or parish council, and opportunities for other parties, such as local residents, to make representations. A recommendation is then made by the planning officers to the local planning committee, composed of elected councillors, which approves or disapproves the application. An applicant has the right of appeal to central government against either a disapproval or conditions attached to an approval. Thus, in the words of Cherry (1988, p. 151), 'for approaching half a century British cities have been publicly regulated by a system designed to guide, shape and control the form and appearance of the urban enviroment.' A major aim of the remainder of this chapter will be to assess, by means of case studies, the extent to which this objective of the planning system has been met as far as ordinary residential landscapes are concerned. It is necessary first, however, to outline some of the salient characteristics of post-war urban development as a context for these more detailed studies.

By the end of the Second World War, housebuilding in Great Britain had been at a virtual standstill for over six years and nearly half a million houses had been either destroyed or damaged beyond economic repair (Cherry, 1988, p. 152). In the initial post-war years priority was given to subsidized local authority housing and restrictions were placed on private housebuilding until 1954. Between the end of the war and the beginning of 1953 well over a million houses were built including, in the initial period, temporary, prefabricated houses (Mitchell and Deane, 1962, p. 239). Although some of the inter-war stylistic influences on residential architecture were still apparent, the cottage style that had characterized council housing in that period became less evident, as did the semi-detached house. Layouts became less formal, the gable roof replaced the hipped roof, and the front-garden fence became less common. One of the forces at work was the Ministry of Health *Housing Manual 1949*, prepared with the assistance of a panel of architects (Ministry of Health, 1949). The mixture of stylistic influences, notably Scandinavian, functionalist and pseudo-vernacular, gave rise to what Edwards (1981, pp. 162–3) has termed the Anglo-Scandinavian style (figure 4.1D).

By the mid-1950s the housing shortage had been reduced and attention reverted to the long-standing problem of sub-standard housing: a legacy of the nineteenth century that still characterized extensive zones surrounding the commercial cores of nearly all major British cities. The economic return on the renewal of this huge, largely rented housing stock, whether by refurbishment or redevelopment, was generally small by comparison with that on alternative investments, even where units of property ownership were sufficiently extensive for large-scale redevelopment to be practicable. In the majority of cases it was in the economic interest of landlords to operate a policy of minimum maintenance. Few voices of objection were raised to the widespread assumption that the solution to this problem lay in the acquisition of these areas by local authorities, the demolition of existing dwellings and the comprehensive redevelopment of their sites. In the period 1955–74, nearly 1.5 million dwellings were demolished in Great Britain (Cherry, 1976, p. 59), removing from the urban landscape all but a small fraction of the hitherto still substantially intact pre-1875 industrial housing (figure 4.2). In its place, and on large sites at the urban fringe, local authorities erected modern style, often functionalist, housing. In the inner areas of cities in particular, much of this took the form of flats, often of many storeys. At the urban fringe, terraces were

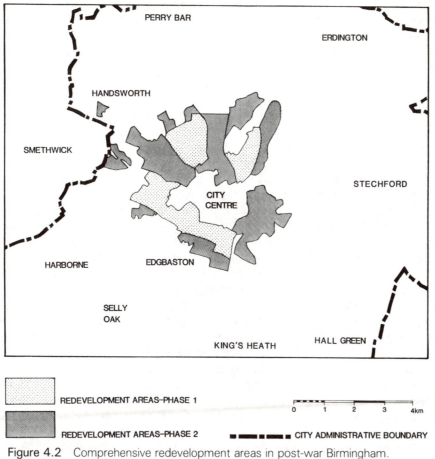

Figure 4.2   Comprehensive redevelopment areas in post-war Birmingham.
Source: City of Birmingham, 1973, fig 4.

more common. Brick and local stone became rare by comparison with concrete, glass, and other materials that paid no respect to the *genius loci*. In the redeveloped areas the contrast with the domestic scale of the mainly terrace houses that had been replaced was often sharp. And it was emphasized by the multiple-lane ring roads and radial roads that were simultaneously constructed.

Meanwhile, private housebuilding, constrained by the designation of green belts around the major cities and obliged to toe the line of development control, resumed its outward spread in a more orderly manner than it had done in the inter-war period. It was less scattered, and ribbon development along arterials, hitherto a major feature of its progress, was greatly reduced. There were stylistic changes too. Although privately-built semi-detached houses continued to be constructed in the 1950s and 1960s, they tended to take on the Anglo-Scandinavian style, as bay windows, imitation timber framing, hipped roofs and leaded lights declined in popularity. Eventually, they were largely supplanted in the speculative builder's repertoire by 'town houses' (a new name for terraces) in Anglo-Scandinavian or neo-Georgian styles or small detached houses in similar styles. Where the speculative builder erected terraces in Anglo-Scandinavian style it became increasingly difficult to distinguish them from the products of local authorities. The association between style and social status that had been so characteristic of the inter-war period had largely disappeared (Edwards, 1981, p. 172).

Going on in parallel with these stylistic changes were changes in the size of 'developers', a title that in residential areas was already almost synonymous with 'builders', owing to the conflation of land-development and building operations. That large, non-local developers were assuming a greater importance in residential development was confirmed by Craven's (1969) study of private residential expansion in Kent. There these firms favoured the area beyond the Green Belt and, within that area, were attracted to large sites, on which they constructed semi-detached houses or terraces. Closer to London, sites tended to be smaller, often undeveloped areas within or adjacent to existing settlements. Here small developments, often by small, local developers, were prevalent. Small sites tended to be developed for either detached houses, as had been the case, for example, in the inter-war period in Bexley, or high-density dwellings (Craven, 1969, pp. 11–12).

National figures for the size of building firms confirm the increasing number of large firms (Bowley, 1966, p. 425). Nevertheless, between 1935 and 1954 the proportion of building firms employing ten or fewer persons fell only from 89 to 82 per cent. For Banstead in particular, comparison of the 1945–72 period with the 1925–39 period reveals an appreciable fall in the proportion of new dwellings constructed by firms responsible for ten or fewer dwellings (Butcher, 1974, app. I), though nearly all firms were still from within a radius of 16 km.

From the standpoint of the early 1990s it is clear that in a number of major respects the residential development of the 1970s and 1980s differed from that of the quarter of a century following the Second World War. But the contrast was less pronounced than in the case of development in commercial cores. A major reason for this was that even at the height of the Modern Movement private residential developers seldom got closer to embracing it than employing an Anglo-Scandinavian style. The residential equivalents of the glass and concrete redevelopments of the 1950s and 1960s in commercial cores were the multi-storey flats of the local authorities.

Some of the post-war changes in residential areas were a consequence of the rapid residential growth of the 1950s and 1960s combined with the designation of green belts. There was a shortage of 'greenfield' sites for housebuilding around major urban areas, especially in south-east England. Furthermore, an aging population of widows and retired couples, combined with an increase in the number of young people forming one-person and two-person households, was fuelling the demand for small dwellings. Such households on the whole favoured proximity to the commercial core over inaccessible urban fringe locations. For these and other reasons, such as the widespread reaction against the inhuman scale of much post-war development and redevelopment (Cherry, 1988, pp. 154–5), there was an increased interest in the reutilization and refurbishment of existing residential areas. 'Slum clearance had begun to look like vandalism and the cry was for conservation' (Esher, 1981, p. 75). The Civic Amenities Act of 1967 made provision for the designation of Conservation Areas by LPAs. These were areas considered to merit special consideration on grounds of architectural or historical interest or both, and within them LPAs now had increased influence over changes to the landscape.

The refocusing of attention on existing residential areas resulted in two main types of changes. One of these was the refurbishing of inner residential areas that had escaped comprehensive redevelopment by local authorities. As Smith (1979) has pointed out in regard to America, although this reflected to some extent a change of fashion, it also reflected a recognition that the dwellings in such areas had declined in value, relative to dwellings in other, especially outer, residential areas, to the point where at prevailing values they constituted a sound investment. The attractiveness of such areas to middle-class 'gentrifiers', as they were misleadingly termed, was further enhanced in Great Britain by the provision of local-authority grants towards the cost of refurbishment. Indeed, so great was the change of policy in Birmingham that by the 1980s the exteriors of privately-owned dwellings in selected areas developed in the few decades before the First World War were being refurbished entirely at the expense of the local authority (Thomas, 1983, pp. 218–20).

The other type of change to existing residential areas that has been particularly characteristic of the most recent post-war decades, though it has much earlier precursors, is the piecemeal infill and redevelopment of middle-class areas. This has particularly affected the middle zones of cities developed between the last decades of the nineteenth century and the Second World War. It has understandably attracted less attention than the abrupt changes associated with slum clearance, the building of major shopping centres, and the large-scale reshaping of rail and road systems. Any particular piece of infill or redevelopment in such areas is seldom a matter of serious concern to more than a score of families living in the immediate vicinity. The cumulative effect, however, of such infills and redevelopments is considerable. Piecemeal infill and redevelopment is particularly characteristic of areas initially developed at very low density, but in areas where sites for housebuilding are scarce its impact is beginning to be felt more widely (Tym & Partners, 1987, p. 6). In the absence of plans for most existing residential areas that go much beyond the maintenance of the *status quo*, it is becoming the normal form of residential change. However, most LPAs, preoccupied as they are with processing individual planning applications, have done little to monitor it. The case studies that follow will be concerned with this type of residential change, but it appears increasingly likely that many of the most important relationships underlying this second cycle of residential development also pertain to the residential development of greenfield sites (Pompa, 1988, p. 267).

CASE STUDIES: CONTEXT

South-east England contains by far the greatest area of low-density detached houses in Great Britain. It has been subject, since the 1950s, to especially high pressures for more-intensive residential development, reflecting in particular a reduction in the average size of households and increases in incomes, population and employment opportunities (Damesick, 1986; Hamnett, 1986; Simmons, 1986). Figure 4.3 shows the area occupied by large detached houses and their gardens in settlements in south-east England outside the main built-up area of London in *c.*1955, at the start of the main resurgence of private housebuilding after the war (Mitchell and Jones, 1971, p. 118). It was largely compiled from the Ordnance Survey Provisional Edition 1:25,000 sheets. Whether or not a detached house is represented by a single symbol on these sheets depends essentially on the distance of the house, including outbuildings, from neighbouring houses. Where average configurations of plots and buildings exist, a density of not more than about seven dwellings per ha is required for detached houses to be separately represented. Figure 4.3 may therefore be taken as a rough indication of the extent of residential development at below this density. Occasionally, small dwellings and detached buildings forming a quite different landscape occur at sufficient distances apart to be separately shown on the Provisional Edition. Doubtful areas were checked in the field, and a number of areas of shacks, bungalows and summerhouses were eliminated in this way. The high incidence of large detached houses to the north-west and south-west of London is a striking feature (Whitehand, 1967a).

Pressure for change

To ascertain the extent of the physical changes that took place between the mid-1950s and the late 1980s in low-density residential areas in south-east England, 25 ha national-grid squares having more than 80 per cent of their areas (excluding roads) occupied by large detached houses and their gardens were identified in the settlements shown in figure 4.3. Settlements having at least one such grid square entirely within 1 km of the edge of the commercial

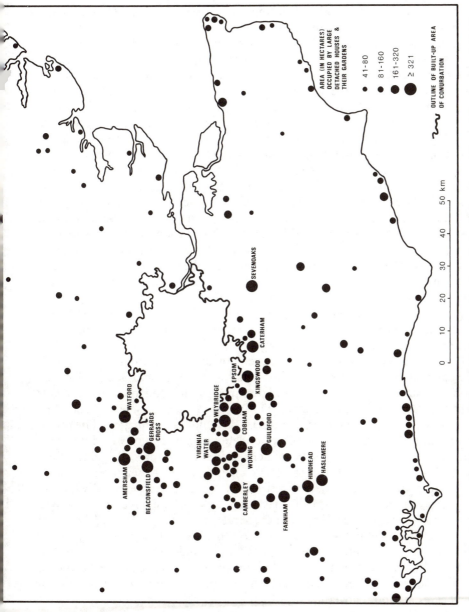

Figure 4.3 Area occupied by large detached houses and houses their gardens in south-east England, outside the main built-up area of London, c. 1955.
Source: field survey and Ordnance Survey 1/25,000 maps.

The following labels appear on the map:

AMERSHAM
BEACONSFIELD
GERRARDS CROSS
WATFORD
VIRGINIA WATER
WEYBRIDGE
CAMBERLEY
COBHAM
WOKING
EPSOM
KINGSWOOD
GUILDFORD
CATERHAM
SEVENOAKS
FARNHAM
HINDHEAD
HASLEMERE

Legend:

AREA (IN HECTARES) OCCUPIED BY LARGE DETACHED HOUSES & THEIR GARDENS

- 41–80
- 81–160
- 161–320
- ≥ 321

OUTLINE OF BUILT-UP AREA OF CONURBATION

Scale: 0   10   20   30   40   50 km

core (an inner square) and at least one such grid square entirely within 1 km of the edge of the built-up area (an outer square) were divided into four groups by a 2×2 matrix according to population in 1971 (approximately the middle of the study period) and distance from the centre of London. One settlement was selected randomly from each cell in the matrix, Guildford representing larger distal settlements (more than 40,000 population), Epsom representing larger proximal settlements, Amersham representing smaller distal settlements (less than 40,000 population) and Gerrards Cross*representing smaller proximal settlements. One inner square and one outer square were selected randomly from within each of these settlements, giving a total of eight sample squares. Plot subdivision and redevelopment since *c*.1955 were mapped in the sample areas from information obtained from a plot-by-plot field survey undertaken in early 1987, Ordnance Survey maps and plans surveyed in the 1930s and 1950s, and local authority building applications and planning applications.

A good deal of each sample area underwent change during the study period (figure 4.4). Even in the case of Gerrards Cross, the smallest settlement, the sample squares contained continuous areas of several hectares in which few plots remained unmodified. A recurrent feature in most of the sample areas was the truncation of corner plots. Although firm conclusions about the variability of features between areas must await a survey of more settlements, within the sample areas the amount of redevelopment and the proportion of it that took the form of flats were highest in the larger settlements, and there was a tendency for both plot subdivision and redevelopment to have a higher incidence on the more-central sites. Examples of residential landscapes associated with these changes, both in the sample areas and elsewhere in south-east England, are shown in figure 4.5.

The influences underlying these developments ranged from national, even international, economic factors and social fashions to local authority policies and the circumstances of individual owner-occupiers. Outer London's high-class residential areas, like those of many Anglo-American cities, are a battleground between powerful opposing forces of preservation and transformation. The preservation camp consists mainly of those residents who own sites with little if any potential for more-intensive development in the near future. Concerned about the effects of such development nearby on the value of their property in its existing use, they exert pressure to restrain that development, especially through their local councillors (Short et al., 1986, pp. 134–5). The forces of transformation – those seeking to benefit from the large profits to be obtained from residential development in these areas because of the high effective demand for new housing – are more heterogeneous. They comprise developers, owners of land with development potential (many of them owner-occupiers), and firms providing finance and services for the development process. Sitting in arbitration in many cases is central government, which in the 1980s shifted the balance of its support in favour of the forces of transformation (Department of the Environment, 1980b). The rapidly changing residential landscape results from the working out of these conflicting interests. The fact that most of the greenfield land immediately outside London is fairly effectively precluded from development by

Figure 4.4 Plot subdivision and redevelopment in low-density residential areas in sample towns in south-east England, c. 1955–1986.
Source: field surveys and Ordnance Survey plans.

Figure 4.5   Infill and redevelopment in low-density residential areas in south-east England (photographs by the author): (A) Unkempt garden awaiting infill, Epsom (photograph 1989); (B) Vehicular access to new houses under construction close behind detached house, Amersham (photograph 1987); (C) Demolition of detached house, Gerrards Cross (photograph 1987); (D) Conversion of existing detached house (to right)) to form part of a block of flats, Amersham (planning application approved 1960; photograph 1988); (E) Flats (to left) in rear garden of detached house, Amersham (planning application approved 1978; photograph 1986); (F) Cul-de-sac to new dwellings at rear of detached house, Northwood (planning application approved 1981; photograph 1989).

its designation as Green Belt heightens the pressure for the redevelopment or more-intensive development of existing settlements (especially the gardens of large houses) and of land immediately beyond the Green Belt. Some of the pressures and conflicts are suggested by aggregate statistics compiled by the Department of the Environment (DOE) and other organizations; others can only be uncovered by teasing out relationships existing locally.

One index of the pressure for residential development exerted by house purchasers is the comparatively high house prices in the region, those in the Outer

Metropolitan Area being second, within the United Kingdom, only to those in Greater London. A crude measure of the overall pressure for development is the proportion of planning applications on which an appeal is made to the Secretary of State for the Environment against the refusal of planning permission. Figure 4.6 clearly shows, despite the failure of some local authorities to make returns, the relatively high percentages for areas in a broad zone surrounding London. (The fact that the majority of planning applications are for minor, non-controversial matters, such as small changes to individual houses, accounts for the generally low percentages in figure 4.6.) Arguably, another indicator of development pressure, though it may also reflect other factors, such as the infrequency of planning committee meetings, is the length of time taken to decide planning applications. In 1982/83 in large parts of south-east England, including Greater London, over one-third of applications took more than the statutory eight-week period to decide (figure 4.7), a considerably higher proportion than the national average. This was despite the fact that south-east England had a relatively high percentage of 'householder' applications, which tend to be decided more quickly than applications for major developments (Association of County Councils et al., 1982, esp. annex A. p. 30, table A14).

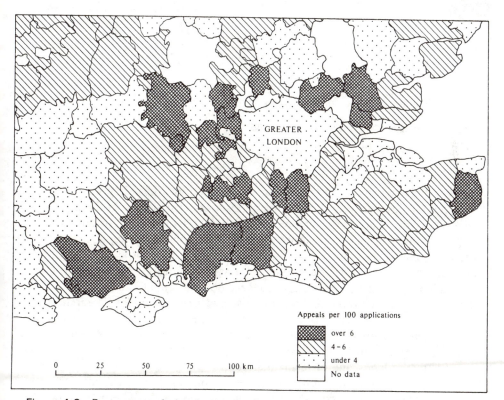

Figure 4.6 Percentage of planning applications upon which an appeal was lodged in south-east England 1984/5.
Source: CIPFA 1985 9–51.

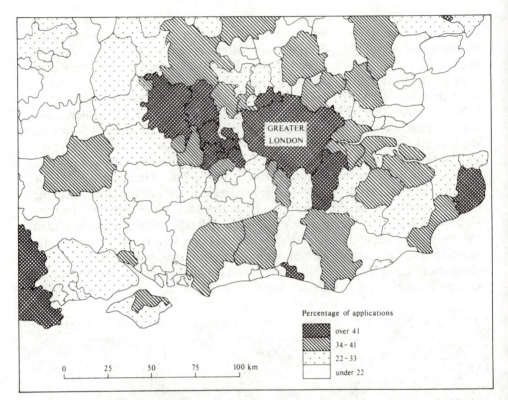

Figure 4.7 Percentage of planning applications taking over eight weeks to decide in south-east England 1982/3.
Source: Department of the Environment, 1985,65–87.

Research questions

These official statistics, even if viewed in conjunction with policy statements of local authorities and central government, leave concealed most of the processes at work. If these are to be uncovered, studies at a finer scale of analysis are required, involving examination of individual planning applications and therefore small areas. Since planning applications are a central element in the development-control procedure, they are a natural unit for recording purposes, especially for LPAs but frequently also for applicants and others concerned with development. It is therefore both rational and convenient for researchers to treat individual applications as entities for analytical purposes. Here, the information they provide will form the basis for an examination of two groups of interrelated questions that relate directly to the activities underlying physical changes to the landscape of residential areas.

The initial group of questions relates to planning applications for new dwellings treated as self-contained development proposals. There are similarities here to the approach adopted in the study of commercial cores. First, what are the characteristics of, and interactions between, the parties (individual and corporate) involved in attempts, successful and unsuccessful, to effect such physical change? Secondly, what is the relationship between the characteristics of these parties and the types of urban landscape elements, especially the building types, that they seek to create? Thirdly, what are the characteristics of failed attempts to bring about change and what is the role played in these attempts by LPAs and the DOE? Of particular interest in this regard is the relationship between the policies and attitudes adopted by LPAs in their attempts to resist development pressures and the actions of the other main parties.

The second group of questions is concerned with the histories of attempts to develop individual residential sites. Here, proposals to bring about a physical change to the landscape of a residential area are examined as a series, in an attempt to unravel the often complicated sequence of events between the initial decision to develop, or redevelop, a site and the eventual change in the landscape or decision to abandon the project. The questions addressed are therefore concerned less with the characteristics of individual planning applications and the individuals and organizations concerned with them, and more with relationships between key events in a complex historical process.

There are three questions in this group, each to some extent compound. First, to what extent are the intentions of property owners, developers and LPA officers realized as far as the outcome in the landscape is concerned? Secondly, what are the bases for planning officers' recommendations to their planning committees, and what would be the effects on the landscape of the requirements they seek to impose? Finally, to what extent are site histories in general, and the implementations of proposals in particular, influenced by the types (especially the sizes) of residential developments proposed and the characteristics of those responsible for the proposals?

The answers to these two groups of questions for two particular study areas provide the basis for a review and assessment of the characteristics of infill and redevelopment in low-density residential areas, including a discussion of how these characteristics differed between areas and of the implications of the processes involved for the understanding and managing of residential landscape change. A matter that is given particular attention is the extent to which the successions of proposals that were characteristic of attempts to develop sites led to the creation of types of landscapes that were unintended and unforeseen, rather than provided a means of working towards improved schemes.

Study areas

The penumbra of low-density suburban settlements fringing London provides a large number of potential study areas. However, the time-consuming nature of the necessary data compilation severely limits both the size and the number of areas that it is practicable to investigate in a single study. In view of the well-attested correlation between intensity of residential development and accessibility to commercial cores in general, and to Central London in particular (Lever, 1974, pp. 30–2), two study areas were chosen that were differentiated primarily in terms of these aspects of accessibility. These were selected from the eight previously surveyed areas, though the boundaries of the chosen areas were adjusted in the light of the survey; for example, to minimize the inclusion of non-residential land. It was decided to examine an area adjacent to the commercial core of a settlement close to the built-up area London and an area in a comparable location in relation to a commercial core but within a more distal settlement. The final choice of the two study areas from those possessing the requisite characteristics was largely based on the nature and accessibility of the available local authority records.

One of these areas is just north-west of the commercial core of Amersham-on-the -Hill, some 40 km north-west of the centre of London. The other, an area affording better access to London for commuters, is just south-east of the commercial core of Epsom (figure 4.8), some 20 km south-west of the centre of London. In the 1950s the Amersham study area consisted almost entirely of detached houses in large gardens (figure 4.9A), most of them having been constructed during the first 40 years of this century, following the opening of the railway station. The Epsom study area contained many similar houses, but also a considerable number of detached and semi-detached Victorian houses of various sizes (figure 4.9B) and a few detached Georgian houses on the site of the medieval village of Epsom.

For these study areas, LPA files were inspected for all planning applications for new dwellings received between the beginning of 1960 and the middle of 1987, the precise end date being that when the LPAs' card indexes of applications were inspected. Sites only partially within the study areas were included. Decisions, including those on appeals to the Secretary of State for the Environment, were incorporated up to 30 June 1988. Applications submitted before 1960 were included if they were part of a series of related applications the most recent of which was received within the study period. In addition to the information gained from the examination of planning files, it was possible to obtain information from a variety of other sources, including developers, owners and estate agents, about certain sites both within the study areas and in their vicinity. These informants occasionally provided very detailed information on individual cases, which, although their selection was largely determined by the opportunities for obtaining extra information that arose in the course of the main data collection, provided valuable supplementary evidence.

The study areas yielded almost identical numbers of applications – 140 for the Epsom study area and 141 for the Amersham study area. These applications were considered by the LPAs in relation to local and national policies and intentions, ranging from the standards existing at the time for such matters as parking provision and highway specifications to notions, which sometimes changed in the course of an application's being considered, about whether certain types of dwellings should be approved. In neither study area had the LPA adopted a Local Plan, as envisaged in the Town and County Planning Act of 1971, by the end of the study period. In Amersham the relevant formal plan was a Town Map, approved in 1958, on which primarily residential areas were differentiated only in terms of gross polulation densities calculated for areas

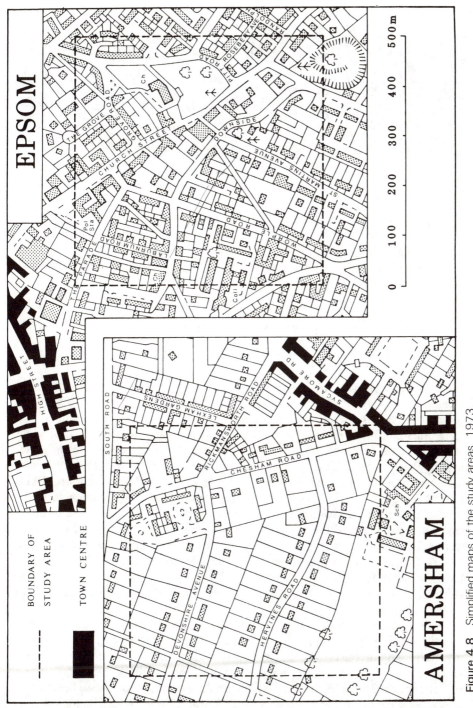

Figure 4.8 Simplified maps of the study areas, 1973.
Source: Ordnance Survey 1/10,000 maps, planning applications and building applications.

Figure 4.9   (A) Inter-war detached house at Amersham (photograph by the author, c. 1959). (B) Mid -Victorian detached house at Epsom (photograph by the author, 1988).

much larger than the study area. A similar Town Map was approved for Epsom in the same year but this was later replaced by a revised version prepared in 1965 and approved in 1971. Large parts of the northern half of the Epsom study area were included in a Conservation Area, which was designated in 1973 and extended in 1976.

CASE STUDIES: DEVELOPMENT PROPOSALS

Participants in development

With few exceptions, the initiative for residential development in the study areas came from existing owner-occupiers, the large majority of whom were private individuals. There is considerable evidence, albeit fragmentary and sometimes circumstantial, to suggest that it arose, in large part, out of individual family circumstances, especially the old age or death of the owner-occupier (cf. Booth, 1989, p. 140). This accords with previous findings for different types of area and much earlier periods (Slater, 1978; Goodchild and Munton, 1985, p. 101). In some cases the decision to initiate or consider initiating development was influenced by decisions by owner-occupiers of adjoining properties or by communications from other individuals and organizations, notably estate agents and developers, seeking to develop or promote development, or by both of these factors. DOE circulars (Department of the Environment, 1980a, 1984) required LPAs to identify sites to accommodate DOE targets for new housing but, although this served to draw attention to sites, the key decision-makers remained the owners.

Once a decision was taken to explore the possibilities of development (usually infill or redevelopment), a number of other interested parties became involved. The precise way in which this happened was rarely recorded. However, access to an owner's files on applications for the development of one site of about 0.35 ha in the vicinity of the Amersham study area allowed the interactions between interested parties to be traced in great detail. Included in the files were approximately 400 items of correspondence, mainly between the owner's agent and developers, estate agents, legal, architectural and planning advisers, local residents, contractors, the LPA and the DOE, and notes made by the owner's agent during or following some 100 telephone conversations concerned with the proposed development (figure 4.10). It is not suggested that this single example is representative either in the detail of the record it provided, which was quite exceptional, or in the relative strengths of the interactions between individuals and organizations that it revealed. However, it does indicate the high level of involvement in such dealings not only by LPAs, the DOE and owners themselves, but also by developers, architects, estate agents and legal advisers. An analysis of the contents of LPA planning files frequently provides at least some information about all of these participants except the last.

Having decided to initiate some kind of development of his land, an owner is faced with three main possibilities. The first is to sell the piece of land outright to a developer at a price that includes 'hope value' based on the chances of the developer's obtaining planning permission. Though it is favoured by developers this course is relatively infrequently taken, since under it the owner loses all control and sells at a lower price than he would have got if planning permission had already been obtained. The second is to enter into an agreement with a developer, perhaps granting an option to purchase if the developer obtains planning permission or entering into a contract with the

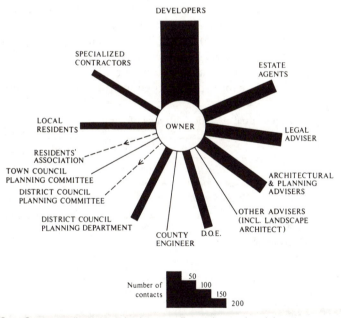

Figure 4.10 Contacts (letters, telephone calls and meetings) between an owner and other parties during and just after attempts to gain outline planning permission for the development of a site of about 0.35 ha at Amersham between August 1983 and March 1986. A broken line indicates one-way communication.
Source: owner's files

developer that is conditional upon planning permission's being granted. Thirdly, the owner can himself apply for planning permission, usually through an agent, before selling to a developer.

The third of these methods has the attraction for the owner that, if planning permission is obtained, he can sell the land for its full value for development. In fact, 44 per cent of the applications in the study areas were made by private individuals (practically all of them owner-occupiers), or by executors or trustees acting on their behalf. Most of the remaining applications were made by developers, applications by non-local developers (that is, developers from outside the towns in which the study areas were located) outnumbering those by local developers in the ratio of 3 to 2. Many of the developers were seeking either a detailed permission or a different permission after purchasing land from a private individual with outline permission. In the case of 55 per cent of the applications made by developers the site had already been purchased by the developer by the time of the application.

The connections between the types of applicant and the types of agents they employed showed a strong neighbourhood effect. Individuals employed local agents in 43 per cent of their applications. In contrast, local developers employed local agents in only 20 per cent of their applications, the comparative figure for non-local developers being as low as 13 per cent. However, the main feature of the relationship between the types of applicants and the types of agents they employed was the different types of agents mainly used by developers and individuals. Architects were by far the most important type of agent used by developers, the large majority of the architects being non-local (in contrast to the finding of Larkham (1988, p. 155) for the West Midlands), whereas estate agents were the main type of agent used by individuals, most of the estate agents being local (table 4.1). Nearly all the applications for which estate agents were the agents were in outline. The majority of those for which architects were the agents

Table 4.1   Types of agent used by different types of applicant

Type of agent		Type of applicant				
		Local developer (n = 55) %	Non-local developer (n = 81) %	Individual (n = 124) %	Other (n = 21) %	All (n = 281) %
Architect	Local	15	4	2	5	5
	Non-local	56	46	21	33	36
Estate agent	Local	0	9	32	33	19
	Non-local	2	9	15	5	10
Other*	Local	5	0	9	0	5
	Non-local	2	11	10	5	9
None		20	22	10	19	16

*Includes cases in which the agent's profession was unknown
n = number of applications

were full applications. These differences in the main type of agent employed may be connected to some degree with the fact that applications by individuals were on average for smaller developments (median 4 dwellings) than those for which applications were made by developers (median 7.5 dwellings). They reflect above all, however, the fact that most individuals became drawn into development purely because they found themselves in possession of land with development potential. An estate agent, often introduced by the family solicitor (cf. Booth, 1989, pp. 144–5), provided the individual's point of contact with the development industry. In contrast, for developers direct contacts with architects were an integral part of their professional activities.

Owners, developers and the urban landscape

As far as the possible impact on the urban landscape is concerned the effect of proposals on existing buildings is a major consideration. An important distinction in this regard can be made between proposals to demolish main buildings and those involving their retention. In the case of both study areas, the different categories of applicant differed considerably in this respect (Figure 4.11). Individuals were the most conservative (cf. Pompa, 1988, p. 250). Only about one-third of their appllications involved proposals to demolish main buildings, or plot dominants, to use the term employed by Conzen (1969, p. 128). This often reflected the desire of the owner to continue to occupy an existing house on the site, particularly where it was proposed to add a single dwelling in the garden. Even when an owner was moving elsewhere, however, it may well be that he adopted a less radical attitude towards his former home

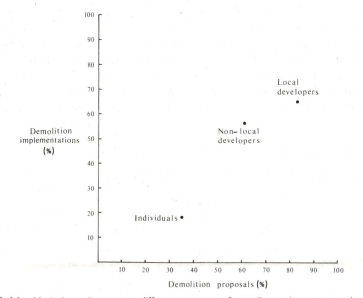

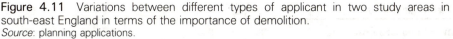

Figure 4.11 Variations between different types of applicant in two study areas in south-east England in terms of the importance of demolition.
Source: planning applications.

than a developer would have done. When individuals did seek to demolish main buildings, the proposals were rarely implemented without the submission of a subsequent application by a developer.

Developers, in contrast, were much more demolition prone, some 70 per cent of their applications involving main-building demolition. Assuming local developers to be more sensitive to the existing urban landscape than non-local developers (McNamara, 1982, p. 68), one might have expected that, in the case of the two study areas, they would have been less disposed towards demolition in their proposals. In reality the opposite was the case (figure 4.11). This is consistent with the conclusion of Pompa (1988, p. 253), in the case of suburban Birmingham, that local developers, as distinct from individuals, showed little concern for the character of the existing urban landscape. However, the proportion of local developers' implementations that involved main-building demolitions differed little from the comparable proportion for non-local developers' implementations (figure 4.11). This reflected the fact that applications by local developers to demolish main buildings had a lower rate of implementation (23 per cent) than those by non-local developers (35 per cent), though not nearly as low as in the case of individuals (5 per cent).

The Dwelling types proposed also varied by type of applicant (table 4.2). Detached houses were rarely proposed by local developers, 93 per cent of the dwellings they proposed being terraces or flats/maisonettes. In contrast, between about one-fifth and one-quarter of the dwellings proposed by individuals and non-local developers were detached houses. The contrast between individuals and local developers was even more pronounced in the case of implemented proposals (table 4.3).

Underlying these broad differences in these figures were those that existed between on the one hand attempts by individual owner-occupiers to gain permission to develop their gardens, often with the aid of a local estate agent and often retaining an existing house, and on the other hand attempts by developers to initiate more radical change, frequently after an initial outline application by an owner-occupier had been approved. Attempts by individuals to initiate relatively small-scale change often led eventually to more substantial change.

Table 4.2   Dwelling types proposed by different types of applicant

Type of dwelling	Type of Applicant				
	Local developer (n = 607) %	Non-local developer (n = 947) %	Individual (n = 697) %	Other (n = 293) %	All (n = 2544) %
Detached	0	24	21	11	16
Semi-detached	7	4	3	0	4
Terrace	22	6	6	28	12
Flat/maisonette	71	65	71	61	68

n = number of dwellings

Table 4.3 Dwelling types implemented by different types of applicant

Type of dwelling	Type of applicant				
	Local developer (n = 153) %	Non-local developer (n = 245) %	Individual (n = 43) %	Other (n = 52) %	All (n = 493) %
Detached	1	18	58	6	14
Semi-detached	4	5	0	0	4
Terrace	12	11	0	6	10
Flat/maisonette	84	66	42	88	72

n = number of dwellings

These findings suggest the importance in determining the form taken by land-scape change in these areas of both the characteristics of the interested parties and their relationships one to another. They also indicate both the pressure for change, in particular by owners and developers, and the need to distinguish between initial proposals and eventual outcomes in the landscape. The plans of owners and developers have clearly been met by strong countervailing forces, and it is to the extent of, and form taken by, this resistance that attention will now be turned.

Resistance to development

Perhaps the most obvious manifestation of resistance by the LPAs responsible for the study areas was the comparatively low percentage of applications approved: 47 per cent compared with an annual average of 66 per cent for major residential developments (generally having ten or more dwellings) in south-east England as a whole over the years 1979/80 to 1982/83, the comparative figure for the whole of England being 68 per cent (Department of the Environment, 1985, pp. 6–9, 33–4). A further indicator of resistance, although it may also have reflected other factors, was the length of the planning gestation period. This is defined as the time-lag between the receipt of the initial application and the approval of the development, in cases where the proposals were imple-mented, or the most recent rejection or approval, in cases where no development took place. In the study areas the median planning gestation period was no less than 15 months. Furthermore, the proportion of appeals allowed, 9 per cent, was small compared with an anual average of 29 per cent for England as a whole over the period 1974–83 (Department of the Enviroment, 1985, p. 95). Although the number of appeals (34) was too small to allow comparisons between different types of appellant, the rates of approval of applications were clearly lower for individuals (41 per cent) than for developers (non-local developers 53 per cent; local developers 51 per cent). The proportion of proposals by individuals that were implemented was as low as 10 per cent, compared with 37 per cent for non-local developers and 29 per cent for local developers.

The relatively low rate of approval of applications by individuals accords with the findings of other studies (Simmie and Hale, 1978, p.17; Goodchild and Munton, 1985, p. 80; Rydin, 1985, p. 45). The lack of sophistication of individuals in negotiation, especially in comparison with major (almost entirely non-local) developers, may have been a factor. Furthermore, by comparison with developers, many of whom would have been paying interest on loans with which they had purchased the sites (cf. Fleming, 1984, pp. 54–6), owner-occupiers would have had less financial incentive to negotiate a speedy planning permission. However, there were also factors that might have been expected to produce higher acceptance rates for individuals. For example, it is plausible that estate agents, by far the main agents of individuals, encouraged their clients' compliance with LPAs in order to speed the passage of the land on to the market. It was not uncommon for permissions secured by estate agents on behalf of individuals to be followed by applications by developers for more-profitable developments on the same site. Estate agents may have seen applications by individuals as a first stage leading to the sale of the land to a developer and eventually to the sale by the developer through the estate agent of the new dwellings, dwellings that were more valuable, and therefore yielded a larger commission to the estate agent, than those originally applied for. This scenario of estate agent behaviour is consistent with the low proportion of proposals by individuals that were actually implemented.

The differential rates of approval and implementation associated with the various types of applicants should be viewed in the more general context of the approach of LPAs to unwelcome development proposals. This in turn provides a necessary background for understanding specific cases of restraint within the study areas. In the face of pressures for development, LPAs have improvised an assortment of devices for impeding development. Some of these bear no apparent relation to either local development plans or guidance from central government. In many cases the Local Plans envisaged in the Town and Country Planning Act of 1971 were still, at the end of the study period, in course of preparation. The planning documents still in force were often the Town Maps, prepared well over 20 years previously, which indicated little more than the types of land use permissible in different areas. More up-to-date documents generally existed on such practical matters as parking standards and the dimensions of private gardens. Local planning objectives to restrict further residential development generally have a weak statutory basis within existing settlements. For example, Chiltern District Council adopted a housing restraint policy in December 1984 whereby applications for residential development would be refused unless the proposed development provided accommodation in small units, a type of accommodation favoured by the DOE (Department of the Enviroment, 1980b, annex A, para. 2). However, like much LPA policy, this policy was not subject to any form of statutory process or public consultation, and it was soon overthrown by DOE inspectors when developers appealed against the refusal of their applications on this ground (Bowhill, 1985, 1986).

More important are less explicit attempts to minimize the number of dwellings approved. Some of the evidence for this is hard to quantify, often not susceptible to succinct summary, and open to different interpretations. Without inside knowledge it is frequently difficult to distinguish between inefficiency on the part of an LPA and deliberate attempts to block the progress of applications. Pre-application negotiations are encouraged by the DOE, but the onus is upon the applicant and an LPA's tardiness in responding to letters and queries can delay the actual submission of an application by many months. An LPA determined to restrain development has little to gain by providing information to applicants, and it runs the risk that views expressed in letters will be used as evidence against it at a subsequent appeal (Punter, 1985, p. 50). If repeatedly pressed for information, an LPA may resort to irrelevancies and obfuscation. Outline applications, intended to establish whether a particular type of development is acceptable in principle, are particularly vulnerable to delays, owing to their susceptibility to demands from LPAs for more information. Although strongly discouraged by the DOE (1980b, para. 9), such demands may ultimately proceed to the point of requiring detailed information on all the matters that have been reserved for subsequent approval, including floor plans. For many LPAs the request for an extension beyond the statutory eight-week period for making a decision is practically a normal occurrence in the case of applications for new buildings. After an application has been in the hands of an LPA for many months, at the point of decision it is not uncommon for a deferral to be made in order for the planning committee to make a site visit (Witt and Fleming, 1984, pp.88–91). If the applicant resorts to an appeal, as is frequently the case, the LPA can with virtual impunity delay every stage in the procedure. Such tactics are more than a means of deferring development; since for most developers delay means increased interest payments, they are also a means of putting pressure on developers to modify their proposals, notably to reduce their dwelling densities. Nevertheless, where a developer has acquired a potential infill site the restraints exercised by an LPA are seldom so great as to render development unprofitable.

It would be wrong, however, to attribute solely to LPAs the moderate pace of actual landscape change relative to the number of applications. In the study areas developers were far from being impotent bystanders helplessly watching as their schemes became entangled in a wed of bureaucratic obstructionism. Most notably, on the developers' part, implementations were delayed while further applications were submitted concerning the same sites in attempts to gain permission for more-profitable schemes than those for which outline permission had already beeen obtained: revised applications were submitted for, among other things, the demolition of existing houses that were previously scheduled to remain, the addition of more houses, the substitution of larger dwellings and the removal of more trees and hedgerows. For example, in the Epsom study area a developer, having gained planning permission for, and begun building the office part of, a scheme comprising part offices and part flats near the edge of the commercial core, sought to substitute (more-profitable) offices for the residential component. The fact that offices now existed on part of the site weakened the LPA's case for refusing the revised application; a case that became untenable once an appeal against an enforcement notice to complete the development as previously approved had been allowed.

CASE STUDIES: SITE CHRONOLOGIES

The emphasis so far on planning applications as free-standing units of analysis has left unanswered questions about the way in which outcomes in the landscape are the product of a series of decisions relating to particular sites. What happens in reality is frequently the product of a complicated sequence of events rather than the outcome of the lodging of a single planning application. Viewing planning applications as part of a series of events allows a different set of interrelated questions to be addressed. To seek answers to these questions the data need to be analysed by site. For this purpose a site is defined as a plot or a group of contiguous plots that at some point in the study period was treated as an entity for the purposes of undertaking development. There were 45 such sites in the Epsom study area and 28 in the Amersham study area.

Actual and intended developments

In the case of ordinary developments, as distinct from major public works, analyses of the events taking place between an initial idea for development and the actual landscape change face the problem that the schemes considered before the lodging of a formal planning application are seldom readily available for inspection. However, once proposals enter the formal process of development control by an LPA they are better documented and more amenable to systematic analysis. In the case of the study areas even outline applications generally provide information about dwelling type (which can be categorized as detached, semi-detached, terrace or flat/maisonette), density, access, and whether existing buildings were to be demolished. Although building elevations are often lacking, and density, in terms of floor space per unit of site, may need to be estimated from block plans at scales as small as 1/1250, it is possible to examine in some detail the relationship between applicants' apparent intentions and subsequent proposals and outcomes. In the course of attempts to develop sites in south-east England it is common for several successive schemes to be put forward. It is possible to assess the amount of change between each scheme in terms of each of the four variables just mentioned. Moreover, a distinction can be made between schemes that are the same in respect of all four variables (discounting minor differences in the line and width of roads) and those that are not.

In the case of the two study areas, a comparison between developments proposed in initial applications and actual developments reveals substantial differences (table 4.4). Actual developments that differed from those proposed in initial applications exceeded in number those that did not in both areas. In the Epsom study area only one-third of actual developments were the same as those proposed in the initial application. In both areas changes in density

Table 4.4 Comparison between development proposed in initial application and actual development

	Development type		Applicant		Type of difference			
	Different	Same	Different	Same	Demolition	Density	Access	Building type
Amersham	10	8	14	4	3	7	5	7
Epsom	21	10	14	17	8	16	5	14

(mainly reductions) and building type were the most numerous differences. Least numerous, but still significant, were changes in whether existing buildings were to be demolished and changes to the vehicular access. Changes in the block plans of buildings were often pronounced: sometimes this was associated with an increased density of dwellings (figure 4.12), which usually

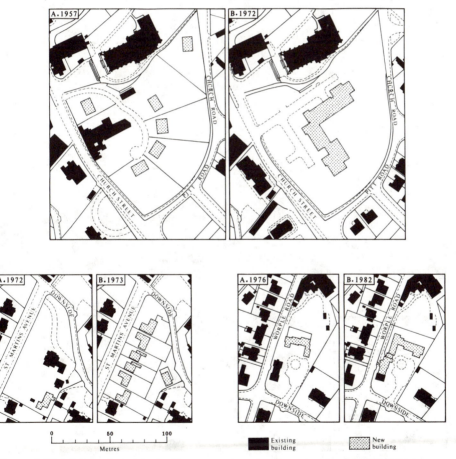

Figure 4.12 Selected sites in the Epsom study area where the density of dwellings was increased between development proposed in initial application (A) and actual development (B). The date shown is the year in which the planning application was submitted.
Source: planning applications.

entailed an increase in building coverage, but more often density of dwellings and building coverage were reduced (figure 4.13). Sometimes the layout bore a resemblance to that proposed in the initial application, but more often it was completely different. If sites on which there resulted no development at all are added (10 sites in the Amersham study area and 13 in the Epsom study area, excluding one where a decision on an application was still pending on 30 June 1988), only on 18 out of 72 sites in the two study areas combined did a development take place that was the same as that proposed in the initial application.

Figure 4.13   Selected sites in the Epsom study area where the density of dwellings was reduced between development proposed in initial application (A) and actual development (B). The date shown is the year in which the planning application was submitted.
Source: planning applications.

The fact that on many of the sites that were developed the actual development took a form different from that of the development for which permission was initially sought is to be explained in part by the fact that an initial application was sometimes merely an attempt by an owner to gain planning permission as a basis for selling to a developer who then proposed a different, usually more profitable scheme. That there is more to the explanation than this is evident, however, from tables 4.4 and 4.5. In the case of the majority of sites in the Epsom study area the initial applicant was the eventual developer (table 4.4), and only about one-half of the instances of a difference between the development proposed in the initial application and the actual development coincided with a difference between the eventual developer and the initial applicant (table 4.5). In the Amersham study area a much higher proportion of the instances in which there was a difference between the development proposed in the initial application and the actual development were associated with a change of applicant, and in a much smaller proportion of cases was the initial applicant the eventual developer. This latter finding reflects the fact that here sites were on average sold by owner-occupiers to developers at a later stage in the pre-development process, often only after one or more applications had already been lodged.

Table 4.5   Extent to which change between development proposed in initial application and actual development was associated with a change of applicant

	Amersham		Epsom	
	Same applicant	*Different applicant*	*Same applicant*	*Different applicant*
Same development type	3	5	7	3
Different development type	1	9	10	11

LPA influences

Uncovering the role played by the LPAs in these events is of central concern here. In nearly all cases in which a development did not take place, or was different from that initially proposed, the initial application was refused. About one-half of the applications approved (discounting second or subsequent approvals) differed from the application initially submitted despite the fact that in the large majority of cases in both study areas the applicant was unchanged (table 4.6). The most important single source of difference was density. Where there was a density difference, on 80 per cent of sites in the two study areas combined the approved density was lower than that proposed in the initial application. Such reduced densities suggest that the LPAs exercised a significant restraining influence on development. But it is important to look beyond the differences between what was applied for and what was approved to consider both the planning activities, formal and informal, that provided the basis of the LPAs influence and the extent to which initial planning approvals were translated into actual developments in the landscape.

Table 4.6   Comparison between development proposed in initial application and development plan initially approved

	Development type		Applicant		Type of difference			
	Different	Same	Different	Same	Demolition	Density	Access	Building type
Amersham	9	9	4	14	1	7	5	4
Epsom	16	16	8	24	4	13	6	7

Planning decisions in the case of the study areas were based to a considerable extent on the views of individual case officers. These views were strongly influenced by then current practice within the particular planning office. Only rarely were plans that had been formally approved for the areas a significant factor. Documents on such matters as the standards relating to highways, parking, garden sizes and dwelling sizes were referred to in reasons for refusal and conditions of approval, as, in the case of the Epsom study area, was the inclusion of large parts of it in a Conservation Area. Putative highway and town centre plans played a role in the Amersham study area in that the risk that development would fail to accord with them was used as a ground for refusing planning permission, though neither plan materialized within the study period and there is evidence to suggest that preparation of a town centre plan was never begun (Internal memorandum from County Planning Officer, Planning Application Am/1629/69). The majority of the formal reasons given for refusing planning permission related to the detailed circumstances of specific sites.

Whatever the legitimacy of the LPAs' formal reasons for refusing planning permission, they clearly succeeded in precluding the implementation of many schemes. That they performed this preventive role did not, however, mean that actual developments largely accorded with the LPAs' wishes. That they frequently did not is suggested by a comparison, for those sites developed, of the developments envisaged in the positions initially taken up by planning officers, as expressed in their initial recommendations to their planning committees (and in the large majority of cases endorsed by those committees), with the developments that eventually took place (table 4.7). In the Epsom study area there was a roughly equal split between sites on which actual development accorded with the planning officers' initial position and sites on which there

Table 4.7   Comparison of development envisaged in planning officers' initial recommendation to Planning Committee and actual development

	Development type		Type of difference				
	Different	Same	Demolition	Density	Access	Building type	Other*
Amersham	4	14	0	1	0	1	3
Epsom	14	17	7	10	2	6	0

*Opposition by officers to redevelopment either on principle or on the grounds that it was premature or piecemeal

was a difference. Only two of the fourteen cases in which there was a difference were accounted for by successful appeals against the LPA's refusal of planning permission. In two further cases the developer allowed houses that the LPA wanted to be retained to fall into serious disrepair, one of them eventually being destroyed by fire. The majority of the other cases can be attributed to the eventual acquiescence by the planning officers in the developers' schemes, usually owing to their adjudging their position unsustainable. In some cases they considered that there was a risk that intransigence on their part would lead to a successful appeal and an outcome even further removed from that envisaged in their initial position. In eight of the ten cases in which there was a difference of density the development took place at a higher density than the planning officers initially favoured, and in all but one of the seven cases in which there was a difference in respect of demolition, actual development involved demolition of buildings (two of them requiring 'listed building consent') that the planning officers would have preferred to be retained. The discrepancies in regard to building types were various.

In the Amersham study area there was greater conformity with the positions initially taken up by the planning officers. This relates in large part to the LPA's success in resisting development on the ground that there was a need for comprehensive schemes compatible with road improvements. Of eighteen apeals on this issue only one (a proposal for infill by a single dwelling) was upheld, eleven being dismissed and six withdrawn. Although by the end of the study period the actual road improvements that had been made were minimal, most of the sites in question had been occupied by, or were in the process of being occupied by, 'comprehensive' schemes with access to the main road (Chesham Road) via existing side roads (figure 4.14). There were but four cases in the Amersham study area in which developments took place that were not in accord with the planning officers' initial position. In the first of these, which arose at the beginning of the study period, the Planning Committee overturned its officers' recommendation to refuse permission for the erection of a block of flats. This occurred before attitudes on resisting development had hardened. The second concerned the building of an old people's home, a development which took place following conflicting LPA decisions, one a permission for a single house on the site and the other, six years later, a permission for a comprehensive scheme that included other properties. The other two cases of development that was not in accord with the planning officers' initial position involved compromises by the planning officers on their stand on the primacy of comprehensive redevelopment and highway considerations.

In comparing actual developments with those envisaged in the initial positions adopted by planning officers, it is important to appreciate that an initial LPA position arrived at independently of the specific proposal being considered rarely, if ever, existed. Little previous thought by the relevant LPAs appears to have been given in the case of the study areas to the form that the development of specific sites might take or to principles that might be adopted in dealing with the landscape problems that different types of proposals frequently presented. The initial positions adopted by planning officers were

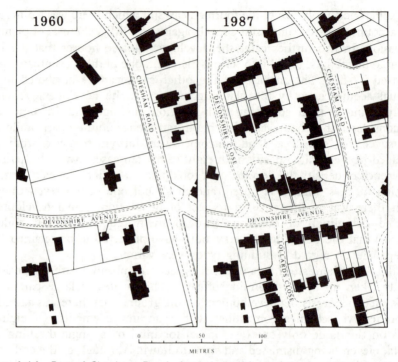

Figure 4.14 Part of Chesham Road, Amersham. Most of the large detached houses existing in 1960 had been replaced by estates of smaller dwellings by 1987.
Source: planning applications.

invariably prompted by a prospective or actual application, and were influenced in some cases by a response to an earlier application relating to a nearby site. Planning stances were therefore taken up in reaction to practical situations; they were expediences rather than attempts to apply urban design principles, and were far removed from a theory of urban landscape management. With the types of development considered here, planning, other than of a reactive type, scarcely existed.

In the case of both study areas, the first formal indication of the LPA's attitude towards the development of a specific site was generally the decision notice that it issued in response to the first application. Just over three-fifths of such notices were refusals. Formal reasons for refusal set out in a decision notice sometimes suggested whether a different form of development might be viewed with favour. A decision notice of approval provided a positive, usually clear, indication of what was acceptable to the LPA. However, this was frequently far from being identical in form to the development that eventually took place. Indeed, the discrepancies were of a similar magnitude to those between the developments envisaged in planning officers' initial positions and the eventual developments. They mainly related to building type and density (table 4.8). The existence of such differences may be attributed in part to the use of planning applications as a means of eliciting an expression of the LPA's attitude to development on a particular site, perhaps to establish the value of the site. Having had the right to develop approved, applicants then sometimes sought permission for a different type of development (table 4.9). Similarly, where developers had purchased a site with planning permission, they sometimes subsequently sought permission for a different, usually higher-density, development.

Table 4.8 Comparison between development envisaged in initial approval and actual development

	Development type		Applicant		Type of difference				
	Different	Same	Different	Same	Demolition	Density	Access	Building type	Other
Amersham	5	13	12	6	2	4	2	3	1
Epsom	12	19	12	19	4	7	2	8	0

Table 4.9 Extent to which change between development envisaged in initial approval and actual development was associated with a change of applicant

	Amersham		Epsom	
	Same applicant	Different applicant	Same applicant	Different applicant
Same development type	3	10	12	7
Different development type	3	2	7	5

Density and size of development

The tendency for density to be reduced between an initial application and a first approval, and for it to be increased between the first approval and the actual development may be seen in terms of the following sequence: first, there was an initial attempt to gain permission for as much development as possible on a site; secondly, in the face of LPA objections, often on the grounds of 'overdevelopment', a compromise permission was eventually arrived at, often following one or more rejections; thirdly, this permission was used, either by the same applicant or by another applicant to whom the site had now been sold, to obtain a permission for a more profitable, usually higher-density, development. Consistent with this sequence, dwellings favoured for retention in planning officers' initial recommendations were frequently demolished in actual developments, and it was common for the building types constructed to be different from those originally approved.

Perhaps the most basic distinction between the types of development attempted within the study areas was between sites on which only the insertion of a single additional dwelling was attempted, by frontage division or plot truncation, and sites (often larger and formed by the amalgamation of several gardens or parts of gardens) where an attempt was made to construct more than one dwelling, often flats or a small estate of houses. *Prima facie* the former would appear to be simpler developments (figure 4.15). But, they were not more

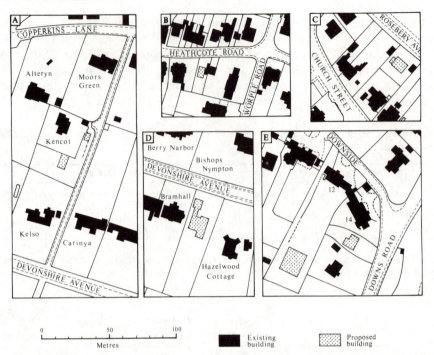

Figure 4.15 Examples of proposals for the construction of a single additional dwelling within an existing plot. (A) Amersham, 1965 (permission refused); (B) Epsom, 1960 (permission refused); (C) Epsom, 1960 (permission granted, development implemented); (D) Amersham, 1986 (permission granted, development implemented); (E) Rear of 12 Downside, Epsom, 1962 (permission refused), and rear of 14 Downside, Epsom, 1981 (permission refused).
Source: planning applications.

straightforward if judged by the proportion that were implemented. A lower proportion of single-dwelling sites were developed than sites for which more than one dwelling was proposed (table 4.10). This reflected a lower proportion of successful planning applications for single-dwelling sites. However, these sites were subject to a shorter planning gestation period. In the Amersham study area the longest planning gestation period for those sites for which there were single-dwelling proposals was actually shorter than the median planning gestation period for those for which more than one dwelling was proposed

Table 4.10   Relationship between maximum number of dwellings proposed for a site and whether development took place

	Amersham		Epsom	
	Developed	*Not developed*	*Developed*	*Not developed*
1 dwelling	5	6	1	4
>1 dwelling	13	4	30	9*

*Excludes site on which LPA decision still pending on 30 June 1988

Table 4.11 Relationship between maximum number of dwellings proposed for a site and planning gestation period*

| Maximum no. of dwellings proposed | Time-lag (months) | | | | | |
| | Amersham | | | Epsom | | |
	Median	Mean	Range	Median	Mean	Range
1	8.0	18.6	1–54	4.0	19.4	2–67
>1	71.5	85.7	3–314	13.5	30.6	1–187

*Excludes site on which LPA decision was still pending on 30 June 1988 and two sites for which the most recent application was withdrawn

(table 4.11). More striking, however, was the difference between the two types of site in the number of applications and appeals. In both study areas the mean and median number of planning applications for sites for which more than one dwelling was proposed exceeded the maximum number of applications recorded for sites for which there were single-dwelling proposals (table 4.12). Furthermore, appeals were comparatively rare in the case of sites for which there were only single-dwelling proposals (table 4.13). While some of these sites were arguably cramped, and therefore intrinsically less suitable for development, it seems probable that the private individual owner-occupiers who made up the large majority of the applicants for planning permission for these sites were more readily deterred than developers would have been by LPA resistance and the prospect of an appeal. In the case of sites for which more than one dwelling was proposed, applications and appeals were both considerably more numerous in the Amersham study area than in the Epsom study area. This would appear to be accounted for mainly by the LPA's resistance, largely

Table 4.12 Relationship between maximum number of dwellings proposed for a site and number of applications submitted

| Maximum no. of dwellings proposed | No. of applications | | | | | |
| | Amersham | | | Epsom | | |
	Median	Mean	Range	Median	Mean	Range
1	2.0	1.8	1–3	1.0	1.4	1–2
>1	5.0	7.1	1–23	3.0	3.3	1–10

Table 4.13 Relationship between maximum number of dwellings proposed for a site and number of appeals lodged

| Maximum no. of dwellings proposed | No. of appeals | | | | | |
| | Amersham | | | Epsom | | |
	Median	Mean	Range	Median	Mean	Range
1	0	0.1	0–1	0	0.2	0–1
>1	0	1.1	0–7	0	0.4	0–2

supported at appeal, to the piecemeal development of sites fronting the main road that ran through the Amersham study area.

Types of applicant

Prima facie there would seem to be a useful distinction between sites for which applications were submitted entirely by firms or organizations (mainly developers) and those where private individuals were applicants on at least one occasion. Although there is no evidence to suggest that this distinction had a bearing on whether or not a site was ultimately developed (table 4.14), it does appear to have had a bearing on the length of the planning gestation period. Where the applicants were, or included, private individuals the planning gestation period was longer (table 4.15): in the Amersham study area it was particularly long (a median length of some eight years) where permission was being sought for the construction of more than one dwelling on a site. This general finding accords with the fact that in both study areas sites that were at some stage the subject of applications by private individuals generated more applications on average than other sites (table 4.16). It also accords with the relatively high rate of planning application refusal suffered by individuals and the fact that private owner-occupiers are less likely than developers to suffer financial loss if negotiations for planning permission are protracted. In this light it is not surprising that in both study areas appeals were less frequent where the applicants were, or included, private individuals (table 4.16). Moreover, many

Table 4.14   Relationship between type of applicant and whether development took place

Type of applicant	Amersham		Epsom	
	Developed	Not developed	Developed	Not developed
Entirely firms or organizations	2	2	13	7*
Partly or entirely private individuals	16	8	18	6

*Excludes site on which LPA decision still pending on 30 June 1988

Table 4.15   Relationship between type of applicant and planning gestation period*

Type of applicant	Median time-lag (months)					
	Amersham			Epsom		
	All	Max. 1 dwelling	Max. >1 dwelling	All	Max. 1 dwelling	Max. >1 dwelling
Entirely firms or organizations	10	†	†	9	†	12
Partly or entirely private individuals	40	13	95	15	†	14

*Excludes site on which LPA decision was still pending on 30 June 1988 and two sites for which the most recent application was withdrawn
†Less than 4 observations

Table 4.16   Relationship between type of applicant and number of applications and appeals

Type of applicant	No. of applications				No. of appeals			
	Mean		Median		Mean		Median	
	Amersham	Epsom	Amersham	Epsom	Amersham	Epsom	Amersham	Epsom
Entirely firms or organizations	3.0	2.7	2.0	3.0	1.8	0.4	0	0
Partly or entirely private individuals	5.4	3.5	3.0	3.0	0.5	0.3	0	0

of the appeals relating to sites that were the subject of one or more applications by private individuals were actually made after the sites had passed into the hands of developers.

CASE STUDIES: CONCLUSION

Differences between study areas

Although the two sets of findings, one for each of the two study areas, are similar, there are noteworthy differences between them. In morphological terms these relate to on the one hand proneness to demolition and on the other density. These differences are related to differences in the character of the two towns.

First, the Amersham study area was less demolition prone than the Epsom one, in terms of both applications and implementations, even though non-local developers were actually more disposed towards demolition there than they were in the Epsom study area (table 4.17). Accounting for this fact, to a large extent, was the high proportion of planning applications for sites in that area from individuals, the type of applicant least disposed towards demolition. This also accounts for the higher proportion of outline applications for sites in that area, since a relatively high proportion of individuals were concerned in the

Table 4.17   Numbers of applications and implementations entailing demolition of a main building, and numbers not doing so

Type of applicant	Applications				Implementations			
	Demolition		No demolition		Demolition		No demolition	
	Amersham	Epsom	Amersham	Epsom	Amersham	Epsom	Amersham	Epsom
Local developer	19	29*	5	5	3	8*	2	4
Non-local developer	25	23	6	25	8	9	4	9
Individual	21	21*	56	23	0	2*	6	3
Other	1	7	8	8	0	1	4	2
All	66	79	75	61	11	19	16	18

*Includes a joint application with another category of applicant

first place to establish whether development would be permitted in principle so that they could ascertain the value of their sites. Moreover, not only did the Amersham study area have a lower proportion of the applications made by developers but a lower proportion of those developers owned the sites for which they were making applications. On average, land there passed out of the hands individuals and into those of developers (both local and non-local) and other organizations at a later stage in the pre-development process than it did in the Epsom study area, often only after one or more planning applications had been lodged. Protracted struggles with the LPA, involving a series of applications made by or on behalf of the same individual, though a feature of both study areas, were more characteristic of the Amersham study area. This was a major factor accounting for the longer planning gestation periods for the Amersham study area – a median planning gestation period of 23 months, compared with only 13 months for the Epsom study area. Probably at least part of the explanation for these differences is the greater size and proximity to London of Epsom. This appears to have stimulated there a greater 'professionalization' of the development process and a much greater use of London agents (for 24 applications, compared with only 7 in the Amersham study area), most of whom were architects. And it is also consistent with the higher proportion of applications for sites in the Epsom study area emanating from outside the town (40 per cent, compared with 27 per cent for the Amersham study area) and the higher proportion of such applications in which the owner was from outside the town (29 per cent, compared with 17 per cent for the Amersham study area).

Secondly, over the study period as a whole, the Epsom study area experienced even greater development pressure than the Amersham study area. Indicative of this was the small size of the developments that non-local developers were prepared to undertake there, and the dwelling type that was favoured. Fifty-eight per cent of their applications for sites there were for developments of four or less dwellings, whereas only 25 per cent of their applications for sites in the Amersham study area were for developments as small as that. Since the median numbers of dwellings per site proposed by local applicants (both individuals and developers) were similar for the two study areas, one possible inference is that development was so profitable in Epsom that, more than in the case of the Amersham study area, outside developers were attracted even to the smaller sites. The difference between the two study areas in numbers of dwellings per application by non-local developers was not accounted for by larger dwelling sizes in the Epsom study area. On the contrary, there a higher proportion of the dwellings applied for by non-local developers were flats/maisonettes (75 per cent, compared with 57 per cent for the Amersham study area). This relative preponderance was consistent with the higher proportion of flats/maisonettes applied for by all applicants there. Furthermore, flats/maisonettes made up as much as 79 per cent of the dwellings erected in the Epsom study area, compared with only 59 per cent in the Amersham study area. These differences were consistent with both Epsom's closer proximity to London and its greater importance as a centre in its own right. In accordance with this greater pressure on land in the Epsom study area (as measured by dwelling types), a higher proportion of the applications made for sites there were implemented (26 per cent, compared with 19 per cent for the Amersham study area), although the percentages of applications approved (47 and 48 per cent respectively) were almost identical.

Reflections and implications

Many of the findings about development decisions that have been made in the case of the two residential study areas are fairly clear-cut. And they may well apply to other low-density residential areas that have undergone or are undergoing strong pressures for more-intensive development. There remains a need, however, to review the main findings in a slightly broader perspective and to reflect upon their implications.

Judged by planning applications, the original intentions of property owners and developers concerning the precise nature of the development on their sites were frequently unrealized. A significant minority of prospective development sites were not developed at all and the eventual outcome on those that were developed was often different from that first envisaged, especially with regard to dwelling density and building types. These findings are even more striking when it is realized that, by the time that a planning application was submitted, original intentions had in some cases already been modified: for example, as a result of discussions with planning officers.

It would be wrong, however, to assume that revision on this large scale reflected the incompatibility of proposals with either formally approved plans or the preconceptions of planning officers about the future of the sites concerned. It is true that increasingly the overriding concern of the LPAs was to restrain development, but unless stimulated by planning applications little thought was given to the future of particular sites. The positions of the LPAs were formulated as reactions to specific proposals by owners or developers. However, many sites were ultimately developed in ways that did not accord with those positions. This reflected both inconsistencies in the attitudes of planning officers during the course of the often lengthy period during which attempts were made to develop sites (including cases in which planning approval was obtained for a site and then an alternative approval was sought), and in rare cases the overturning of officers' recommendations either by planning committees or at an appeal. Most often, discrepancies between the developments envisaged in the initial positions taken by planning officers and the eventual developments reflected a retreat by the LPAs, sometimes from positions that they themselves had regarded as negotiating postures that were ultimately unlikely to be sustainable, in the face of pressure from developers.

These pressures on the LPAs, whose committees, strongly supported by local residents, were increasingly committed to restraining development, led to lengthy conflicts. They were especially protracted where multiple-dwelling developments were attempted. Most of the longest conflicts were cases in which private individuals initially attempted to gain planning permission themselves and became entangled in a web of delay and obfuscation which left some sites in a state of uncertainty for many years, occasionally decades. Developers mostly had more resources and experience than owner-occupiers and were thus better able to cope with the development-control process. They more readily resorted to appeals and their struggles for planning permission rarely lasted more than a few years.

With on average nearly six planning applications (for new dwellings) per implemented development, the energy spent on 'planning' in the study areas was considerable, particularly when it is borne in mind that even the largest sites barely exceeded 2 ha. Ideally, the expenditure of this energy would have been reflected in a progression through a series of improved schemes. However, examination of the sequence of events on each site suggests that, as far as the landscape was concerned, this was often far from being the case. Communications between applicant and LPA consisted overwhelmingly of proposal and objection. With the exception of a few of the applications to construct single dwellings, the motivations of applicants appear to have been largely economic. Planning officers saw their task as being primarily to minimize consequent damage to certain aspects of the physical enviroment. They were influenced heavily by their planning committees, who were in turn sensitive to the prevailing anti-development stance of their constituents. The exercise of restraint by LPAs was viewed by planning officers predominantly in terms of limitations on amounts of development (often measured in dwellings, or 'habitable rooms', per unit area) and constraints on vehicular access, though the appearance of developments played a significant role in those parts of the Epsom study area that were in a Conservation Area. This approach was generally supported at appeals. Attempts by applicants to meet or obviate density and highway objections were often at a cost to the landscape in terms of both the relationship between buildings and the survival of trees and hedgerows. It is true that references to the desirability of minimizing the loss of trees and hedgerows, a fundamental aspect of the landscapes of the study areas, were not uncommon in planning officer's recommendations. But this often amounted to little more than lip-service. In practice, where such losses were side-effects of practical requirements, concerning such matters as the provision of car-parking space and the positioning of road junctions, they were rarely key issues (cf. Havers, 1985). Once the principle of development permission had been conceded, the losses of trees and hedgerows tended to be regarded as regrettable but bearable sacrifices, a finding that accords with Beer's (1983) evidence that developers make light of LPA conditions concerning landscaping and that low priority is given to their enforcement.

Underlying many of these findings was the lack, as far as the management of the landscape was concerned, of an integrated approach, either to individual sites or to larger areas (cf. Beer, 1983, p. 391; Booth, 1989, p. 147). This is not to suggest that there was an absence of a desire for comprehensive redevelopment in the sense of redeveloping several adjacent sites. Indeed, in part of the Amersham study area that was a major objective of the LPA throughout the study period. What was absent was an underlying theory of how changes that were almost inevitably, and in many cases desirably, piecemeal should be fitted together to the enhancement of the landscape. In this respect the processes going on in the study areas differed greatly from the ideals of urban landscape management envisaged by Conzen (1966; 1975). Whereas in Conzen's approach the *genius loci* is the fundamental criterion upon which urban landscape change should be founded, in the study areas outcomes in the landscape were in large part by-products of conflicts between LPAs and applicants. The unforeseen and often unsatisfactory consequences of this kind of process require more consideration, as does the preparation of a more responsible substitute. It is to these subjects that attention is directed in the next chapter.

5

Urban Landscape Management

Conzen's approach to the management of the urban landscape, with its emphasis on the long-term relationship between landscape and society, has been largely overlooked outside academe. Even among academic urban planners who know of Conzen's work, there is scant knowledge of the basis that he has suggested for appraising proposals for change to the urban landscape. Essentially historico-geographical, this basis is derived to an important extent from morphogenetic ideas, especially Conzen's own ideas, about the nature of urban landscape change. These ideas have undergone a revival in terms of academic interest in the past decade. They stand apart, however, from the perspectives of practising planners, which are heavily constrained by political pressures from both central and local government. The gulf between Conzen's standpoint and the standpoints of those most directly involved in urban landscape change – developers and, in some circumstances, property owners – is probably larger still. This chapter is an exploration of these different perspectives by means of detailed case studies of individual developments.

CONZEN'S IDEAS

Conzen's ideas about urban landscape management have been developed in relation to the cores of historic towns and cities. Bandini (1985), one of the few architects familiar with Conzen's work, believes that the successful promulgation of these ideas and the propositions that have stemmed from them will depend on their suitability for much wider application, including application to the modern urban periphery. Before examining actual cases in the light of these ideas, it is necessary to restate briefly Conzen's argument about urban landscape management.

Quintessentially, for Conzen, the past provides the key to the future. Fundamental to this view is the idea that urban landscapes embody not only the efforts

and aspirations of the people occupying them now but also those of their predecessors. It is this, it has been argued, that creates the sense of place and feeling of
continuity that enable individuals and groups to identify with an area. Respect
for these qualities is therefore of prime importance in urban landscape management. A major practical implication of this is that proposals for managing the
urban landscape should place great stress on the way in which new developments
fit into, and in a sense are almost an organic growth from, existing landscapes.

Although the theoretical development of this perspective is still in its early
stages, and the practical problems of its application in planning are likely to be
great, Conzen has indicated the main elements of it to which theoretical and
practical consideration needs to be given (Conzen, 1975, pp. 98–102). It is on the
historical expressiveness or historicity of the urban landscape that he places most
emphasis. It is accordingly the nature and intensity of the historicity of the urban
landscape that provide his main basis for devising proposals for its management.
This basis is articulated in practical terms by utilizing his division of the urban
landscape into three basic 'form complexes' – town plan, building forms and
land use. These are regarded as to some extent a hierarchy in which building
forms are contained within plots or land-use units, which are in turn set in the
framework of the town plan. These three form complexes, together with the site,
combine at the most local level to produce the smallest morphologically homogeneous areas, which might be termed 'urban landscape cells'. These cells are
grouped into urban landscape units, which in turn combine at different levels of
integration to form a hierarchy of intra-urban regions. Since the three form
complexes change at different speeds, their geographical patterns within an urban area frequently differ. Particularly in old urban areas, the delimitations of
cells, units and regions are complex, although the commercial core, fringe belts
and different types of residential accretion are recurrent features. The hierarchy
of areal units is the geographical manifestation of the historical development of
urban form and encapsulates its historicity. It is the reference point for all proposals for change to the urban landscape. The approach, therefore, is essentially
conservative. The accent is on the historically and geographically informed
transformation, augmentation and conservation of what already exists.

It is not the intention here to consider the philosophical basis of this
perspective or examine the technical problems of translating Conzen's accounts
of the constituents of urban landscape regions into actual delimitations on the
ground. Instead, attention here will be devoted to an examination of major
issues in the actual development process in low-density residential areas in
south-east England with a view to assessing them from Conzen's standpoint.
The task is to compare ideal and reality.

ISSUES AND STUDY SITES

Prima facie it would seem reasonable to suppose that the attitudes towards
landscape change taken by the various parties to development will vary both
within and between urban areas. For example, a local authority seeking to

attract development may well adopt a more flexible stance towards the landscape changes that developers propose than a local authority struggling to restrain development. Since attention devoted to the landscape may well entail additional costs, it is likely to prove less attractive to developers where profit margins are low, as was the case during much of the 1980s in large parts of northern England and Scotland. Similarly, it might be supposed that landscape considerations would be an important issue in high-class residential areas in south-east England, that pressure there on local planning committees to restrain further development and maintain exclusiveness would be high. In such areas the parties to development would it would seem be likely to be more concerned about the landscape. It is in relation to this ostensibly favourable environment in south-east England that an attempt will be made to uncover the processes underlying urban landscape change at the micro-scale, to assess the extent to which changes may be construed as 'planned', and to compare them with Conzenian ideals.

Four interrelated questions will be addressed. First, how do parties who have a potential management role in the urban landscape become involved in specific developments and to what extent does this involvement affect the outcome in the landscape? Secondly, as a means of managing change in the urban landscape, how effective does the process of interaction between the parties to development appear in the light of Conzen's philosophy? For example, does the LPA have a coherent strategy that integrates that process; to what extent is it managing the urban landscape, as distinct from reacting to pressures from other parties? Thirdly, given the fundamental importance of the *genius loci* to Conzen's viewpoint, to what extent do the different parties seeking change, especially owner-occupiers and developers, vary in their sense of place? Finally, how much awareness of urban landscape regions, a key feature of Conzen's perspective, is shown by the parties to change?

Discussion will be limited to four sites, ranging in size from about 0.1 ha to about 1.5 ha, that since the 1950s have been the subject of proposals for substantial change and have been subject to the initiation of a second cycle of residential development clearly distinguishable from their original develop-ment. The four sites were within, or in the vicinity of, the study areas examined in chapter 4. Their selection was based in particular on the quality of the development records that were available. They are therefore not a random sample in a statistical sense, but inspection of over 500 planning applications for residential development in south-east England suggests that many of the key issues that arose in connection with these sites recur widely in those mature areas with large gardens in which pressures for more-intensive development are strong. Information has been derived from the files of the main parties involved in the further development of these sites, especially the LPAs, and from correspondence and discussions with individuals who played a significant role.

In the 1950s each site consisted of predominantly large residential plots (0.1–0.5 ha) within 400 m of a commercial core, and was thus particularly subject to pressures for more-intensive development. Two of the sites, just to the south-east of the commercial core of Epsom, were initially developed for residential purposes in Victorian times (figure 5.1C). The other two sites, one located just to the north-west and the other just to the east of the commercial core of Amersham, mostly underwent their initial development as residential areas during the first 30 years of the twentieth century (figure 5.1A,B). The two Epsom sites had frontages onto minor roads whose alignments dated from the pre-railway era. They were set in a larger area that contained numerous mid- to late-Victorian villas, often built of a yellowish brick which had weathered almost grey, and a

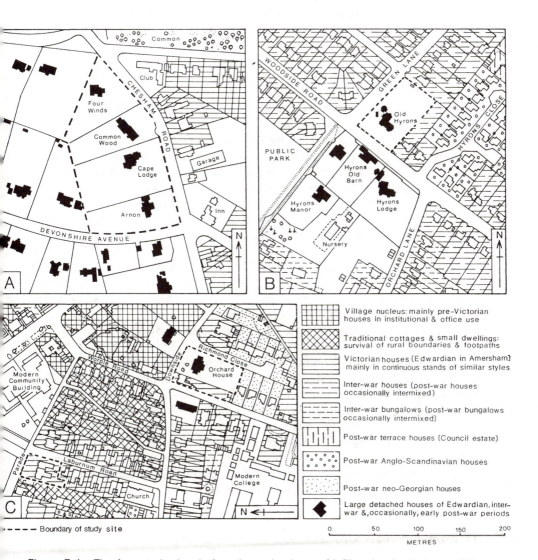

Figure 5.1 The four study sites before the main phase of infill and redevelopment: (A) Devonshire, Amersham *c.*1960; (B) Hyrons, Amersham *c.*1980; (C) Parade and Downside, Epsom *c.* 1977.
Source: field surveys, planning applications and Ordnance Survey plans.

scattering of pre-railway cottages faced in white weatherboard. Both of the Amersham sites had frontages onto busy main roads. In one case, Hyrons, the surrounding mature Stockbroker's Tudor landscape incorporated pre-urban hedgerows and buildings. This landscape abutted onto a 'Metroland' of small detached and semi-detached houses (figure 5.1B). On the other site, Devonshire, similar houses faced small, Edwardian, detached and semi-detached dwellings, not unlike the somewhat older, Victorian buildings in Epsom. All four sites retained a 'rural' atmosphere, consciously and very successfully contrived in the case of Amersham's pseudo-vernacular residences. In Amersham especially, tree and hedgerow planting by initial owners had augmented existing trees to give, by the 1950s, an almost woodland landscape from the air.

The settings of the four study sites in terms of urban landscape regions are shown in figure 5.1. Although a completely objective means of delineating such regions has not been worked out, and may not be feasible in every respect, it is possible, using the guidance that Conzen (1966, 1975, 1988) provides, to produce a delineation consistent with Conzenian principles. Indeed, it is easier to do so in landscapes still retaining most of the features they acquired when first urbanized than in the medieval cores examined by Conzen. Whereas Conzen was dealing with urban landscapes that had in many parts been adapted and redeveloped several times over, the upper-middle-class residential areas of south-east England have mostly only entered a first phase of major redevelopment since the 1950s. In town plan, building forms and land use, many of them, until then, closely resembled their original urban state.

The problem of managing landscape change in low-density residential areas was, however, far from new in the 1950s. In areas of Victorian villas and mansions near major city centres, a wide variety of types of infill and redevelopment had taken place earlier in the century, some paying scant regard to the existing urban landscape, while others were Conzenian in their sympathy with the *genius loci*. Similarly, for each of the four study sites in the 1950s a variety of solutions to the problem of managing landscape change can be retrospectively envisaged. Those in which the new grows out of the old, range from the insertion of individual houses in existing gardens to extensions of existing houses to form a number of dwellings. Dealing with the problem can be seen as much in Conzenian terms as can the much-longer-standing problems of adaptation and redevelopment in medieval cores on which Conzen has focused attention. The art in both cases is to graft sensitively the new onto the old. The actual processes by which more-intensive development was brought about on the study sites will be examined in this light, and obstacles to a Conzenian approach in practice will be discussed.

THE INITIATION OF CHANGE

By the 1960s, if not earlier, three of the sites to be examined – Devonshire, Hyrons and Downside – had become 'ripe' for more-intensive development. They had densities of less than five dwellings per ha, were adjacent to areas of

much higher density and had road frontages on two sides (figure 5.1). The fourth
site – Parade – was more problematic. It was subsequently to be designated as
part of a Conservation Area and had a much higher density – about 15 dwellings
per ha. But it too had the advantage for development of having road frontage on
two sides. In the first three cases a formal proposal for more-intensive development was triggered by the death of an owner-occupier. In the case of Parade it
was the circumstances of a developer, rather than an owner-occupier, that were
particularly important in the initiation of change. A firm of developers who had
acquired much of the land in the vicinity of the commerical core was seeking a
site to which a church could be relocated from another potential redevelopment
site. The owner-occupiers of one of two matching pairs of mid-Victorian semi-
detached houses were bought out for this purpose. The project was, however,
delayed and eventually abandoned owing to changes in a number of factors affecting its viability, including the putting forward of a proposal by the LPA for
the construction of a ring road south of the commercial core through large areas
of the developer's land. The eventual proposal to redevelop Parade for residential, rather than religious, purposes was thus a by-product of changes elsewhere.

For Devonshire the first planning application, for one of the plots, was
submitted by the executors of a deceased owner-occupier; owner-occupiers of
adjoining properties (in one case the trustees of the owner-occupier) then
following suit. For Hyrons the widow of the owner-occupier submitted the first
application. For Downside a prospective developer submitted an application
after purchasing for his own occupation one of the two properties in
anticipation of purchasing the other.

Apart from the fact that the study sites had been designated by the LPAs to
continue in residential use, there is no evidence to suggest that the issue of their
more-intensive development, let alone the form that such development might
take, had been considered by the LPAs before they received a planning
application or informal approach. The executors and the widow employed
agents to prepare and submit outline planning applications for Hyrons and
Devonshire respectively on their behalf, the executors employing a local estate
agent and, later, an architect from a nearby town, the widow employing a
member of her family. They expected that obtaining outline planning
permission would enable them to realize a development value that was
appreciably greater than the existing use value of the properties. In the case of
Downside, the initial development proposal, which was a detailed application,
was submitted on behalf of the developer by a Central London architect,
whereas in the case of Parade, the initial application, also detailed, was prepared
'in-house' by the prospective developer.

INTERACTIONS BETWEEN MAIN PARTIES

It is important to appreciate, at least in outline, the interactions between the
main parties with interests in the study sites. For it is these interactions that
provide the framework within which an outcome in the landscape is to be
understood.

For Devonshire an initial outline application, prepared in 1963, proposed the addition of three dwellings to one side of an existing detached house (Cape Lodge in figure 5.2A) to provide a courtyard development. Although another application for this type of development near to Devonshire had been refused in 1961, precedents for courtyard development had been created by planning approvals on two sites closer to the commercial core in 1960 and 1961 (near the southern edge of figure 5.3). The first had been approved by the Planning Committee despite the view of their planning officers that the density was too high. The planning officers also pointed out that the site had not been programmed for further development. However, since this was true of practically all existing residential areas in the town, it hardly added weight to their argument for recommending that the application be disapproved.

The Planning Committee refused permission for the first application for a courtyard development at Devonshire on the formal grounds that it would increase traffic on the already busy main road and that it was desirable that either this land should be part of a comprehensive redevelopment scheme or that one dwelling only should be constructed adjoining the existing house. Since the planning files on comparable developments closer to the commercial core make no mention of the desirability of comprehensive redevelopment, it is a reasonable inference that this statement of its desirability reflected a belated recognition of the wider implications of those earlier developments and of developments of that kind, such as the one now proposed. There followed in 1965 and 1966 a flurry of seven outline applications (six for courtyard developments) on this plot of land and adjacent parts of the Devonshire site. In five cases the agent employed for planning application purposes was the same architect, from the nearby town of Rickmansworth, who had secured planning permission for the first two courtyard proposals. Appeals to the Minister of Housing and Local Government against the LPA's refusal of the first two of these applications were dismissed, but the Minister considered it unreasonable to delay development until all the plots of land became available that would be necessary for a comprehensive redevelopment with a single access to the main road. It became clear to the four owners that co-ordination of their proposals was likely to increase the chances of gaining permission, and eventually there were approved in quick succession, between August 1966 and March 1967, a number of schemes in which courtyards shared a single access road (see, for example, figure 5.2B). At this stage two developers (prospective purchasers), interested in the potentialities of the site, but not in the intricate scheme of interconnected courtyards that had evolved piecemeal, submitted applications for the comprehensive redevelopment of as much of all four plots as would be consistent with the desire of one or two owners to retain parts of their plots. Figure 5.2C shows one of the schemes put forward. The applications were refused. Ironically, in the light of the LPA's reaction to the first courtyard proposal at Devonshire, a major reason given was that a courtyard-type development was considered to be the most appropriate. However, after further proposals for 'estate' developments by several developers who had in turn purchased, or were prospective purchasers of, part or all of the site, two similar

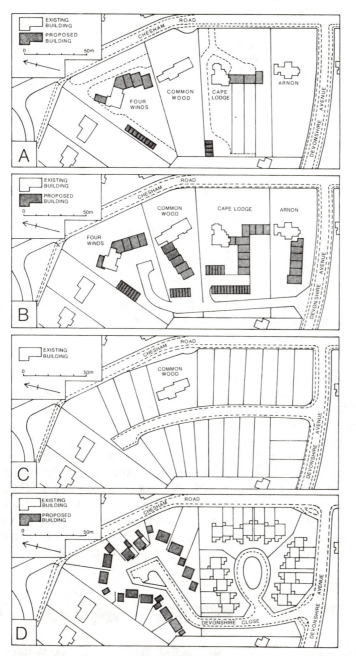

Figure 5.2 Proposed developments at Devonshire: (A) Individual courtyards at Cape Lodge, 1963, and Four Winds, 1965; (B) Co-ordinated courtyard scheme, 1966; (C) Comprehensive redevelopment, 1967; (D) Comprehensive redevelopment in stages (to south – stage 1, constructed 1968/9; to north – revised stage 2, disapproved 1970). *Source*: planning applications.

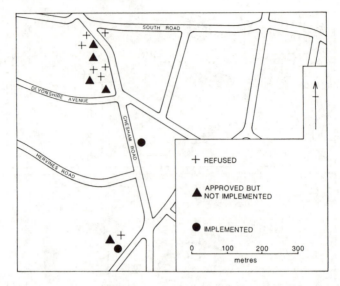

Figure 5.3   Formal proposals for courtyard developments incorporating an existing house close to central Amersham, 1959–70. The number of proposals (fourteen) exceeds the number of planning applications (twelve) since in two cases a single application related to two separate site.
Source: planning applications.

estates of terrace houses in an Anglo-Scandinavian style were built in the late 1960s and early 1970s (for example, figure 5.2D, southern side, and figure 5.4). Thus, a landscape was created that was quite out of character with both its predecessor and the surviving landscape surrounding it.

At Hyrons, where a large, neo-Tudor detached house existed (figure 5.5), there was a similar absence of consideration of the future of the area before informal discussions about development were initiated by the owner in 1983. The planning officer dealing with the matter apparently had virtually no previous knowledge of the site. Again, 'management' of the development consisted of a protracted and complex interaction between the owner (and the owner's agent), the LPA and central government. An initial draft outline proposal from the owner to the LPA was for the demolition of the existing

Figure 5.4   Terrace houses in an Anglo-Scandinavian style at Devonshire, approved 1968.
Source: planning application.

Figure 5.5   Old Hyrons in 1955
(photograph by Ronald E. Haddock).

house and the building of a single block of 20 flats/maisonettes (figure 5.6A), while retaining virtually all the surrounding tree screen. The LPA's response after some two months delay was to recommend 12 flats in three small blocks (figure 5.6B), though as a result of a misunderstanding between officers dealing with the matter it cited as an example of acceptable development an existing block of flats nearby upon which the owner's initial proposal had to a large extent been modelled in both density and appearance. Furthermore, the LPA communicated the view of the Highway Authority that the access way should be more centrally located on the longest frontage, rather than at one end of it as proposed by the owner, who was seeking to minimize damage to the tree screen. Although the owner's agent wrote seeking clarification, his points were ignored in the LPA's reply, which recommended the submission of a formal outline application. When such an application was duly lodged (figure 5.6A) it was rejected by the Planning Committee without discussion, essentially on grounds of excessive density, inadequate car parking, and the unwelcome precedent that would be created. It was followed by an outline application for a lower-density development comprising four blocks, one of which was to be the existing house converted into two dwellings (figure 5.6C). But the LPA officers were in no hurry to expedite an approval. The rate of housebuilding in their area was greater than that specified by the County Planning Authority and they

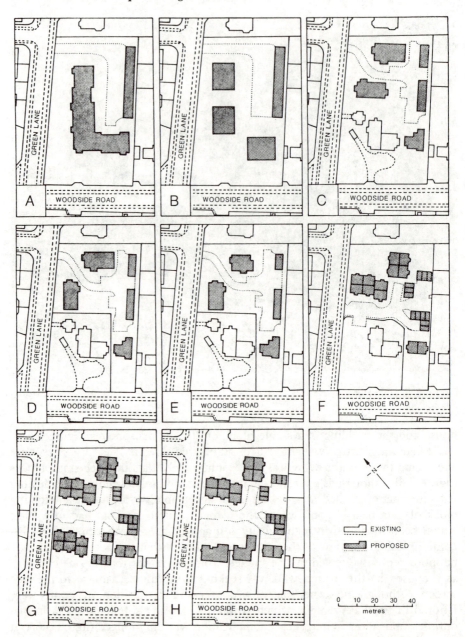

Figure 5.6 Proposed developments at Hyrons: (A) Draft proposal by owner, August 1984, later submitted as first formal application by owner, February 1985; (B) Scheme envisaged by planning officer, October 1984; (C) Second application by owner, May 1985; (D) Second application by owner, revised June 1985; (E) Third application by owner, August 1985; (F) Application by developer, March 1986; (G) Informal proposal by developer for modifying the scheme, November 1986; (H) Formal proposal by developer for modifying the scheme, March 1987.
Source: owner's files.

were only too aware that their Planning Committee was under great pressure from local residents to restrain further development. They therefore insisted on the submission of information on all five matters that the outline application specified as being reserved for subsequent approval. Having received this information and a revised layout (figure 5.6D), they eventually recommended rejection of the application, citing virtually the same grounds for refusal as previously, but adding the further reason that an adjacent property would be overlooked. The Planning Committee having endorsed this recommendation of rejection without discussion, an appeal against the decision was lodged simultaneously with a third outline application (figure 5.6E), which was much the same as the second application although the density was somewhat lower. The third application was approved, although one of the conditions was that both means of vehicular access to the existing house should be blocked off, thereby virtually necessitating demolition of the main garage block in order for vehicular access to be gained to the existing house.

At this stage the site was sold to a developer, and for a period of over a year, during the early part of which the appeal against the rejection of the second application was dismissed, further interaction took place, this time most importantly between the developer and the LPA. The developer put forward a detailed proposal for an entirely new layout (figure 5.6F), including 12 essentially back-to-back houses (figure 5.7) – termed 'maisonettes' in the application – and this was accepted with modifications. (However, an attempt to get reinstated one of the means of vehicular access to the existing house proved fruitless.) This application was followed by an informal proposal, modifying the approved scheme, to demolish the existing house and replace it with six back-to-back houses (figure 5.6G), its now being argued that it was not economic to convert the existing house into two dwellings. The LPA case officer was unwilling to recommend this to the Planning Committee. Finally, a formal proposal for the substitution in the scheme of two detached houses for the existing house, vandalized while standing empty for some 17 months, was eventually approved in 1987, and the development was completed in the same year (figure 5.6H). By this time the once secluded site had been divested of most of its trees and its ancient hedgerow had been devastated by the insertion of a public road about half way along its length. This was despite a barrage of protest from local residents and the stress placed on the need for tree and hedgerow preservation by all the major parties except the developer.

At Parade, there were significant differences in terms of both interactions and landscape outcome. The site had been brought to the threshold of change as part of the developer's activities elsewhere, and it was, according to the developer, delays and uncertainties in these other activities that were responsible for its remaining unused for some three years. During this time it was included within a Conservation Area, a fact that strengthened the influence that the LPA could exercise. Eventually the developer submitted a detailed planning application for the demolition of the existing houses, which had by now been vandalized, and the construction of seven essentially neo-Georgian terrace

Figure 5.7   Neo-Tudor back-to-back houses at Hyrons, approved 1986.
Source: reproduced from the sales brochure of A. C. Frost & Co.

houses in their place (figure 5.8A), arguing that it was not economic to renovate the existing houses. After resistance from the LPA's case officer and considerable delay in dealing with the matter on the part of the LPA, the developer proposed to reduce the number of dwellings to five – a terrace of three dwellings and a pair of semi-detached houses (figure 5.8B). This second application was submitted some nine months after the original one. After a further seven months of communications, few of them in writing on the part of the LPA, and much lobbying, including that by various amenity bodies, agreement had still not been reached. A further application was then submitted for the construction of five houses. This proposed development was recommended by the planning officers for approval but rejected by the Planning Committee on the grounds that it would constitute over-development and that the parking arrangements were unsatisfactory. An appeal against this decision was dismissed some 13 months later, the Secretary of State for the Environment supporting the view that the proposed scheme would result in 'over-development'. After a further interval of some seven months the developer received approval of a planning application to refurbish the existing houses.

As in the cases of Devonshire and Hyrons, the issuing of planning permission was no guarantee that the scheme would be implemented as long as more-profitable alternatives remained unexplored. It would appear that little, if any, of the work of refurbishment was undertaken, and four months later an application to convert the existing houses into offices was submitted. This was rejected for several reasons, notably the fact that the site was shown on the

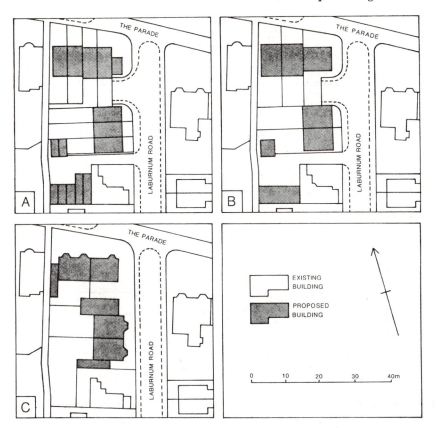

Figure 5.8 Proposed developments at Parade: (A) Application to construct seven dwellings, December 1975; (B) Application to construct five dwellings, August 1976; (C) Application to construct four dwellings, October 1979.
Source: planning applications.

Development Plan as an area that was to continue in residential use. It was followed within three months by an application to construct two pairs of semi-detached houses (figure 5.8C) in a style similar to those then existing (figure 5.9). By this time the existing houses were in a very poor state of repair. Little effective pressure could be brought to bear on the developer to rectify this, and the planning officers again recommended approval, this time securing the acquiescence of the Planning Committee. The new dwellings harmonized with the mid-Victorian character of the area, and, though it was not what had been wished initially by any of the principal parties, the resulting landscape was much more satisfactory in Conzenian terms than those at Devonshire and Hyrons.

In the case of Downside, a plumbing and heating engineer, having expanded his business into house refurbishment and proposing to expand further into small-scale development, purchased one of the two properties involved, after the death of its elderly owner. He did so with the primary purpose of

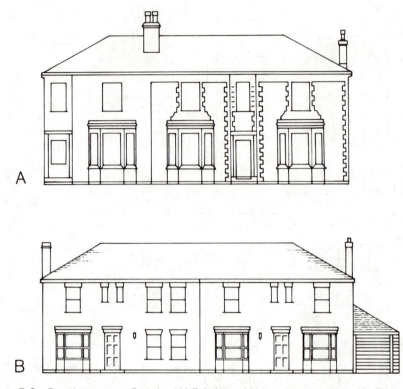

Figure 5.9   Development at Parade: (A) Existing mid-Victorian dwellings; (B) Two of the four replacement dwellings, approved December 1979.
Source: planning applications.

refurbishing the Victorian house, initially for his own occupation, but he was also aware of the possibility of acquiring the larger adjacent property, Orchard House, whose owner had also recently died, which together with the other property would provide him with sufficient land to undertake a small rear-garden development. A much larger individual developer, who some 20 years earlier had developed as Richmond Close the site adjacent to Orchard House on the eastern side, had retained a narrow strip of land (a 'ransom strip') immediately west of Richmond Close (figure 5.10A). In this way he had secured for himself access to Richmond Close, the obvious means of access, if Orchard House came onto the market and he were able to purchase it and planning permission for the redevelopment of its site could be obtained. By the same token, any other developer bidding for the site would need to purchase the ransom strip from him to gain access to the site from Richmond Close.

In the event, the small developer, already in possession of part of the site, managed to negotiate the purchase of Orchard House from the widow of the former owner, having obtained planning permission for a rear-garden development which would retain both existing houses and have a means of access from Worple Road. A significant factor in producing this outcome was the

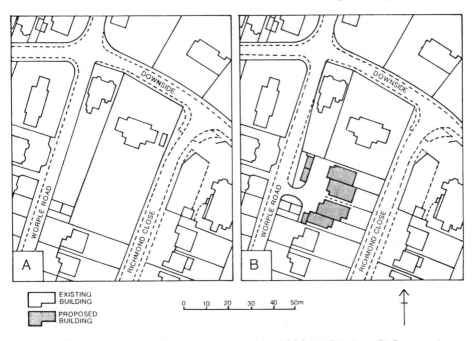

EXISTING
BUILDING

PROPOSED
BUILDING

0   10   20   30   40   50m

Figure 5.10 Proposed development at Downside, 1986 (A) Existing; (B) Proposed.
Source: planning application.

developer's successful negotiations with LPA officers. They were opposed to a
redevelopment for flats such as had been contemplated by the larger developer;
the site was only just beyond a Conservation Area boundary (though there was
a precedent for three-storey flats within 100 metres and within the Conservation Area boundary). The small developer consulted the LPA Highways
Department and, through it, the County Council Highways Department. It was
felt by the LPA officers that, provided the wall along the boundary with Worple
Road was set back, resistance to development on highway grounds would not
be supported if there were an appeal. The success of a planning application was
therefore likely to depend on other matters. On the matter of dwelling density,
the LPA officers preferred no more than three dwellings, but eventually they
seemed willing to accept four dwellings as a compromise. This provided the
small developer with a potentially highly profitable development of an
appropriate scale for his first venture. Trying to obtain a higher density would
have entailed a battle of attrition, almost certainly incurring the delays and
uncertainties of an appeal. Furthermore, if attained it would have diminished
the existing use value of the developer's refurbished house or involved its
demolition. He decided to concentrate on expediting the approval of a detailed
planning application for four dwellings (figure 5.10B). He and his architect
undertook discussions with several planning officers and other interested parties
consulted by the LPA, especially about the preservation of the three screen on
the boundary of the site with Richmond Close, to ensure that objections that
might arise at the meeting of the Planning Committee could be met. The

viability of all existing buildings, including a listed outbuilding to the rear of, and just outside, the site, was ensured and the pseudo-vernacular design was compatible with the styles of the existing buildings.

From the planning officers' standpoint the proposal had the merit of reducing the likelihood of, if not preventing, further pressures for a high-density redevelopment on the site. They reported favourably to the Planning Committee, so much so that they reported the proposed density to be significantly lower than was actually the case. Receipt of the application by the LPA was notified by letter to four local residents only, all of whom had indicated that they wished to be informed in the event of an application being lodged. The objection by the one local resident who opposed the development outright was not mentioned in the written report to the Planning Committee, although the maintenance of the tree screen on one side, which had been the subject of representations by five local residents, was presented as a major issue. Within three months of its having been received, the application was approved by the Planning Committee without discussion. Construction was essentially completed, in the form approved, within a further year.

This remarkably smooth passage for a proposal for a site with considerable development potential just beyond the edge of a major Conservation Area, particularly in contrast to the complex, protracted interactions in the cases of the other three study sites, can be attributed to a number of factors. First, unlike at Devonshire and Hyrons, the developer who was to undertake the development was able to make an integrated assessment of both the various aspects of the development and its likelihood of success well before lodging a formal planning application. He also went to great lengths to ensure that favourable evidence was presented to the Planning Committee. Secondly, the planning officers adopted an acquiescent, even flexible, attitude, contrasting in particular with that taken by the planning officers in the case of Hyrons. Thirdly, the developer had a vested interest in the existing use value of the house that he now occupied on the site. Furthermore, since he was embarking on his first development, he was content for it to be quite small in scale. Thus the circumstances of the developer were of major importance. If the other developer who had been in contention for the site had been successful a quite different scenario can be envisaged.

THE ISSUES REVIEWED

In the light of this brief and necessarily selective account of interactions underlying examples of urban landscape change, a number of findings that bear upon the questions raised earlier in this chapter require discussion.

First, in the cases of Devonshire, Hyrons and Downside the initiation process was largely determined by the domestic affairs of property owners. In the case of Parade it was influenced to a considerable extent by a developer's plans for a larger area. Except perhaps at Parade, the way in which the process of change was embarked on had considerable influence upon the way in which other agents of change, such as estate agents, architects and developers, became involved. In three cases, Downside, Parade and Hyrons, the way in which attempts were initially made to gain permission to develop sites appears to have influenced the outcome in the landscape. A lengthy train of cumulative causation was evident in the case of Hyrons. At Devonshire, in contrast, the legacy of early attempts by owner-occupiers to gain planning permission ultimately had a negligible effect on the landscape.

Secondly, landscape change on the study sites was far from being the outcome of a coherent strategy. Its management was, furthermore, not at all the integrated process of the Conzenian ideal. There was no general underlying theory, and seldom were views and reports on specific matters, such as considerations of access and the preservation of trees, integrated in the light of the personality of the area. Among the bodies and individuals officially consulted for their views on planning applications, for example the local plans section of the LPA, the town or parish council and the highway authority, significant differences of view obtained. These views were frequently transmitted to applicants, either informally or in a formal decision notice, without integration by the officer responsible for handling the application. If to this mélange are added the contributions of planning committees, local pressure groups and the DOE, all of which differed substantially on occasions, it is not surprising that even the most carefully considered application could prove to be only the first step in a protracted conflict between various parties that led ultimately to a landscape change utterly different from that initially envisaged by either the owner, the developer or the LPA. The dominant impression left by the uncovering of the processes underlying landscape change at Devonshire, Hyrons and Parade is of a number of poorly co-ordinated activities. The LPA case officer was a collector and transmitter of views and instructions. He might, usually for his own purposes or those of colleagues, commit to paper a sketch layout, exceptionally a sketch elevation, but his creative role was minimal. Development control was an almost mechanical reaction using predominantly standardized responses. For example, when, as was often the case, such matters as tree screening and access were interrelated, the consequences of the independent treatment of each in terms of mechanically applied rules could create an absurd situation – as at Hyrons, where at one stage the existing house was left without a means of vehicular access.

Thirdly, this study of four sites has provided further support for the view that proposals from owner-occupiers are more sensitive to the *genius* of the existing landscape, and hence to Conzenian precepts, than those from developers. Out of 12 applications for new dwellings by owner-occupiers, or their representatives, spread among six different owners, all but one proposed the retention of the existing house or houses. Furthermore, as far as can be ascertained from the drawings available, all 12 applications seem to have proposed the retention of most of the existing trees and hedgerows. In contrast, of 18 applications for new dwellings from seven developers, all but two proposed the demolition of existing dwellings, and the large majority substantial tree felling. One of the applications that did not propose demolition was submitted by the developer who was refurbishing the existing house for his own occupation. The concern of developers to maximize dwelling densities and the amount of floor space was apparent in their attempts to obtain permission for more dwellings or larger dwellings, or both more and larger dwellings, than had previously been obtained by owner-occupiers when outline permission had been granted to them. A common means proposed by owner-occupiers in Amersham for retaining existing buildings was to incorporate them in a courtyard scheme, a solution to which the LPA was inconsistent in its attitude. Among the reasons for the differences between the proposals of developers and those of owner-occupiers were the personal identification of owners with their property and the fact that they were primarily seeking approval for the principle of development, often for valuation purposes.

Finally, awareness of urban landscape regions was slight among all parties. It was strongest in the case of Parade, where the designation of a Conservation Area served to focus attention on the landscape and virtually ensured the interest of various amenity bodies. Although in relation to the initial planning application for Parade only four of the ten local residents who wrote letters to the LPA actually objected to the demolition of the existing pair of houses, there was an awareness on the part of the planning officers and, when an appeal was eventually lodged, the DOE inspector, that the relation of the site to those around it, especially in regard to the matching pair of houses on the other side of Laburnum Road, was of major importance. Indeed this was one of two reasons – the other being 'over-development' – that were formally given for dismissing the appeal against the rejection of the third application. Although the existing houses were eventually demolished, the replacements were to a considerable extent modelled on them, in contrast to the neo-Georgian design that had been suggested earlier by the Borough Planning Officer. In the case of Downside, there was no explicit awareness of the fact that the site was astride a boundary between urban landscape regions. It is evident, however, that the planning officers and the occupier-developer were aware of the need for sensitive treatment of the site. The letters of all six residents who wrote to the LPA revealed a concern with hedgerows, but other landscape matters were not mentioned. In the case of Devonshire, the owner-occupiers' schemes were consistent with existing urban landscape regions, but those of the developers were not. The LPA vacillated. The DOE inspector agreed that courtyard development, as proposed by the owner-occupiers, was architecturally satisfactory but felt that this consideration was of lower priority than achieving a single means of access to the whole area. In the case of Hyrons, the owner-occupier's schemes were similarly noteworthy for the consideration given to the character of the area, including the preservation of the rural hedgerow (though the first scheme did propose the demolition of the house). The planning officers acknowledged the importance of the hedgerows and the existing house but were more concerned about restricting the density of dwellings. The DOE inspector gave the existing house only a glance on his site visit. His concern was about density, 'noise disturbance' owing to the proximity of the proposed dwellings to their garages, and the risk of undermining part of the tree screen to the site owing to the proximity to it of one of the proposed blocks of flats. Of the written observations on the proposed developments, including letters from some 20 local residents, only two (both from owner-occupiers of neighbouring Hyrons houses) showed any awareness of the group of Hyrons houses as an entity. Of the several objectors to the demolition of the house, all stressed the character of the house itself; none viewed it as one of a distinctive group of houses. The concerns of objectors in fact changed as the threats posed by the successive planning applications changed, a concern with density being succeeded first by a concern over the possible loss of trees and hedgerows and finally by a concern over the proposed demolition of the house.

CONCLUSION

The four sites examined in this chapter have provided information about actual decision-making at the micro-scale. Although each site was unique, it is possible, against a background of the aggregate data presented in the previous chapter, to draw from this study of them certain provisional conclusions of more general significance. Furthermore, it is not too soon to be seeking in these conclusions lessons for planning practice.

In the case of each of the four study sites the main motive for change was unequivocally economic. In three instances the effect of the LPA's actions was to reduce the amount of floor space created to a level below that considered the most profitable by the developer. In the fourth case it suited the purposes of the developer to settle at an early stage for a density below what would have been most profitable. In terms of restraining development it could be argued, therefore, that the LPAs had achieved a measure of success. However, the process by which it was achieved was highly inefficient and the outcome in the two Amersham cases was seriously damaging to the landscape. Although pressures for infill had become evident in Amersham by 1960, the LPA had no policy on the matter. Despite the fact that the landscapes involved were almost invariably in need of sensitive treatment, planning applications relating to the study sites were approached mainly in terms of narrow, technical aspects of development, among which density and access were foremost. There was little attempt to devise or encourage integrated solutions. In a weak position to prevent development, but with their local residents and Planning Committee clamouring for restraints on development, LPA officers resorted to delaying tactics and the giving of spurious reasons for refusing planning permission. The form of the development, particularly its architectural style, tended to be an afterthought, when imbroglios concerning density and access had been resolved. On three out of four study sites the scheme ultimately implemented was inconsistent with that advocated by LPA officers at an earlier stage.

The gulf between Conzenian precept and planning practice is large. Not only was the integrated view of urban landscape development recommended by Conzen almost non-existent in the cases examined but, even if it had been adopted in the preparation of local planning documents, it is hard to see how it could have survived the crude interaction that characterized the decision-making on individual proposals. The nature of this type of interaction and its consequences for the urban landscape need a thorough reappraisal. If an integrated form of urban landscape management is to be achieved, then the role of the LPA case officer must surely be central, especially in ensuring that the character of a development is not determined mainly by a concern with technicalities. This is an important lesson for planning practice. Its application faces serious obstacles in an established context of conflict between the parties to development and its control. But the cost to the urban landscape of its non-application is high.

6

Conclusion

The aim of this last chapter is fourfold. First, it will be shown that a number of the conclusions drawn in preceding chapters fit into a wider pattern of findings from comparable studies just completed. Secondly, returning to the questions posed at the beginning of this study, an attempt will be made, as far as the available information permits, to draw comparisons between the three types of functional area that have been investigated. Thirdly, a number of general conclusions will be drawn about the agents, processes and activities responsible for urban landscape development in Great Britain in the past century, particularly in recent decades. Finally, implications of the findings of this study for planning and, more specifically, urban landscape management will be discussed.

CORROBORATION

The conclusions drawn so far have been based on information of two kinds: first, from diverse secondary sources relating to various areas of Great Britain, many of them small areas; secondly, from detailed analyses of selected parts of urban areas, based on primary sources. In neither case would it be justified to assume that the basis for the findings that have been described is broadly representative. Only when corroborative results are available from further carefully selected comparative studies will a less qualified assessment of the significance of our findings be justified. Two such studies have, in fact just yielded some results of that kind. Brief reference to these is sufficient to reinforce the view that some of the findings described in detail in previous chapters have wider significance.

In the case of commercial cores, Larkham (1991) has undertaken studies of two comparable historic town centres, Henley on Thames in south-east England and Ludlow in the west Midlands, using the same type of analysis used in the studies of residential areas described in this volume. He has also undertaken similar analyses for two residential areas in the west Midlands (Whitehand and Larkham, 1991 a,b). His findings underline those presented in previous chapters. They also indicate, as would be expected, regional variations within Great Britain.

In his studies of commercial cores, Larkham (1991) reveals the expected regional difference in pressure for change. Although the commercial core of Henley is roughly the same size as that of Ludlow, between 1970 and 1986 it was the subject of twice as many applications for new buildings. Furthermore, the proportion of these granted was as low as 37 per cent, compared with 55 per cent for central Ludlow. If all applications over the same period are examined the time-lapse between their receipt by the LPA and the date of the decision was nearly twice as long in the case of central Henley as it was in the case of central Ludlow (a mean of 98 working days for central Henley, compared with 56 working days for central Ludlow). These findings are consistent with those noted earlier concerning the comparatively high degree of LPA restraint in south-east England.

Larkham's two residential study areas in the west Midlands – at Gibbet Hill, on the outskirts of Coventry, and at Tettenhall, on the outskirts of Wolver-hampton – provided data comparable to those for the study areas in Amersham and Epsom (Whitehand and Larkham, 1991a,b). Again, the most noteworthy feature was the tendency for the west Midlands study areas to show, though in more muted form, the characteristics revealed in the detailed studies of areas in south-east England.

First, differences in the numbers of applications per site and the numbers of appeals per site, both of which were lower in the west Midlands study areas, are indicative of differences in development pressure. Similarly, economic factors would seem to account for the fact that the west Midlands study areas were characterized by less demolition, a larger number of detached houses con-structed relative to high-density dwelling types, such as flats and maisonettes, less competition from non-local firms, and the involvement of fewer profes-sional interests in the pre-development process (Whitehand and Larkham, 1991a).

Secondly, for similar reasons, the sequence of events leading to development differed in the case of the west Midlands study areas. The differences between actual developments and those for which initial applications were made were comparatively small, suggesting less LPA intervention. Similarly, nearly all approved applications were the same as those initially submitted, there were fewer attempts by developers to use initial planning approvals as stepping-stones to the approval of more-profitable developments, and the interactions between applicants and LPAs were less protracted (Whitehand and Larkham, 1991b).

Nevertheless, departures from the characteristics identified in the residential study areas in south-east England were of degree rather than kind. The stereotypic residential-site development is one where there are lengthy delays between an initial application and actual development, and where LPA restraint is revealed in formal terms mainly in reasons for refusal relating to particular site circumstances, such as density, the overlooking of other properties, access and parking, rather than in formal plans. In general, sites relating to which permission was sought for the construction of more than one dwelling were associated with longer planning gestation periods and were the subject of more applications than sites for which a single dwelling was proposed. Similarly, planning gestation periods were longer and the number of applications was greater were applicants were private individuals.

The nature of the differences between the west Midlands and south-east England suggests strongly that the supply of and demand for building land are crucial differentiating factors. These factors in turn are related to accessibility to areas of economic prosperity. Thus, current improvements in the accessibility of large parts of the west Midlands and certain other parts of Great Britain to such areas may well be associated with increased development pressures. In such circumstances these parts of the country may take on to a greater degree the characteristics at present more strongly associated with south-east England.

The residential areas studied in detail have been those most susceptible to infill and redevelopment; areas where a single existing house plot may alone provide enough space for redevelopment or infill to be viable. However, less systematic studies of areas of smaller, medium-size plots near the study areas in south-east England have revealed evidence that some of these too are subject to increasing pressure for more-intensive development. Although in such cases the co-operation of two or three adjacent owners is usually necessary to assemble a large enough site, it is likely that the use as residential sites of gardens of less than 0.1 ha will become increasingly common as the supply of larger sites is used up. In due course this practice is likely to extend to other parts of the country where housing demand is high and building land is in short supply.

COMPARISONS BETWEEN TYPES OF AREA

The results of these further studies underline the findings for particular types of area discussed earlier. An attempt will be made now to draw comparisons between the three types of functional area that have been examined. Although the areas that have been studied in detail are few and of limited extent, certain characteristics are sufficiently pronounced to suggest that the findings concerning them may have more than local validity.

A major finding is the differing importance of individuals as initiators of development proposals. In the development of residential areas they remained important as initiators in the post-war period, whereas they had ceased to be a major force by the early 1920s in the development of institutional and public areas and by the late 1920s in the development of commercial cores. As far as the actual process of development is concerned, in the development of residential areas the roles of builder and developer had frequently become indistinguishable by the inter-war period, whereas in the development of commercial cores and of institutional and public areas the builders involved were largely, if not entirely, contractors.

The timing of the release of land for development in residential areas continued to be significantly affected by the family life cycle of individual owners. This was not on the whole a major factor in the development of either commercial cores or institutional and public areas after the First World War. In both commercial cores and residential areas the actual timing of development was related to market factors. These varied in their impact according to the social and economic structures of the particular urban area. Although the development of institutional and public areas was by no means independent of economic factors, the fact that the responsibility for the development of these areas was primarily in the hands of non-profit-making bodies – predominantly private up to the First World War and largely local government after that time – was associated with a low correlation over time, sometimes an inverse relation, between the incidence of that type of development and that of other types (cf. Whitehand, 1981a).

A further difference concerns the provenance of those involved in development. Whereas the large majority of owners in residential areas and institutional and public areas remained local even in recent decades, in commercial cores local owners declined from being in a large majority at the beginning of the century to being in a small minority by the 1970s. The role of estate agents in the development process appears to have been largely confined to the residential areas of south-east England: they were mainly local. Whereas in the mid-nineteenth century non-local architects (especially London-based ones) were already a significant minority of the architects involved in development in institutional and public areas, it was not until the twentieth century that they became a significant force in the design of developments in commercial cores and residential areas. In these types of areas they have predominated since the Second World War in south-east England, although local architects are still frequently in a majority in the west Midlands.

In so far as local individuals and organizations were imbued with a sense of place, it might have been expected, in the light of the longer perpetuation of the activity of these agents of change in residential areas, that the local character of the residential landscape would have been perpetuated longer than that of other kinds of area. However, the influence of owner-occupiers on the local character of the residential landscape, as distinct from the timing of change, was considerably less than might have been supposed from the high proportion of planning applications that they submitted. The form taken by a residential development was more often determined by a scheme reflecting its profitability to a developer, perhaps following a series of applications, than by an initial scheme put forward by, say, a local estate agent on behalf of an owner-occupier.

In both the commercial cores and residential areas there were differences of building form associated with the types of agents involved. In the case of the residential areas the tendency for developers to be more demolition prone than individuals was marked. In the commercial cores, at least during the twentieth century, there were roughly equal numbers of bespoke and speculative developments. The latter tended to be more conservative in architectural style, but the wider validity of this finding remains uncertain in the light of studies of other urban areas. In the residential areas bespoke developments, almost entirely detached houses, were in a small minority. In institutional and public areas nearly all developments were bespoken and therefore usually in some respects unique, albeit they generally conformed to prevailing fashions.

The extent of, and the form taken by, resistance to development pressure was much the same for residential areas as it was for commercial cores. For example, the defensive attitude adopted by Chiltern District Council towards unwelcome proposals for intensified residential development resembled that taken by Reading Borough Council towards proposals for the erection of town-centre offices (Punter, 1985). For both types of areas lags of several years between an initial application and an approval were widespread, and protracted interactions between those seeking to effect change and those attempting to control, and frequently to prevent, it were a major characteristic of the development-control process. Similarities between commercial cores and residential areas were also evident in the stances adopted by developers; indeed, occasionally the same firms were involved. The resulting landscape forms, however, were different, both because of functional differences and because of different physical legacies, especially different building coverages, left by earlier cycles of development.

GENERAL CONCLUSIONS

Three main types of urban landscape – commercial, institutional/public, and residential – have been considered. In each case a historical outline provided the basis for micro-scale studies of individual sites and groups of sites. These studies have revealed some of the distinctive aspects of the processes and activities responsible for the development of each of these types of urban area and have also suggested some of the diversity found within each type. An attempt will now be made to distil some general conclusions, and, more briefly, to offer speculations that may provide a point of departure for further research. In so far as the conclusions drawn are concerned with the micro-scale, they must necessarily be provisional, for the choice of areas and sites upon which the detailed investigations have been based depended to a considerable extent on ease of access to sources of information, a statistically inadequate method of selection. Nevertheless, the points that emerge provide a useful basis for a concluding, albeit somewhat open-ended, discussion of the implications for planning practice of the processes and activities that have been revealed.

First, timing plays an important part in the outcome of attempts to bring about change in the physical fabric of the urban landscape. Most obviously, the success and character of a proposal are influenced by the life cycles of fashions. In the development of commercial cores timing has been particularly influenced by economic factors, many of which are cyclical in character. In the development of residential areas the family life cycles and other circumstances of owner-occupiers have been significant influences. However, there is a variable, sometimes lengthy, time-lapse between initial attempts to bring about change and the actual change. Among the factors responsible for this are changes in economic conditions after a development has been proposed and, largely since the Second World War, the vagaries of development control. A consequence is that developments sometimes take place in conditions markedly different from those in which they were conceived.

Secondly, economic factors were crucial to the form of development in all the areas studied. They seem to be no less important in the 1970s and 1980s than they were at the beginning of the industrial era. Building types and building density have a strong relationship to economic factors, especially land value (cf. Whitehand, 1987), with high-density forms occurring on high-value land. Such factors have underlain significant recent differences between south-east England and the west Midlands. Development-control officers tend to argue that the economics of proposals is not their concern. But economic considerations are so central that it makes little sense for LPAs to respond to proposals as if the financial return to the developer were immaterial.

Thirdly, there has been a long-term increase in the role played by non-local firms; a trend that has continued in the period since the Second World War. Its effects on architectural style were more evident before the war, when in most areas local firms still predominated and non-local firms acted as innovation-diffusion agents. Nationally, the enlargement of the operational areas of firms has been associated with a tendency for activity to be concentrated in the hands of fewer firms. However, increasing concentration was not, on the whole, apparent within the study areas. This reflects the fact that firms operating over a large area, sometimes nationally, were often involved in fewer schemes within each study area considered individually than the local firms that they replaced.

Fourthly, governmental control over development has paid little heed to the appearance of the built environment. The by-laws adopted by local authorities during the course of the second half of the nineteenth century were concerned with building standards, and their successors have had a similar emphasis. The development-control system introduced after the Second World War has, at the scale of individual sites, been concerned primarily with physical standards relating to such matters as building density, car parking, access and the overlooking of neighbouring properties. The appearances of developments, particularly their architectural styles, tend to be afterthoughts, when battles over density and access have been concluded. Landscaping receives lip-service. There is a price to pay in lost cultural assets and the quality of the visual environment. The existing framework of plots and streets acts as a constraint on the process of infill and redevelopment but this is by no means a guarantee that the new landscape forms created respect the existing urban landscape.

Fifthly, conflict is endemic to much of the process of development and attempted development. It almost inevitably arises to some degree where development occurs within existing urban areas, although it may be less where new structures are well separated from neighbouring owner-occupiers. It is particularly acute, though it usually attracts only localized concern, where attempts are made to fit new dwellings into existing residential areas. In the nineteenth century much of the conflict in all types of area was among private individuals and organizations. But as legislation increased so local authorities became more involved. Since the Second World War they have been at the centre of conflict. This partly reflects their role in development control as mediators between private interests, notably between developers and the occupiers of properties in the vicinity of the proposed development sites. In recent decades disputes between developers and LPAs have been particularly prevalent in areas where there is strong development pressure. But in virtually all residential areas there is a wider conflict between the forces of preservation and the forces of change, including, for example, that between residents who own potential development sites and those whose gardens are unsuitable for development.

Sixthly, many more urban landscapes exist on paper than ever come into being on the ground. In the case of institutional and public areas this has been partly a reflection of the extensive use of design competitions, particularly before the First World War. In the case of commercial cores and residential areas the large number of unimplemented schemes since the Second World War is attributable to the way in which the development-control process operates. Modifications and complete transformations of proposals are particularly characteristic of, but by no means confined to, areas where local authorities exercise a strong restraining influence. In so far as the arguments advanced for modifying or abandoning plans are ascertainable, they are often unconvincing. By no means do successions of proposals consist of progressions towards improved solutions. Clearly a great deal of energy, some of it creative, is wasted. The pre-development process is inordinately time consuming for both applicants and LPAs. Whether the quality of the outcome would be worse if development or non-development followed a single planning application processed by the LPA within the statutory eight-week term is a matter for speculation. In the case of institutional and public areas, the amount of non-implementation of proposals reflects in part the long time-span over which some of the more significant of such developments are undertaken. Whereas in residential areas and commercial cores once developments have begun to take shape on the ground it is common for them to be completed according to the plan in use when implementation began, complex plans for large public and institutional sites are commonly overtaken by events and work is stopped in an incomplete state. When it is recommenced, sometimes many years later, the circumstances and agents of change are frequently different. This often gives rise to major inconsistencies, especially stylistic mismatches, between the initial buildings and those planned later. This is not to suggest that the manner in which work is started is irrelevant to the nature of the outcome. The sequence of events between initial thoughts about a project and completion of works on the ground rarely consists of a number of independent events. The causal links are often clear in the light of careful historical reconstruction. Individual episodes within the sequence may even be pre-conceived by one or more of the parties involved. For example, in recent decades it has been common for the acceptance of a planning application for a commercial or residential development in south-east England to be used by a developer as a stepping-stone towards the approval of a more profitable scheme. But the outcome in the landscape results from interactions between the parties over a period during which the influences upon decision-making are changing, and it is commonly different from that envisaged by any of the parties.

Seventhly, greater building density does not necessarily mean more-obtrusive development. For example, small detached houses, such as are characteristic of recent infill and redevelopment in the west Midlands, are sometimes more obtrusive in the landscape than flats, which have been the predominant type of dwelling constructed in existing residential areas in south-east England. The new building type that is potentially the most compatible with the existing landscape of low-density residential areas is the block of flats designed to look like a large detached house.

Eighthly, infill and piecemeal redevelopment often require the employment of particular ingenuity if the visual environment of neighbouring occupiers, and cumulatively the visual environment of the larger community, are not to be adversely affected. The need for that ingenuity is likely to become greater in the development of residential areas as the shortage of land leads to the redevelopment of medium-sized gardens becoming profitable.

Ninthly, the dominant impression given by the present-day decision-making process that leads to development or non-development is that it consists of a number of poorly co-ordinated activities. The LPA case officer emerges as a collector and transmitter of views and instructions. He should be much more of an integrator, with a major role in ensuring that the awareness of the total character of a development and its relationship to the existing urban landscape is not subordinated to a concern with technicalities.

Tenthly, in scarcely any of the time periods or areas examined were there activities that might be described as urban landscape management in the Conzenian sense of that term. At the micro-scale, much of the development control was not 'planning', as this activity is commonly understood. The detailed studies of residential areas in recent decades revealed that the effects of local planning documents were generally small at the scale of individual sites. Even in Conservation Areas little guidance about specific plots or groups of plots was provided. The plans prepared by LPAs have often provided less guidance on the appearance of specific areas in their planning districts than was provided by major landowners planning the development of their estates in the nineteenth century.

Finally, it is important to underline a caveat concerning the general conclusions that have been drawn here. In focusing on detailed site-specific evidence, useful additions have been made to our knowledge of the processes and activities responsible for urban landscape change and the parts played in them by the various agents of change. The representativeness of the chosen sites, however, remains uncertain. Because the collection of information for individual sites is so time consuming, it is likely to be a long while before sufficient studies have been undertaken, and comparisons made, to clear up this uncertainty. Moreover, the comparability of case studies remains a difficulty even when studies are undertaken with comparison in mind. Bridging the gap between the highly aggregated data collected by local authorities and bodies such as the DOE, on the one hand, and the particular actions of individuals that those data reflect, on the other, is far from straightforward but is necessary if case-study comparisons are to contribute fully to both the explanation of urban landscape change in the past and the management of urban landscape change in the future.

PLANNING AND URBAN LANDSCAPE MANAGEMENT

The detailed studies that have been described here have largely been confined to the twentieth century, especially recent decades. They provide evidence of a great deal of change to the urban landscape and in the organizations and individuals responsible for that change. Internal change to urban areas, as distinct from outward growth, reached unprecedented levels in the post-war era. This has been documented in some detail for selected commercial cores. The broader spectrum of aggregate change has been summarized by Cherry (1976). Government intervention in urban change in Great Britain has taken place on a major scale since the Second World War. It was most pronounced in the 1950s and 1960s, when zones of working-class housing surrounding city centres were transformed by massive programmes of comprehensive redevelopment organized by local authorities. More recently the accent has been on piecemeal change. This has been especially so in suburban areas first developed in the last quarter of the nineteenth century and the first half of the twentieth century. In these areas, as has been shown in the previous two chapters, private enterprise has been responsible for bringing about change under the surveillance of LPAs. There remains the need to review the processes at work in this latest phase of change, especially in regard to planning, and to explore a little further some of the issues surrounding attempts to formulate principles of urban landscape management.

The cost of planning

The progression in this volume from a study of traditional commercial cores to a study of institutional and public areas and finally to a study of the more-recent reshaping of residential suburbs has been accompanied by a parallel development – an increasing concern with planning practice. It is clear that to treat planning as just another kind of innovation or as little more than a fine-tuning of the market mechanism is analytically insufficient. There is ample evidence in our case studies that such standpoints under-represent the influence of the planning authorities, albeit that much of what such bodies do is somewhat marginal to popular notions of planning. Ascertaining how different the urban landscape would have been without planning is not feasible. What can be done is to compare the schemes envisaged by owners and developers with what is permitted by LPAs. It has already been shown that in the case of the study areas in south-east England, and to a lesser extent in that of comparable areas in the west Midlands, this comparison reveals contrasts. However, a detailed under-standing of the underlying reasons for such contrasts requires further informa-tion. Particularly important is a knowledge of the economics of development, for in the case of commercial cores and residential areas at least, financial considerations are of primary importance in most proposals. To the outside observer, such information is rarely available, since it is confidential to the parties concerned. However, occasionally it is possible to assemble sufficient information about a particular site to cast light on the economic consequences, particularly for an applicant for planning permission, of the position adopted by the LPA. This has been done for one of the sites discussed in the previous chapter, Hyrons, for which a remarkable collection of records has been compiled by the applicant's agent (Whitehand, 1989a).

Figure 6.1 shows variations in bid prices for this site under various conditions and assumptions. The offer shown for the site with outline permission for 12 flats and the conversion of the existing house into 2 dwellings was the highest of 15 offers received (and was the one finally accepted). The offer shown for the site conditional upon the upholding of an appeal against refusal of permission for 14 flats and the conversion of the existing house into 2 dwellings was the highest of 10 offers received. A correlation between dwelling density and size

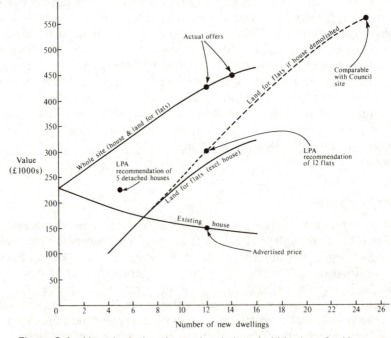

Figure 6.1 Hypothetical and actual variations in bid prices for Hyrons, 1985.
Source: owner's files.

of offer is evident, though an increase from 12 units to 14 units resulted in a less than proportional increase in the total offer. This makes sense in economic terms, since even in the case of flats some loss of environmental quality is almost unavoidable if density is increased beyond a certain point. In this case there was the additional consideration that the value of the existing house would have tended to fall as the density of the proposed new development alongside it was increased.

In this 'bidding' process what seemed profitable to developers was intermixed with what was, or was expected to be, acceptable to the LPA and the DOE. In most cases where pressure on land is great, the LPA endeavours to reduce densities below those sought by developers. The effect is generally to reduce land values on the sites concerned, though in south-east England this may be more than compensated for by the inflation in land values caused by the fact that the presence of the Green Belt has greatly reduced the supply of housebuilding sites. In the case of Hyrons the extent of the reduction in bid prices attributable to LPA action may be assessed by making comparisons between the bid prices for the site under the constraint of upper limits on density with those for a nearby site owned by the Council itself which were not constrained in this way. On its own site the LPA had granted itself planning consent for residential development at a *minimum* of 35 units per ha. It would appear that the bid price for the Hyrons site based on planning permission for 12 new dwellings and the conversion of the existing house into 2 dwellings was 76 per cent of what it would have been based on the much higher density approved for the Council's site (figure 6.1).

It is also possible to estimate the bid prices for the site based on various proposals made by the LPA in the course of its processing of applications. One recommendation was that 12 flats be constructed, utilizing the whole of the site. Assuming a constant relationship between the number of dwellings and bid price, an assumption which, at least at such a low density, would seem to accord with the practice of most developers, the bid price would have been 71 per cent of that actually obtained (figure 6.1). If five detached houses had been constructed, which was to be the LPA's recommendation if its policy of restricting planning permission to small dwellings were rescinded, then the bid price would have been 53 per cent of that actually obtained. This assumes that the market value of such houses in this location would have been £125,000 each (an estimate based upon the study of advertised house prices in Amersham) and that the land value would have been 36 per cent of the sale price of the completed dwellings (A. G. Wilson, Martin Grant Homes, personal communication).

These calculations are concerned with exchange value or market value. In this case exchange value is the value of land for development based on the profit that a developer could be expected to realize by converting that land to a more intensive use. The exchange value of the Hyrons site if a large part of the grounds were utilized for the construction of twelve flats/maisonettes and the existing house were converted into two dwellings or retained as a single dwelling was about twice the existing-use value, judging by estate agents' estimates and prices of similar properties that were apparently being sold for owner-occupation. This difference was largely academic until the owner's changed family circumstances led to the decision to sell the property. Then it became of practical significance to the variety of firms and individuals seeking a share in the realization of the exchange value through development.

Clearly, the financial interests involved in this type of development are fundamental, at least to owners, developers and estate agents. For them the planning process is generally viewed as a cost. For others, notably many residential neighbours, by preventing development, or minimizing its effects, planning generally helps to mitigate cost. For some neighbours it enhances the development value of their own potential sites in that the granting of permission establishes a precedent in the area for more-intensive use. Indeed, in the case of a commercial core, the granting of planning permission and the consequent enhanced prospect of attracting potential customers to the vicinity might increase the existing use value of nearby sites. Most damage to the landscape reduces to some extent the existing-use value of sites in the vicinity. But such damage is almost always associated with the enhanced use value of the site on which it takes place. Indeed the increased value of the developed site is likely to exceed, sometimes greatly, any reductions in the aggregate value of other sites in the vicinity. Consequently, what is frequently a net loss in landscape terms is usually associated with a net gain in total property values. The landscape is an element in use value, but its importance varies greatly. Moreover, this importance mainly relates to the more-obvious attributes such as the screening of other properties. The significance of landscape qualities with a less practical bearing such as historicity varies considerably depending on their importance to potential occupiers. Historicity is probably of minimal importance to some.

To most of those involved in the development process, sometimes even local residents seeking to prevent the development of sites, the delay that the development-control process involves is a cost. Delay gives rise to uncertainty about the future, which may discourage investment in maintenance, and for developers delay may well entail a financial penalty in terms of an extended period of interest payment on a loan. The case studies of residential areas have revealed that delays of several years between the lodging of an initial planning application and the granting of planning permission are common. In south-east England further delays often ensue while attempts are made to obtain permissions for more-profitable schemes. It has not been possible to detail for a wide range of sites the reasons for such delays. It is only in exceptional circumstances, such as those of the Hyrons case, that documentation makes this feasible for a particular site. The delay in the application process in regard to the Hyrons site occurred in an area where an attempt was being made to restrain development and in circumstances in which there was a mismatch between central government policy and local opinion. The following outline of the main stages in the interchange between applicant and LPA up until the sale of the site to a developer (cf. figure 5.6) suggests that a significant part of the delay was due to the operation by the LPA of unofficial restraint procedures.

August 1983:	Preliminary discussion between owner and development-control officer on site.
16 August 1984:	Submission by owner of draft outline application, at suggestion of LPA.
19 October 1984:	After two months without acknowledgement of draft application, despite reminder letter, LPA reports to owner in writing the views of its local plans section and other bodies. A development nearby is recommended to owner's attention.
6 November 1984:	Owner raises by letter queries about the development referred to by LPA and about other matters discussed in its letter.
30 November 1984:	LPA responds, ignoring most of the queries raised by owner (including one about the development previously recommended) and recommending submission of a formal outline application.
14 February 1985:	Formal outline application (for 20 dwellings) submitted.
18 April 1985:	Application rejected by Planning Committee, on recommendation of Chief Planning Officer, without discussion. Reasons for refusal: excessive number of dwelling units; out of scale with surroundings; insufficient amenity space and parking space; and creation of a precedent.
17 May 1985:	Second outline application (for 16 dwellings, including conversion of existing house) submitted in the light of the reasons given for rejection of first application.
31 May 1985:	LPA writes to owner requiring further information, including floor plans, despite the fact that Circular 22/80 (Department of the Environment, 1980b, para. 9) states that LPAs should 'ask for additional information on outline applications only if the information is indispensable in reaching a decision'.
20 June 1985:	Additional information submitted. Accompanying letter from owner invites comment and notes that the additional information shows only tentative ideas of how the development might be carried out and that according to 'Notes for applicants' supplied by Council it does not form part of the application.
24 July 1985:	After delay of five weeks, despite reminder letter, the eventual acknowledgement of receipt of the additional information states that Chief Planning Officer is recommending refusal but gives no reasons.

27 July 1985:   Owner writes to LPA requesting reasons for recommendation of refusal and a meeting with development-control officer dealing with application, but receives no reply.

1 August 1985:   Second application rejected by Planning Committee, on recommendation of Chief Planning Officer, without discussion.

2 August 1985:   Owner arranges meeting with development-control officer and receives formal reasons for rejection. These are virtually the same as those for rejection of first application, with the added reason that the adjacent property in Green Lane would be overlooked.

12 August 1985:   Simultaneous submission of third outline application (for 14 dwellings, including conversion of existing house) and appeal to Secretary of State for the Environment on second application.

23 September 1985:   Six weeks after receipt by Council of the appeal and after date by which representations should have been received by DOE, Council invites representations from local residents and other bodies.

27 September 1985:   In response to owner's enquiries about progress of third application LPA initiates negotiation by telephone on proposed conditions to be attached to a recommendation of acceptance by Chief Planning Officer.

4 October 1985:   Council requests one month extension beyond statutory period for making a decision.

10 October 1985:   Third application approved by Planning Committee, on recommendation of Chief Planning Officer, following about four minutes discussion.

16 October 1985:   Two months after Council's receipt of appeal on second application, DOE informs it that its Statement, due within four weeks, has not been received.

18 October 1985:   Council sends to owner incorrect decision notice on third application.

21 October 1985:   DOE forwards Statement of Council to appellant, now one month behind DOE's target timetable. This degree of lateness is the norm for Chiltern DistrictCouncil, but some 25 per cent of local authorities are as slow or slower (Wakeford and Heywood, 1985, pp. 116–17).

27 October 1985:   Appellant sends comments on Council's Statement to DOE and Council.

30 October 1985:   Following a request from owner, Council sends correct decision notice on third application.

25 November 1985:	A fortnight after DOE Inspector's site visit DOE receives Council's response to comments submitted by appellant one month previously.
5 December 1985:	DOE sends Council's response to appellant.
7 December 1985:	Appellant responds.
3 January 1986:	DOE Inspector's decision letter, dismissing appeal, sent to appellant.

If the ultimate outcome of this process had been a better landscape than would otherwise have been the case, this would have been an important consideration to be set against the costs incurred, both financial and in human energy. But, as has been shown, there were in fact serious detrimental effects on the landscape, and few of those involved in the development were satisfied with the outcome. Although this example may be somewhat extreme, the conclusions drawn from it are not out of character with those drawn from a range of sites in previous chapters. It is far from clear from these studies that, at the micro-scale, the benefits of the planning process are commensurate with their costs, and in some cases there have undoubtedly been significant costs.

How justified is this conclusion more generally? Unfortunately, there are few comparable studies of the effects of planning on landscape development. A notable exception is the work of Punter (1985, 1986b). As has been mentioned, this focuses attention on office building in the commercial core of Reading. The scenario of protracted interaction between applicants and LPA that it presents is consistent in its essentials with that for the areas under severe development pressure examined here. But Punter's conclusion concerning the value of development control is different. He suggests that 'perhaps half of the major office applications since 1974 have been significantly improved in design terms by passage through the control process' (Punter, 1986b, p. 209). However, he also notes that, 'what is difficult, if not impossible, to assess is the extent to which planning control, and specifically aesthetic control, has been responsible for this' (Punter, 1986b, p. 209). Nevertheless, his judgement on the effects of the entire process to which planning proposals are subjected is at least less equivocal than that of the present study, and it is reiterated in a later study of office development in central Bristol (Punter, 1990, p. 365). The difference may reflect the different types of area being examined. The study by Larkham (1988) of a mixture of residential and commercial Conservation Areas in the west Midlands, although avoiding value judgements, concluded that in those cases the influence of the LPAs has often been minor. Specifically referring to the LPA's influence on the design and architectural style of developments in a suburban area of Birmingham not dissimilar to our residential study areas, Pompa (1988, p. 265) concluded that it was very limited. There is clearly a need for more investigations of the way in which the development-control process influenced, and is influencing, urban landscape change.

People and urban landscapes

The place of the main users of urban areas, the general public, in relation to urban landscape change generally, and the process of decision-making that underlies it in particular, remains poorly understood. Groat has investigated several aspects of this matter in regard to urban areas in the American Mid-West. Of particular interest is her examination of public reactions to the view that 'architecture should be treated as an historic document' (Groat, 1986). She concludes that this view has little support. One inference to be drawn would seem to be that considerations of the historical associations or historical expressiveness of buildings are, to say the least, a less significant part of the landscape appreciation of those interviewed than other considerations. Of overriding importance, Groat concluded, is the visual compatibility of new buildings with those existing. This conclusion is consistent with the findings of Punter (1986b, p. 208) for central Reading. The view that for most people it is outward appearances, rather than historicity, that is crucial is supported by the work of Bishop (1982, p. 263) on Guildford in Surrey. He found that residents of that town who mistakenly believed several twentieth-century neo-Tudor buildings to be genuinely Tudor were not at all disturbed to find that they were fakes. That the appreciation of an architectural style is independent of an awareness of its historical associations or expressiveness is, however, a much more dubious proposition. It is hard to see how 'fakes' in the landscape can be appreciated independently of the cultural context which includes the historically redolent originals they seek to copy. For those who know anything about the history or historical associations of a style, an ahistorical appreciation is impossible.

The views displayed in surveys of attitudes to the urban landscape should not be confused with those that inform the actual participation of users of urban areas in the process of decision-making concerning landscape change. A number of aspects of the behaviour of those affected by particular landscape changes deserve attention. First, there is the amount and geographical distribution of public participation. Secondly, there is the nature of the views fed into the decision-making process through public participation. Thirdly, there is the impact of those views on the decisions taken.

Perhaps the most noteworthy feature is the highly localized nature of public interest in proposals for change. Figure 6.2 shows the location of those making representations at the appeal against the refusal of the third planning application for Hyrons. They were tightly clustered around the application site, and represented a small minority of the occupiers to whom the LPA sent letters giving notice of the appeal. Similarly, Burnett and Moon (1983) demonstrated that the distribution of objectors to the conversion of premises to hostels for single homeless men in Portsmouth was largely limited to within a radius of 200 m of the proposed sites, despite the noxious image of this land use. This particular land use is not, of course, to be taken as representative of the broad category of institutional and public land use discussed in chapter 3: some of the sites considered there were themselves larger than the distribution area of

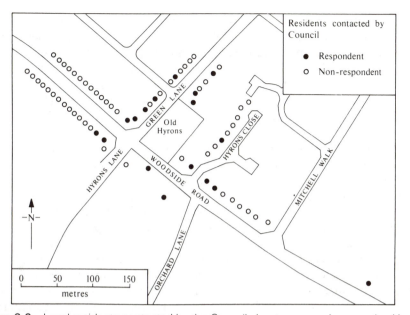

Figure 6.2 Local residents contacted by the Council about an appeal concerning Hyrons in 1985, and those making representations.
Source: owner's files.

objectors just referred to. Nevertheless, the distribution area of objectors to proposals for infill on such large sites tends to be relatively limited, indeed such proposals are on average less contentious than those for sites in residential areas or commercial cores, because the new buildings proposed are often well removed from boundaries with neighbouring sites.

Analysis of the representations made in the Hyrons case sheds light both on the perception of the Hyrons area by local residents and by other parties and on the extent of the area that was considered the appropriate context for judging the development proposal (Whitehand, 1989a, pp. 16–18). In offering judgements, all but five parties compared the character of the proposed development with the character of the area in which it was to be located, but this area of comparison was seldom clearly defined. The distinctive character of the Hyrons area received hardly any mention. Since the plots surrounding Old Hyrons itself were varied in their character, the ascription of qualities and densities to an unspecific area such as 'the locality', 'the neighbourhood', 'the vicinity', 'the area', 'the surrounding area', and 'the immediate vicinity', was almost meaningless. It is possible, however, to recognize differences between the parties in the way in which the areal context of the development was identified.

For the Amersham and District Residents' Association the context was broadly 'the Amersham and Chesham Bois area, ('our area'). One resident (a planning consultant), whose property had a frontage practically onto the proposed entrance to the development in Green Lane, stated that 'the neighbourhood of which the appeal site forms part lies to the north of Woodside

Road': thus, so far from recognizing the Hyrons area as an entity, he actually divided it into two parts. The DOE Inspector in his decision letter also identified for comparative purposes 'the northern side of Woodside Road', meaning, it can be inferred, Green Lane and the roads leading off it (figure 6.2). He made no reference to the rest of the Hyrons area, arguing that 'the proposal need have only a very slight effect' on the Woodside Road frontage, though it was the relationship of the proposed development to this area that was of greatest concern to the LPA.

Clearly, most of these different viewpoints were permeated by self-interest. In the case of most local residents there was little to be gained from the development and, according to one estate agent, for some a fall in the value of their property might be expected. But the effects of the development were likely to be far from evenly spread. All but one of the local residents who made representations occupied plots that were unsuitable for profitable redevelopment or filling in. The one exception, the owner-occupier of Hyrons Lodge (figure 5.1B), was also the only local resident to make representations in favour of the proposed development. A land surveyor by profession, he was well aware that it would enhance the exchange value, though not the existing-use value, of his property, which extended over about 1.2 ha, including a commercial nursery of about 0.8 ha at the rear. Furthermore, having been retired for some years, he had family reasons, similar to those of several owners who had just sold, or were in the process of selling, their land for development in the inner area of Amersham, for prizing exchange value more than existing-use value. He had in the past, like the owner of Old Hyrons, received several approaches from estate agents to sell for development, but had preferred to retain the existing-use value of the site. His ambivalence was characteristic of such owners. It is frequently only in old age that family circumstances cause a concern with exchange value to override the interest in existing-use value.

The contribution of the public to the development-control process is of interest for the light it sheds on their attitudes to development proposals. But quantifying the impact of public participation is difficult. Its direct influence on individual outcomes would seem to be small. Probably more significant is the influence of the weight of public opinion more generally on local councillors' attitudes owing to its importance at local elections. In his study of office development in central Reading, Punter (1986b, p. 208) describes as 'minute' the effects of public participation in aesthetic control.

Towards urban landscape management?

The process of working towards a change to the urban landscape that has been described is characterized by muddle and incoherence. The appearance of developments is a by-product of considerations other than design, especially the economics of density and highway considerations. From the first days of 'aesthetic control' early in the twentieth century, central government circulars have discouraged the local authorities from taking an interest in design details (Punter, 1986a, p. 56). They have consistently advised that design is primarily a matter for developers and their architects. Thus development-control officers are constrained from adopting an open, constructive attitude towards planning applications. In addition, they frequently lack either the requisite skills to contribute to the design of buildings or the time to spend on a matter that their paymasters regard as inessential, or both. As far as developers are concerned, there is an understandable preoccupation with the profitability of their developments. In so far as the appearance of a development is a consideration, they will not want to risk offending potential purchasers and tenants with styles that depart from the mainstream of architectural fashion (Punter, 1986b, pp. 202–3).

How does the low priority given to the urban landscape appear from a broader perspective? Although the influence of local authorities and central government on urban deveopment has increased greatly since the nineteenth century, governmental impact at the scale of the streetscape is often less than that of major nineteenth-century estate owners exercising control over the development of their land. At this scale, LPAs and central government exercise supervisory powers over change, but they do this for the most part by reacting to proposals whose initiation and specific formulation are outside their control. The characteristics of these proposals are explicable to a considerable degree in terms of the characteristics of the relevant property owners and the various firms and organizations that make up the development industry, though these in turn need to be viewed in the context of market forces and changing fashions, neither of which are free from governmental influences. Unlike major nineteenth-century landowners, LPAs plan specific landscapes only rarely. In response to specific proposals they seldom suggest, except in the most general terms, the type of landscape that they regard as desirable. They state what is unacceptable according to their rules and procedures, but their creative role is, in the majority of cases, minimal. Like most bereaucracies, LPAs rely heavily on a battery of standardized responses. Elusive qualities of a landscape, such as the *genius loci*, pale into insignificance as determinants of development-control decisions by comparison with measurements of building density and the dimensions and geometry of highways.

A major underlying problem is that much of the formal and informal power of LPAs is directed at restraining the profit-maximizing proposals of developers. This emphasis on restraint is more evident in some localities than in others, for profitability has a far from even distribution. In some localities where development is deemed to be socially desirable a more receptive attitude is necessary on the part of a LPA if development is to occur at all. In south-east England, in contrast, resistance to change is pervasive, and leads to an atmosphere of confrontation. This is especially evident in the interchanges between on the one hand developers, often with a small and, as time goes on, diminishing commitment to the local landscape, and on the other hand LPAs representing to a large extent the interests of those experiencing the landscape on a daily basis. Within residential areas, owner-occupiers of sites with development potential often have a somewhat ambivalent attitude, embodying both a concern to retain their site's existing-use value and a concern to capitalize on its development potential. This would seem to be a factor underlying the tendency for proposals by owner-occupiers for developing their land more intensively to involve the retention of more of the existing landscape than those by developers. The atmosphere of conflict between LPAs and those seeking to carry out developments sometimes has seriously detrimental effects on the landscape. Indeed, the concern of LPAs with employing the tactics of restraint, rather than with taking an integrated view of developments that ultimately they are unlikely to be able to prevent in some form, can lead to the creation of urban landscapes much less satisfactory than many of those created in the past by powerful private landowners whose development activities were relatively untramelled by government controls.

These findings and others, such as the fact that urban development proposals and intentions seldom give rise to the physical forms that were initially conceived, and that outcomes in the landscape are frequently unsatisfactory in important respects, give this study a temper that differs considerably from that of most planning-historians' studies of the urban landscape. Relying heavily on plans and documentation relating to policies and legislation, their findings usually fall far short of offering explanations for the actual development of urban landscapes at the micro-scale. Our findings are also a salutary reminder of the realities of which account needs to be taken when seeking to apply academics' ideas on urban design. More theory is necessary but it needs to be viewed in the light of the problems of real-world application.

The processes at work in the development of urban areas and the built-forms that are emerging on the ground and seem likely to emerge in the future must ultimately be evaluated according to the quality of the environment, and in particular the landscape, that they provide. The interests that are crucial here are those of the people using urban areas. However, despite their fundamental importance, these interests have received comparatively little attention in our discussion so far, since on the whole they impinge on the processes creating urban landscapes only indirectly: the interests of those living and working in urban areas are filtered by the various parties with a formal role. When these interests are examined, however, a number of problems come into sharper focus.

Despite the fact that individual owner-occupiers remain an important force in the initiation of major landscape changes within existing residential areas, even here the character of such changes is not determined primarily by how they fit into the existing fabric or by the needs of the inhabitants. Moreover, the activities of non-local concerns, which tend to have less sense of place, are becoming increasingly important. This is especially the case in commercial cores. There, the incidence and the type of landscape change are influenced by events far removed from what is visible to the average user of these areas, notably the investment decisions of insurance companies and not least the changes in the attractiveness of overseas investment to pension-fund managers, in comparison with investment in property in Great Britain. Landscape problems are minor influences by comparison. This all results in, among other things, the destruction long before they are worn out physically of buildings into which enormous amounts of economic and cultural capital have been invested and, in commercial cores in particular, their replacement by structures out of scale with the existing landscape. In city centres in particular these processes have led to cultural impoverishment. They have been aggravated by the enlarged scale, and impersonalization, of land- and property-ownership, which stemmed in part from the increased powers of local authorities to acquire land. This increased the facility with which major road-system changes were implemented in conjunction with redevelopment and gave scope to a kind of functional logic that was all too frequently divorced from intimate human experience of the landscape.

The main reaction to these developments has taken the form of a conservation movement. Unfortunately, the effectiveness of this movement has been hampered in two crucial respects, both of which reflect a national propensity to put short-term economic gains before long-term social and cultural ones. First, conservation policy lacks an effective means of implementation: although the conservation emphasis in local planning documents is unmistakable, local authorities lack both the financial means and the staff with the requisite skills to give effect to it. Secondly, and even more fundamentally, it lacks a theoretical basis – a theory of urban landscape management that can give direction and coherence to the way in which conservation problems are tackled. The first of these problems raises issues beyond the scope of this study, but the second can be treated as an extension of our main theme.

The effects in the landscape of the processes and activities that have been discussed have a number of important attributes that a theory of urban landscape management needs to take into account. In addition to having a considerable life-span relative to the individual human life-span, each change in the landscape embodies something of the efforts and aspirations of the society responsible for creating it. This asset is increasingly under threat. This is partly because so many of the agents of change are now intrusive rather than being outgrowths of the local economy and society. Furthermore, in commercial cores at least, the scale of many individual developments has become so large that they cannot readily fit harmoniously into a landscape founded on a system of traditional plots and their derivatives. In the case of commercial cores, this enlarged scale, by no means always in accord with the interests of the occupiers of premises, has been engendered to a considerable extent by changed investment policies in combination with the enlarged scope of local authority powers. The consequent discord in the landscape is accentuated by the increasing role of consulting engineers and associated changes in constructional materials. Until the 1960s the keynote of city-centre development was transition: in cases of abrupt change, and there were many, the scale of new developments was often sufficiently similar to that of previous developments for them to blend in. The combination of a heavy concentration of investment funds in commercial property, local authority involvement (and hence large areas under single, impersonal ownership), and the use of new materials and technology has changed this.

The problems that this situation poses for the management of the urban landscape are of major proportions even by comparison with those faced in the Victorian era. Their significance is not lessened by the fact that the landscape asset that is at risk is often experienced unconsciously and is not susceptible to direct measurement in terms of economic benefit. The problems have been widely recognized, particularly in the last 20 years, and there has been an increasing concern that the appearance of new developments should be compatible with that of existing buildings. But the way in which this should be achieved has rarely been discussed by academics, and in practice development has been characterized by crude attempts to reproduce historical styles with little reference to the historicity of the particular urban landscape.

Given this theoretical vacuum, the Conzenian approach to managing urban landscapes merits close examination. Although it does not provide a complete solution, it does suggest a way forward. However, in the light of the findings of this study it is apparent that a great deal more groundwork by academics will be necessary if it is to be pursued successfully by practising planners in Great Britain. An important part of that groundwork is being undertaken by Kropf (1986). A glimpse along the paths he is treading provides an appropriate ending to this study and a prospect of an important research task still to be accomplished.

If the detailed studies described in this volume are to contribute to a more coherent development of both the theory of urban landscape management and planning practice, a firm grip must be taken on the baton of urban morphology. The strategy that is being pursued by Kropf is to explore both the trail mapped by Conzen, which we have discussed in practical terms in chapter 5, and that followed by the Italian architect Gianfranco Caniggia. The positions reached by these two scholars, though arrived at independently and from quite different disciplinary starting-points, have much in common. For Kropf they afford the means of pursuing, and eventually articulating, a philosophical position that underpins the relationship between the historico-geographical explanation of the development of urban forms and the prescription of urban design.

Fundamental to the thinking of Caniggia, as to that of Conzen, is the view that the intelligibility of the city depends on its history. On the way to establishing a basis for managing urban landscapes it is a short step from this fundamental belief to regarding the city as a source of accumulated wisdom, and from there to utilizing this wisdom as the basis for prescribing change. This is not to argue that there are neither new problems nor new solutions. Possible solutions may be 'read' from the existing landscape, provided that the 'language' of the landscape is understood, but they must be assessed to ensure that they are appropriate to new problems.

In looking to the past for guidance and finding it in the historical unfolding of the urban landscape, we are firmly back in the intellectual milieu that provided the starting-point for this volume. The Conzenian perspective recognizes new functional needs but requires that the ways in which they are met respect the existing landscape as a tangible record of the endeavours of past societies in a particular locale. It is founded on a long-term view of human endeavour. By emphasizing the historical and geographical context of each change in the landscape, and by laying stress on the long-term repercussions of decisions affecting the landscape, it draws attention to the responsibility that a society has to future generations. In a sense it seeks to restore that sense of geographical identity that was once taken for granted but which the industrial revolution and its aftermath have partially destroyed. The view of urban landscapes that is recommended is thus essentially conservative, the accent being not on wholesale clearance and comprehensive redevelopment but on historically and geographically informed transformation, augmentation and conservation. This is not a panacea for the many problems outlined earlier. The piecemeal approach that is to some extent necessary entails financial costs as well as social gains. In practice a balance has to be struck, and Alexander (1974) has suggested ways in which this may be effected.

Whilst it is inevitable that in the foreseeable future the pace of change will to a considerable extent be determined by economic conditions, in the light of the processes at work and in particular their character and outcome in the post-war period it would be irresponsible effectively to leave decisions about long-term social assets largely in the hands of organizations whose concern for history is slight and whose connections with the landscape effects of their actions upon those who live and work in urban areas are frequently tenuous. There is thus a large gap between the way in which the landscapes of British towns and cities appear to have developed in recent times and our suggestions as to the principles that should govern the management of the urban landscape. Nevertheless, the mood in general is far more receptive to a concern for the visual environment than it has been for many decades. It is the responsibility of academics and practising planners to take advantage of this to harness potentially powerful, but still incipient, theory to the task of at least limiting damage to urban landscapes and, more optimistically, enhancing them.

References

Alexander, I. 1974: City centre redevelopment: an evaluation of alternative approaches. *Progress in Planning*, 3, 1–81.

Allsopp, B. (ed.) 1967: *Historic Architecture of Newcastle upon Tyne*. Newcastle upon Tyne: Oriel Press.

Ambrose, P. and Colenutt, B. 1975: *The Property Machine*. Harmondsworth: Penguin.

Aspinall, P. J. 1977: *The Size Structure of the House-building Industry in Victorian Sheffield*. University of Birmingham Centre for Urban and Regional Studies Working Paper 49.

Aspinall, P. J. 1982: The internal structure of the house-building industry in nineteenth-century cities. In J. H. Johnson and C.G. Pooley (eds), *The Structure of Nineteenth Century Cities*, London: Croom Helm, 75–105.

Aspinall, P. J. and Whitehand, J. W. R. 1980: Building plans: a major source for urban studies. *Area*, 12, 199–203.

Association of County Councils, Association of District Councils, Association of Metropolitan Authorities 1982: *Interim Report of the Joint DOE/Local Authority Associations Planning Statistics Analysis Working Group on the Determinants of Efficiency in Development Control in England*. London: National Development Control Forum.

Bandini, M. 1985: Urban morphology: the British contribution. Unpublished report for the French Ministry of Urbanism, Housing and Transport, commissioned by the Institute of Urbanism at the University of Paris VII.

Barnard, R. W. (comp.) 1948: *A Century of Service: the story of the Prudential 1848–1948*. London: Prudential.

Barras, R. 1979a: *The Returns from Office Development and Investment*. Centre for Environmental Studies Research Series 35.

Barras, R. 1979b: *The Development Cycle in the City of London*. Centre for Environmental Studies Research Series 36.

Bateman, M. 1971: *Some Aspects of Change in the Central Areas of Towns in West Yorkshire since 1945*. Portsmouth Polytechnic Department of Geography Occasional Paper 1.

Beer, A. R. 1983: Development control and design quality. Part 2: attitudes to design. *Town Planning Review*, 54, 383–404.

Bennison, D. J. and Davies, R. L. 1980: The impact of town centre shopping schemes in Britain: their impact on traditional retail environments. *Progress in Planning*, 14, 1–104.

Bentley, I. 1987: The social production of housing design: layout, appearance and concepts of 'good design' in British interwar estates. Unpublished paper, Joint Centre for Urban Design, Oxford Polytechnic.

Beresford, M. W. 1975: Red brick and Portland Stone: a building history. In P. H. J. H. Gosden and A. J. Taylor (eds), *Studies in the History of a University 1874–1974*. Leeds: E. J. Arnold & Sons, 133–80.

Bishop, R. 1982: The perception and importance of time in architecture. Unpublished PhD thesis, University of Surrey.

Booth, P. N. 1989: Owners, solicitors and residential development: the case of a Manchester suburb. Unpublished MPhil thesis, University of Birmingham.

Borsay, P. 1984: The rise of the promenade: the social and cultural use of space in the English provincial town *c*.1660–1800. Unpublished paper presented to the Urban History Group Colloquium on Urban Space and Building Form, London, 21 September.

Bowhill, A. 1985: Briefing planning law. *Chartered Surveyor Weekly*, 13, 603.

Bowhill, A. 1986: Briefing planning law. *Chartered Surveyor Weekly*, 14, 532.

Bowley, M. 1966: *The British Building Industry: four studies in response and resistance to change*. Cambridge: Cambridge University Press.

Boyd, C. W. (ed.) 1914: *Mr Chamberlain's Speeches*. London: Constable, 2 vols.

Broaderwick, R. F. 1981: An investigation into the location of institutional land uses in Birmingham. Unpublished PhD thesis, University of Birmingham.

Burgess, E. W. 1925: The growth of the city. In R. E. Park, E. W. Burgess and R. D. McKenzie, *The City*, Chicago: University of Chicago Press, 47–62.

Burnett, A. and Moon, G. 1983: Community opposition to hostels for single homeless men. *Area*, 15, 161–6.

Burnett, J. 1978: *A Social History of Housing, 1815–1970*. London: Methuen.

Burstall, F. W. and Burton, C. G. 1930: *Souvenir of the Foundation and Development of the Mason Science College and of the University of Birmingham 1880–1930*. n.p.

Butcher, K. E. 1974: Spatial patterns of urban growth in the commuter settlement of Banstead, 1900–1972. Unpublished BA dissertation, University of Birmingham.

Callis, S. E. 1986: Redevelopment in Epsom commercial centre, 1898–1984: a spatial analysis of agents and architectural styles. Unpublished BSc dissertation, University of Birmingham.

Cannadine, D. 1977: Victorian cities: how different? *Social History*, 4, 457–82.

Cannadine, D. 1980: *Lords and Landlords: the aristocracy and the towns, 1774–1967*. Leicester: Leicester University Press.

Carr, M. C. 1982: The development and character of a metropolitan suburb: Bexley, Kent. In F. M. L. Thompson (ed.), *The Rise of Suburbia*, Leicester: Leicester University Press, 212–67.

Carter, H. 1970: A decision-making approach to town-plan analysis: a case study of Llandudno. In H. Carter and W. K. D. Davies (eds), *Urban Essays: studies in the geography of Wales*, London: Longman, 66–78.

Casson Conder & Partners 1964: University of Birmingham Academic Site: 1964 development plan. Unpublished plan, in Estates and Buildings Department, University of Birmingham.

Casson, H. and Conder, N. 1957: Report on proposed developments for Birmingham University. Part I – The University site. Unpublished MS.

Central Statistical Office 1964–81: *Financial Statistics*. London: HMSO.

Chalklin, C. W. 1974: *The Provincial Towns of Georgian England: a study of the building process 1740–1820*. London: Edward Arnold.

Chalklin, C. W. 1980: Capital expenditure on building for cultural purposes in provincial England, 1730–1830. *Business History*, 22, 51–70.

Cherry, G. E. 1976: Aspects of urban renewal. In T. Hancock (ed.), *Growth and Change in the Future City Region*. London: Leonard Hill, 53–71.

Cherry, G. E. 1988: *Cities and Plans: the shaping of urban Britain in the nineteenth and twentieth centuries*. London: Edward Arnold.

CIPFA 1985: *Planning and Development Statistics 1985–86 Estimates*. London: Chartered Institute of Public Finance and Accountancy.

City of Birmingham 1973: *City of Birmingham Structure Plan: written statement*.

Birmingham: City of Birmingham.

City of Birmingham 1980: *Birmingham Central Area District Plan: draft written statement.* Birmingham: City of Birmingham.

City of Liverpool 1980: *Shopping: trends and opportunities.* Liverpool: City of Liverpool.

Clifton-Taylor, A. 1972: *The Pattern of English Building.* London: Faber and Faber.

Collier, R. N. 1981: A study of the residential growth of Amersham and Chesham Bois, Buckinghamshire and the influence of architects and builders 1919–1929. Unpublished BSc dissertation, University of Birmingham.

Conway, H. 1985: The Manchester/Salford parks: their design and development. *Journal of Garden History,* 5, 231–60.

Conzen, M. R. G. 1958: The growth and character of Whitby. In G. H. J. Daysh (ed.) *A Survey of Whitby and the Surrounding Area,* Eton: Shakespeare Head Press, 49–89.

Conzen, M. R. G. 1960: *Alnwick, Northumberland: a study in town-plan analysis.* Institute of British Geographers Publication 27. London: George Philip.

Conzen, M. R. G. 1962: The plan analysis of an English city centre. In K. Norborg (ed.), *Proceedings of the IGU Symposium in Urban Geography Lund 1960,* Lund: Gleerup, 383–414.

Conzen, M. R. G. 1966: Historical townscapes in Britain: a problem in applied geography. In J. W. House (ed.), *Northern Geographical Essays in Honour of G. H. J. Daysh,* Newcastle upon Tyne: University of Newcastle upon Tyne, 56–78.

Conzen, M. R. G. 1969: *Alnwick, Northumberland: a study in town-plan analysis.* Institute of British Geographers Publication 27. London: Institute of British Geographers. Revised Edition.

Conzen, M. R. G. 1975: Geography and townscape conservation. In H. Uhlig and C. Lienau (eds), *Anglo-German Symposium in Applied Geography, Giessen-Würzburg-München,* Giessen: Lenz, 95–102.

Conzen, M. R. G. 1988: Morphogenesis, morphological regions and secular human agency in the historic townscape, as exemplified by Ludlow. In D. Denecke, and G. Shaw (eds), *Urban Historical Geography: recent progress in Britain and Germany,* Cambridge: Cambridge University Press, 253–72.

Corey, K. E. 1969: A spatial analysis of urban houses. Unpublished PhD dissertation, University of Cincinnati.

Council of the Stock Exchange 1940: *Stock Exchange Official Year-book, 1940.* London: Council of the Stock Exchange.

Craven, E. 1969: Private residential expansion in Kent 1956–64: a study of pattern and process in urban growth. *Urban Studies,* 6, 1–16.

Cunningham, C. 1981: *Victorian and Edwardian Town Halls.* London: Routledge & Kegan Paul.

Daily Chronicle 1909: 15 June.

Damesick, P. J. 1986: The M25 – a new geography of development? I. The issues. *Geographical Journal,* 152, 155–60.

Daunton, M. J. 1977: *Coal Metropolis: Cardiff 1870–1914.* Leicester: Leicester University Press.

Daunton, M. J. 1984: Introduction. In M. J. Daunton (ed.), *Councillors and Tenants: local authority housing in English cities, 1919–1939,* Leicester: Leicester University Press, 1–38.

Department of the Environment 1975: *Commercial Property Development.* London: HMSO.

Department of the Environment 1980a: *Land for Private Housebuilding.* DOE Circular 9/80. London: HMSO.

Department of the Environment 1980b: *Development Control: policy and practice.* DOE Circular 22/80. London: HMSO.

Department of the Environment 1984: *Land for housing.* DOE Circular 15/84. London: HMSO.

Department of the Environment 1985: *Development Control Statistics: England 1979/80–1982/83.* London: Government Statistical Service.

Department of the Environment, Scottish Development Department, Welsh Office 1972: *Housing and Construction Statistics*. London: HMSO.

Department of the Environment, Scottish Development Department, Welsh Office 1980: *Housing and Construction Statistics*. London: HMSO.

Duffy, F. 1980: Office buildings and organizational change. In A. D. King (ed.), *Buildings and Society: essays in the social development of the built environment*, London: Routledge & Kegan Paul, 255–80.

Dyos, H. J. 1968: The speculative builders and developers of Victorian London. *Victorian Studies*, 11, 641–90.

Economist Intelligence Unit 1977: *An Analysis of Commercial Property Values 1962–1976*. London: Economist Intelligence Unit.

Edwards, A. M. 1981: *The Design of Suburbia: a critical study in environmental history*. London: Pembridge Press.

Esher, L. 1981: *A Broken Wave: the rebuilding of England 1940–1980*. London: Allen Lane.

Fleming, S. C. 1984: *Housebuilders in an Area of Growth: negotiating the built environment in central Berkshire*. University of Reading Department of Geography Geographical Paper 84.

Forster, C. A. 1972: *Court Housing in Kingston upon Hull: an example of cyclic processes in the morphological development of nineteenth century bye-law housing*. University of Hull Occasional Papers in Geography 19.

Freeman, M. 1986: The nature and agents of central-area change. Unpublished PhD thesis, University of Birmingham.

Freeman, M. 1987: Property development in the CBD: concentration or dispersal? *Area*, 19, 123–9.

Freeman, M. 1988: Developers, architects and building styles: post-war redevelopment in two town centres. *Transactions of the Institute of British Geographers*, NS 13, 131–47.

Gad, G. and Holdsworth, D. 1984: Building for city, region and nation. In V. L. Russell (ed.), *Forging a Consensus: historical essays on Toronto*, Toronto: University of Toronto Press, 272–319.

GLC 1975: *The Museums Area of South Kensington and Westminster*. Survey of London, 38. London: Athlone Press.

Gomme, A. and Walker, D. 1968: *Architecture of Glasgow*. London: Lund Humphries.

Goodchild, R. and Munton, R. 1985: *Development and the Landowner: an analysis of the British experience*. London: George Allen and Unwin.

Gordon, G. 1981: The historico-geographic explanation of urban morphology: a discussion of some Scottish evidence. *Scottish Geographical Magazine*, 97, 16–26.

Gordon, G. 1984: The shaping of urban morphology. *Urban History Yearbook*, 1–10.

Groat, L. N. 1986: Contextual compatibility: a study of meaning in the urban environment. Unpublished paper presented to the Annual Meeting of the Association of American Geographers, Minneapolis.

Hamnett, C. 1986: The changing socio-economic structure of London and the South East, 1961–1981. *Regional Studies*, 20, 391–406.

Harper, R. 1977: The conflict between English building regulations and architectural design 1890–1918. *Journal of Architectural Research*, 6, 24–33.

Harvey, J. 1972: *Conservation of Buildings*. London: J. Baker.

Havers, J. 1985: Development control in villages – the highways factor. *Journal of Rural Studies*, 1, 253–66.

Hennock, E. P. 1973: *Fit and Proper Persons: ideal and reality in nineteenth-century urban government*. London: Edward Arnold.

Hillier Parker Research 1979: *British Shopping Developments*. London: Hillier Parker May and Rowden.

Hobhouse, H. 1971: *Thomas Cubitt: master builder*. London: Macmillan.

Horsey, M. 1985: Speculative housebuilding in London in the 1930s: official control and popular taste. Unpublished paper presented to the Fourth Annual Seminar of the Construction History Group, London, 12 September.

Hutton, W. 1783: *A History of Birmingham*, 2nd edn. Birmingham: Pearson and Rollason.

Jefferys, J. B. 1954: *Retail Trading in Britain 1850–1950*. Cambridge: Cambridge University Press.

Jencks, C. A. 1975: *The Language of Post-Modern Architecture*. London: Academy Editions.

Johns, E. 1971: Urban design in Dawlish and Chelston. In K. J. Gregory and W. Ravenhill (eds), *Exeter Essays in Geography in Honour of Arthur Davies*, Exeter: University of Exeter, 201–8.

Jones, A. N., Booth, P. N., Larkham, P. J., Pompa, N. D. and Whitehand, J. W. R. 1988: *The Management of Planned Residential Townscapes*. University of Birmingham School of Geography Working Paper 43.

Jones, J. H. 1935: Introduction. In British Association, *Britain in Depression: a record of British industries since 1929*, London: Sir Isaac Pitman & Sons, 1–21.

Jones, J. T. 1940: *History of the Corporation of Birmingham*, vol. 5. Birmingham: Corporation of Birmingham.

Jones, K. R. 1971: *Companion around Watford*. n.p.

Kaye, B. 1960: *The Development of the Architectural Profession in Britain*: London: George Allen & Unwin.

Kelly & Co. 1917: *Kelly's Directory of Hertfordshire*. London: Kelly & Co.

Kelly & Co. 1929: *Kelly's Directory of Hertfordshire*. London: Kelly & Co.

Kelly's Directories 1914: *Kelly's Directory of Bedfordshire, Huntingdonshire and Northamptonshire*. London: Kelly's Directories.

Kelly's Directories 1920: *Kelly's Directory of Bedfordshire, Huntingdonshire and Northamptonshire*. London: Kelly's Directories.

Kelly's Directories 1924: *Kelly's Directory of Bedfordshire, Huntingdonshire and Northamptonshire*. London: Kelly's Directories.

Kelly's Directories 1928: *Kelly's Directory of Bedfordshire, Huntingdonshire and Northamptonshire*. London: Kelly's Directories.

Kelly's Directories 1931: *Kelly's Directory of Bedfordshire, Huntingdonshire and Northamptonshire*. London: Kelly's Directories.

King, A. D. 1984: *The Bungalow: the production of a global culture*. London: Routledge & Kegan Paul.

Knox, P. L. 1991: The restless urban landscape: economic and socio-cultural change and the transformation of Washington D.C. *Annals of the Association of American Geographers*, 81, 181–209.

Kropf, K. S. 1986: Urban morphology considered. Unpublished MA thesis, Oxford Polytechnic.

Larkham, P. J. 1986a: Conservation, planning and morphology in West Midlands conservation areas, 1968–1984. Unpublished PhD thesis, University of Birmingham.

Larkham, P. J. 1986b: *The Agents of Urban Change*. University of Birmingham Department of Geography Occasional Publication 21.

Larkham, P. J. 1988: Agents and types of change in the conserved townscape. *Transactions of the Institute of British Geographers*, NS 13, 148–64.

Larkham, P. J. 1991: *The Changing Urban Landscape in Historical Areas*. University of Birmingham School of Geography Occasional Publication 30.

Larkham, P. J. and Freeman, M. 1988: Twentieth-century British commercial architecture. *Journal of Cultural Geography*, 9, 1–16.

Lee, F. 1953: A new theory of the origins and early growth of Northampton. *Archaeological Journal*, 110, 164–74.

Leech, M. and Cook, C. F. 1951: *David Greenhill: master printer*. n.p.

Lever, W. F. 1974: Planning standards. In J. Forbes (ed.), *Studies in Social Science and Planning*, Edinburgh: Scottish Academic Press, 9–53.

Ley, D. 1988: From urban structure to urban landscape. *Urban Geography*, 9, 98–105.

Lichtenberger, E. 1970: The nature of European urbanism. *Geoforum*, 4, 45–62.

Luffrum, J. M. 1980: Variations in the building fabric of small towns. *Transactions of the Institute of British Geographers*, NS 5, 170–3.

MacGregor, G. S. 1984: The roles of owners, architects and builders in the development of selected streets in two dormitory towns, 1919–39. Unpublished BA dissertation, University of Birmingham.

McNamara, P. 1982: *Land Release and Development in Areas of Restraint*. Oxford Polytechnic Department of Town Planning Working Paper 76.

McNamara, P. F. 1985: The control of office development in central Edinburgh, 1959–1978. Unpublished PhD thesis, University of Edinburgh.

Marriott, O. 1967: *The Property Boom*. London: Hamish Hamilton.

Massey, D. 1967: *Ruislip-Northwood: the development of the suburb with special reference to the period 1887–1914*. Eastcote, Middx: The Ruislip, Northwood and Eastcote Local History Society.

Massey, D. and Catalano, A. 1978: *Capital and Land*. London: Edward Arnold.

Ministry of Health 1949: *Housing Manual 1949*. London: HMSO.

Mitchell, B. R. and Deane, P. 1962: *Abstract of British Historical Statistics*. Cambridge: Cambridge University Press.

Mitchell, B. R. and Jones, H. G. 1971: *Second Abstract of British Historical Statistics*. Cambridge: Cambridge University Press.

Morris, A. E. J. 1979: *History of Urban Form: before the industrial revolution*. London: George Godwin.

Morris, D. S. and Newton, K. 1970: Profile of a local political elite: businessmen as community decision-makers in Birmingham, 1838–1966. *The New Atlantis*, 1, 111–23.

Moser, C. A. and Scott, W. 1961: *British Towns: a statistical study of their social and economic differences*. Edinburgh: Oliver and Boyd.

Northampton Civic Society 1975: *Northampton '75*. Northampton: Northampton Civic Society.

Northampton and County Independent 1930: Obituary – Councillor A. P. Hawtin, 25 January, 14.

Northampton and County Independent 1968: September, 44.

Northamptom Independent 1944: Mr Frank Panther's will, 3 November, 6.

Northampton Independent 1949a: Obituary – Mr F. H. Allen, 25 February, 9.

Northampton Independent 1949b: Obituary – Mr W. Lawson Carter, 13 May, 17.

Northampton Independent 1956: Obituary – Mr C. H. Dorman, 24 February, 7.

O'Donoghue, R. 1983: A Victorian suburb: some aspects of town planning in 19th -century Norwich. *Norfolk Archaeology*, 28, 321–8.

Openshaw, S. 1974: Processes in urban morphology with special reference to South Shields. Unpublished PhD thesis, University of Newcastle upon Tyne.

Pain, R. J. 1980: Changes to the building fabric of the town centre of Boston, Lincolnshire, 1918–1977. Unpublished BA dissertation, University of Birmingham.

Pevsner, N. 1966: *The Buildings of England: Warwickshire*. Harmondsworth: Penguin.

Pompa, N. D. 1988: The nature and agents of change in the residential townscape: South Birmingham, 1970–85. Unpublished PhD thesis, University of Birmingham.

Prest, A. R. 1948: National income of the United Kingdom 1870–1946. *Economic Journal*, 58, 31–62.

Prudential Pensions 1981: *Report to Policy Holders for the Year Ended December 1980*. London: Prudential Pensions.

Punter, J. 1986a: Circular arguments: Central Government and the history of aesthetic control in England and Wales. *Planning History Bulletin*, 8, 51–9.

Punter, J. 1986b: Aesthetic control within the development process: a case study. *Land Development Studies*, 3, 197–212.

Punter, J. V. 1985: *Office Development in the Borough of Reading 1954–1984: a case study of the role of aesthetic control within the planning process*. University of Reading Working Papers in Land Management and Development Environmental Policy 6.

Punter, J. V. 1989: Development control: case studies. In M. Hebbert (ed.), *Development Control Data: a research guide*, London: Economic and Social Research Council, 55–71.

Punter, J. V. 1990: *Design Control in Bristol 1940–1990: the impact of planning on the design of office development in the city centre*. Bristol: Redcliffe.

Rasmussen, S. E. 1960: *London: the unique city*. Harmondsworth: Penguin.

Redfern, P. 1938: *The New History of the CWS*. London: J. M. Dent & Sons.

Redmayne, R. (ed.) 1950: *Ideals in Industry*. Leeds: Montague Burton.

Rees, V. O. 1949: University of Birmingham: key plan of future developments. Unpublished plan, in Estates and Buildings Department, University of Birmingham.

Richardson, H. W. and Aldcroft, D. H. 1968: *Building in the British Economy between the Wars*. London: Allen and Unwin.

Ross, G. R. 1979: The interaction of function and form in the pattern of building replacements in central Newcastle under Lyme, Staffordshire 1920-1975. Unpublished BA dissertation, University of Birmingham.

Rydin, Y. 1985: Residential development and the planning system: a study of the housing land system at the local level. *Progress in Planning*, 24, 1-69.

Samuels, I. 1985: Urban morphology in developed countries. Unpublished paper, Joint Centre for Urban Design, Oxford Polytechnic.

Schwind, M. 1951: Kulturlandschaft als objektivierter Geist. *Deutsche geographische Blätter*, 46, 5-28.

Short, J. R., Fleming, S. and Witt, S. J. G. 1986: *Housebuilding, Planning and Community Action: the production and negotiation of the built environment*. London: Routledge and Kegan Paul.

Simmie, J. M. and Hale, D. J. 1978: The distributional effects of ownership and control of land use in Oxford. *Urban Studies*, 15, 9-21.

Simmons, M. 1986: The M25 - a new geography of development? III. The emerging planning response. *Geographical Journal*, 152, 166-71.

Simpson, M. A. and Lloyd, T. H. 1977: Introduction. In M. A. Simpson and T. H. Lloyd (eds), *Middle Class Housing in Britain*, Newton Abbot: David & Charles, 7-11.

Slater, T. R. 1978: Family, society and the ornamental villa on the fringe of English country towns. *Journal of Historical Geography*, 4, 129-44.

Slater, T. R. (ed.) 1990: *The Built Form of Western Cities*. Leicester: Leicester University Press.

Smith, N. 1979: Toward a theory of gentrification: a back to the city movement by capital, not people. *Journal of the American Planning Association*, 45, 538-48.

Spensley, J. C. 1918: Urban housing problems. *Journal of the Royal Statistical Society*, 81, 161-228.

Springett, J. 1986: Land development and house-building in Huddersfield, 1770-1911. In M. Doughty (ed.), *Building the Industrial City*. Leicester: Leicester University Press, 24-56.

Sutcliffe, A. and Smith, R. 1974: *Birmingham 1939-1970*. London: Oxford University Press.

Tate, B. 1983: Alterations to the physical fabric of selected streets in central Glasgow, 1886-1905. Unpublished BA dissertation, University of Birmingham.

Thomas, A. D. 1983: Planning in residential conservation areas. *Progress in Planning*, 20, 178-256.

Thomas, D. 1963: London's Green Belt: the evolution of an idea. *Geographical Journal*, 129, 14-24.

Thompson, F. M. L. 1974: *Hampstead: building a borough, 1650-1964*. London: Routledge & Kegan Paul.

Thompson, I. A. 1987: An investigation into the development of the building fabric of Huddersfield's CBD 1869-1939. Unpublished PhD thesis, University of Birmingham.

Thorne, R. 1984: Office building in the City of London 1830-1880. Unpublished paper presented to the Urban History Group Colloquium on Urban Space and Building Form, London, 21 September.

Treen, C. 1982: The process of suburban development in north Leeds, 1870-1914. In F. M. L. Thompson (ed.), *The Rise of Suburbia*, Leicester: Leicester University Press, 158-209.

Trowell, F. 1983: Speculative housing development in the suburb of Headingley, Leeds, 1838-1914. *Publications of the Thoresby Society*, 59, 50-118.

Tym, R. & Partners 1987: *Land Used for Residential Development in the South East: a*

    summary report. London: R. Tym & Partners.
University of Birmingham 1925: Council Minutes 9086, 4 February. Unpublished MS.
University of Birmingham 1928a: Council Minutes 10900, 3 October. Unpublished MS.
University of Birmingham 1928b: Council Minutes 11013, 5 December. Unpublished MS.
University of Birmingham 1928c: Council Minutes 11014, 5 December. Unpublished MS.
University of Birmingham 1929a: Council Minutes 11043, 23 January. Unpublished MS.
University of Birmingham 1929b: *University of Birmingham Twenty-ninth Yearly Meeting of the Court of Governors, 21 February 1929. Report of the Proceedings of the Council of the University.*
University of Birmingham 1929c: Council Minutes 11105, 6 March. Unpublished MS.
University of Birmingham 1930: Council Minutes 11721, 7 May. Unpublished MS.
University of Birmingham 1945: Meeting of the Developments Committee, 4 July. Unpublished MS. File 741 in the Senate Store Room, University of Birmingham.
Vilagrasa, J. 1990: Morphological transformations of historical and commercial cores in England and Spain: a comparative study. Unpublished paper presented to the International Conference on the Urban Landscape, Birmingham, 9–10 July.
Wakeford, R. and Heywood, R. 1985: *Speeding Planning Appeals: a review of the handling of transferred written representation planning appeals*. London: HMSO.
West Herts and Watford Observer 1917: Obituary – Mr F. Fisher, 4 August, 5.
Whitehand, J. W. R. 1967a: The settlement morphology of London's cocktail belt. *Tijdschrift voor Economische en Sociale Geografie*, 58, 20–7.
Whitehand, J. W. R. 1967b: Traditional building materials in the Chilterns: a survey based on random sampling. *Oxoniensia*, 32, 1–9.
Whitehand, J. W. R. 1972: Building cycles and the spatial pattern of urban growth. *Transactions of the Institute of British Geographers*, 56, 39–55.
Whitehand, J. W. R. 1974: The changing nature of the urban fringe: a time perspective. In J. H. Johnson (ed.), *Suburban Growth: geographical processes at the edge of the Western city*, London: John Wiley, 31–52.
Whitehand, J. W. R. 1978: Long-term changes in the form of the city centre: the case of redevelopment. *Geografiska Annaler*, 60B, 79–96.
Whitehand, J. W. R. 1981a: Fluctuations in the land-use composition of urban development during the industrial era. *Erdkunde*, 35, 129–40.
Whitehand, J. W. R. 1981b: Background to the urban morphogenetic tradition. In J. W. R. Whitehand (ed.), *The Urban Landscape: historical development and management*, Institute of British Geographers Special Publication 13. London: Academic Press, 1–24.
Whitehand, J. W. R. 1983a: Land-use structure, built-form and agents of change. In R. L. Davies and A. G. Champion (eds) *The Future for the City Centre*, Institute of British Geographers Special Publication 14. London: Academic Press, 41–59.
Whitehand, J. W. R. 1983b: Renewing the Local CBD: more hands at work than you thought? *Area*, 15, 323–6.
Whitehand, J. W. R. 1984a: Commercial townscapes in the making. *Journal of Historical Geography*, 10, 174–200.
Whitehand, J. W. R. 1984b: Architecture of commercial redevelopment in post-war Britain. *Journal of Cultural Geography*, 5, 41–55.
Whitehand, J. W. R. 1984c: *Rebuilding Town Centres: developers, architects and styles*. University of Birmingham Department of Geography Occasional Publication 19.
Whitehand, J. W. R. 1987: *The Changing Face of Cities: a study of development cycles and urban form*. Institute of British Geographers Special Publication 21. Oxford: Basil Blackwell.
Whitehand, J. W. R. 1988: The changing urban landscape: the case of London's high-class residential fringe. *Geography Journal*, 154, 351–66.
Whitehand, J. W. R. 1989a: *Residential Development under Restraint: a case study in London's rural-urban fringe*. University of Birmingham School of Geography Occasional Publication 28.
Whitehand, J. W. R. 1989b: Development pressure, development control, and suburban

townscape change: case studies in south-east England. *Town Planning Review*, 60, 403–21.

Whitehand, J. W. R. 1990a: Makers of the residential landscape: conflict and change in outer London. *Transactions of the Institute of British Geographers*, NS 15, 87–101.

Whitehand, J. W. R. 1990b: Townscape management: ideal and reality. In T. R. Slater (ed.), *The Built Form of Western Cities*, Leicester: Leicester University Press, 370–93.

Whitehand, J. W. R. and Larkham, P. J. 1991a: Housebuilding in the back garden: reshaping suburban townscapes in the Midlands and south-east England. *Area*, 22, 57–65.

Whitehand, J. W. R. and Larkham, P. J. 1991b: Suburban cramming and development control. *Journal of Property Research*, 8.

Whitehand, J. W. R. and Whitehand, S. M. 1983: The study of physical change in town centres: research procedures and types of change. *Transactions of the Institute of British Geographers*, NS 8, 483–507.

Whitehand, J. W. R. and Whitehand, S. M. 1984: The physical fabric of town centres: the agents of change. *Transactions of the Institute of British Geographers*. NS 9, 231–47.

Whitehouse, B. P. 1964: *Partners in Property*. London: Birn, Shaw.

Williams, M. 1966: The parkland towns of Australia and New Zealand. *Geographical Review*, 56, 67–71.

Winton, J. R. 1982: *Lloyds Bank 1918–1969*. Oxford: Oxford University Press.

Witt, S. J. G. and Fleming S. C. 1984: *Planning Councillors in an Area of Growth: little power but all the blame?* University of Reading Department of Geography Geographical Paper 85.

Index

Note: References in italics refer to captions to photographs and designs. There are occasionally also textual references on these pages. General maps and diagrams are not indicated by italics.

Related Titles: List of IBG Special Publications